TORONTO

THE UNKNOWN CITY

TORONTO

THE UNKNOWN CITY

Howard Akler
and
Sarah B. Hood

ARSENAL PULP PRESS

VANCOUVER

ARSENAL PULP PRESS
103 - 1014 Homer Street
Vancouver, B.C.
Canada V6B 2W9
arsenalpulp.com

The publisher gratefully acknowledges the support of the Government of Canada through the
Book Publishing Industry Development Program for its publishing activities.

Design by Lisa Eng-Lodge
Production assistance by Judy Yeung
Cover photography by Cosmo Condina/Getty Images

Printed and bound in Canada

National Library of Canada
Cataloguing in Publication Data

Akler, Howard, 1969-
  Toronto: the unknown city / Howard Akler & Sarah B. Hood.

  (Unknown city)
  Includes index.
  ISBN 1-55152-146-6

  1. Toronto (Ont.)–Guidebooks. I. Hood, Sarah B. (Sarah Barbara), 1958-
II. Title. III. Series.

FC3097.18A34 2003   917.13'541044   C2003-911182-2

c o n t e n t s

acknowledgments

This book is dedicated to Nonni and Saul Akler,
and to Noreen Mallory (a.k.a. M.M.M.).

There is a rich and diverse historical tradition in Toronto.
The authors would like to recognize those who have come before
them. This book, and this city, would never have achieved their
present form without the inspiring work of:
Eric Arthur, Rick Bébout, William Dendy, Rosemary Donegan, Mike Filey,
Greg Gatenby, Jane Jacobs, Alfred Holden, Susan Houston, Nicholas
Jennings, William Kilbourn, Patricia McHugh, Peter McSherry, Rick Salutin,
Carolyn Strange, Gwyn "Jocko" Thomas, and the volunteer participants in
our many cultural, heritage, environmental, and historical organizations.

Thanks to:
Winston Abernethy, Daniel Akler, Ed Akler, Matt Akler, Rhea Akler and
Soumen Karmakar, Trudy Akler, Jake Allderdice, Leslie Ashton, Nathalie
Atkinson and Peter Birkemoe, Angela Baldassarre, Steve Beauregard,
Carolyn Bennett, the good folks at Book City, Steve Brearton, Manuel
Cappel, Derek Chadbourne, Rick Conroy, John Consolati, Shannon
Cooney, Ed Drass, Peter Duckworth-Pilkington, Linda Eggerer, Gerry Englar,
Sian Ferguson and John Fraser, Albert Fulton, Nick Gamble, Li-lien Gibbons,
Tanner Helmer, Annie Hillis, Alexandra Hood, John Hood, "Big Al" Howe,
Alex Israel, Rose Jacobson, Cathy Katrib, Doug Lee, Linda Litwack, Tracy
Loverock, Peter Lovrick, Mireille Macia, Sally Mackay, Chris Malcolm,
Geoff MacBride, Jason McBride, Derek McCormack, Kate Minsky,
Modupe Olaogun, Sergio Paez, David Perlman, Kathleen Rea, Janice Reid-
Johnston, the inimitable Jim ("JAMR") Rooney, Allan Ross, John Scully, Mary
Lynn Smith, Bruce Rosensweet, Celeste Sansregret, Rey Stephen, Adam
Sternbergh, Alec Stockwell, Bev Taft, Megan Williams, and Sharon Wilson

Special Thanks to:
Blaine, Brian, and Kiran at Arsenal Pulp, Alana Wilcox, fact checker
Jennifer Yap, and designers Lisa Eng-Lodge and Judy Yeung

Also to Susan Kernohan and Jonathan St. Rose, whose humour,
compassion, and cooking made the writing of this book much, much easier.

introduction

This book is incomplete. Given an extra week, we would have dug up another tunnel, pictured one more artist, bellied up to one last bar. But once that week was up, we'd have clamoured for another and another. We're not the first authors to curse a deadline; such is the nature of publishing. But more to the point, such is the nature of a city. It's a place that is impossible to catalogue once and for all.

Toronto has long struggled with self-definition. Victorian mores saddled us with the epithet "Toronto the Good," a name that was only superficially true. Sometime in the 1970s, we became the City that Works because our social programs and public transportation system appeared to run smoothly. Peter Ustinov compared us to "New York run by the Swiss." More recently, politicians have taken to blurting out World-Class City, an appellation that smacks of insecurity. They point to kitschy Walks of Fame or bravura Olympic bids, but sometimes ignore the most important fact: 44% of our population was born on foreign soil. What could be more world-class than that?

Newcomers inevitably add something to the city. Fresh ideas of community are incorporated into existing ones so Toronto is always in flux. New residents, earnest backpackers, and curious locals are constantly reinventing the city that they want. The writers of this book – a native Torontonian and a not-so-recent arrival – were delighted in seeing their two versions of the city become one. But, as noted earlier, this book is incomplete. This is only our city. Yours awaits.

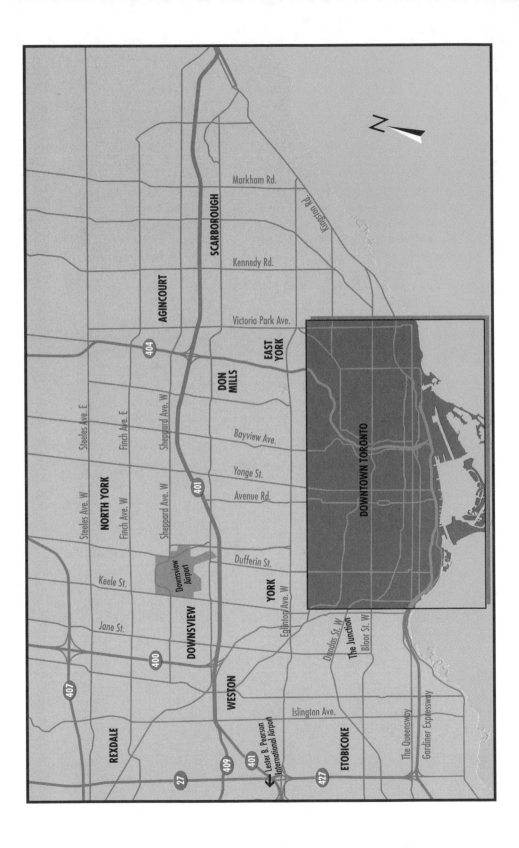

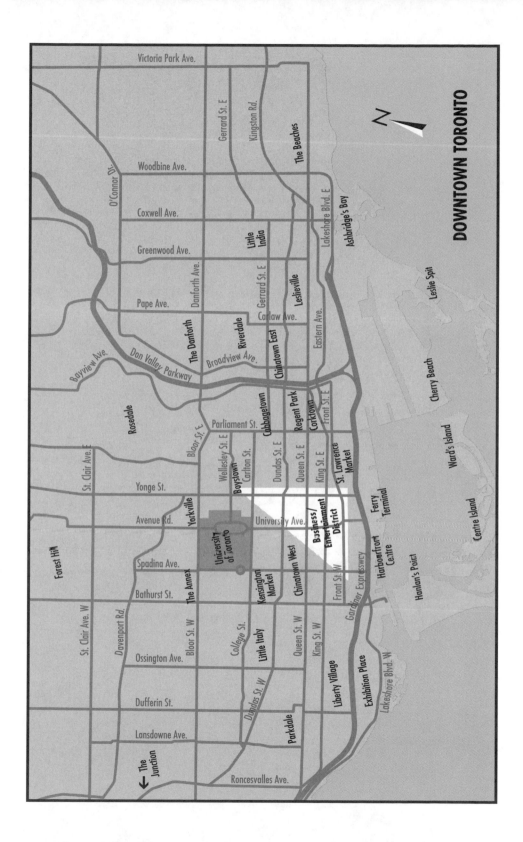

DOWNTOWN TORONTO

Landmarks & Destinations

Toronto, despite frequent photographic evidence to the contrary, is more than just a Tower and a Dome. We have a gilded bank building that was creatively financed and a buried stream that refuses to flow quietly. We've got haunted tunnels, questionable sculpture, and a long-lost bomb shelter. It's a city that is surprising, diverse, and only a single glance away.

Tall Tales

It's taller than five football fields and weighs more than 23,000 elephants. It gets hit by lightning 200 times a year. But the real charm of the CN Tower is its ability to attract eccentrics. The first was "Sweet" William Eustace, part of the original construction team in 1975, who parachuted 465 metres down from a crane. When he landed, he was fired. Then came Patrick Ballie in 1979, who dropped a Grade A egg from the top and set a record when it landed unbroken in a specially-designed net. In 1989, Brendan Keenoy raced up 2,570 stairs in seven minutes and 52 seconds. Most recently, Greenpeace members Steven Guilbeault and Chris Holden staged The World's Tallest Protest in July 2001. Using standard safety harnesses, they scaled the Tower in three hours. Hanging outside the observation deck, they unveiled a banner that read "Canada and Bush – Climate Killers" and conducted cell phone interviews on the topic of greenhouse emissions.

Photo: Ontario Tourism, 10127

In the 1880s, Toronto was a city on the verge. Industry was afoot, taverns were full, and the population was inching towards 100,000. So politicians thought it was time to erect a public building befitting the city's new status. Choosing architect E.J. Lennox, a local boy about to make good, initial plans called for a $200,000 courthouse. By 1887, the plan expanded into a $1.5 million city hall/courthouse. Work started in 1889 and it did not end until ten years later. During that decade, Lennox attended 520 meetings in which he quarreled with city politicians over the project's long delays and mounting costs. Indeed, when City Hall ran $1 million over budget, no one was very impressed. And the real fight was only beginning.

In 1907, Lennox presented his final bill for the job. Meticulously calculated on six sheets of paper, the tab totaled $242,870.82, with $181,255.71 still owing. Jaws dropped, ire was raised. The original fee was supposed to be $68,000 but Lennox, who had taken over as mason, felt his additional duties demanded additional dollars. Lawyers were called in and Lennox eventually pocketed $120,000 in an out-of-court settlement.

That just left the small matter of posterity.

Lennox had insisted on a plaque commemorating his accomplishments, but city officials nixed the idea. Still, like any good architect, Lennox had made careful plans. Cajoling a handful of workers, he had a string of letters carved on all sides of the building. Spelled out, they read: EJ LENNOX ARCHITECT. And there was more, found in the arches above the main door. There, in the middle of a group of dopey-eyed grotesques, is a familiar mustachioed face: E.J. Lennox. And he's smiling.

WATERY WALKWAY

There's an underwater tunnel connecting the Toronto Islands to the mainland, the conduit for all the utilities that serve Island residents and businesses. It's accessed by a manhole in the pavement near the mainland side of the ferry to the Island Airport. But don't try to get down there! It's pressurized with water most of the time. Whenever technicians need to work on the connections, the tunnel must be pumped out, and its air quality is carefully monitored. The last time that happened was when the Island was wired for high-speed computer access in the late 1990s.

Doing Time

The Don Jail is a place of contradictions: a beautiful building that has housed the seamier side of society. A detention centre most famous for its escapees. A virulent hole about to be transformed into a health-care facility.

Built in 1865, the jail sits on a grassy knoll east of the Don River. Classically designed, with a brooding stone face carved over the entrance, the jail has an unquestionably ugly past; whippings and hangings occurred well into the 20th century. Still, the most notorious incident was an escape. Two, actually. On November 4, 1951, bank robber Edwin Alonzo Boyd and two cohorts, Lennie Jackson and Willie Jackson (unrelated), sawed through the cell bars using a file hidden in Lennie's artificial foot. The Boyd Gang then went on a spree, hitting banks and killing a cop. Recaptured, they escaped again on September 8, 1952, before being jailed for good. Lennie Jackson and another member, Steve Suchan, were hanged here for the cop-killing.

In 1977, the original jail was shut down, putting great strain on the still-operating 1960s addition. Overcrowded, rat-infested cells were so common it was said prisoners awaiting trial would plead guilty just to get out. But that's all about to become history because the Don Jail is soon to close and become part of the new Bridgepoint Health Care Campus. The $11 million plan, which will incorporate nearby Riverdale Hospital, will see the exterior of the original Jail restored and the interior modified to become administrative offices. The plan is scheduled for a 2008 completion date.

Liberty Lost and Found

Photo: Sarah B. Hood

Now it's known for condos and creative warehouse occupants, but in the early 20th century the Liberty Village neighbourhood must have seemed a pretty dreary part of town. Just to the north stands the building then known as the Provincial Lunatic Asylum, with the remaining parts of its once-forbidding stone walls built by the patients themselves. From 1880 onwards, the present site of Lamport Stadium (*1155 King St. W.*) housed the grim Andrew Mercer Reformatory for Women, where you could be locked up under harsh conditions just for being unmarried and pregnant. (Area residents believe that the gracious King Street managers' residence next to the Stadium is still haunted.)

Equally cruel was the Central Prison (1874-1915), of which only the chapel still stands (technically at *20 Strachan Ave.*, although it's well back from the road). The main wings of the prison were demolished in 1920; the chapel was eventually incorporated into the (also mostly demolished) John Inglis plant, where they made washing machines in peacetime and Bren guns during the Second World War. There's a faint scrap of ghost writing on the west face of the building that dates from the Inglis era; a much more recent graffiti sunflower cheers up the north. Over the past few years the forlorn two-storey red brick building has lain abandoned, its insides completely gutted, unused except as an oversized tool shed by maintenance crews in the area, and a shelter for the starlings in its eaves and the killdeer nesting below. The area is due to become a townhouse development.

A sad site for a new home: for one thing, the prison was built on swampland and the buried "Asylum

SUBTERRANEAN PASSAGEWAYS

From time to time one hears the rumour that the Wheat Sheaf Tavern at King and Bathurst was connected by secret passageway to Fort York, ostensibly to facilitate the drinking excursions of the soldiers. The Wheat Sheaf is certainly old enough; it opened in about 1848 under the proprietorship of Irish immigrant Bernard Short and his wife Rose. Although some point to the fireplace in the east wall of the basement as the original entrance, there probably never was a tunnel, since the now-buried Garrison Creek would have proved a formidable obstacle to the most determined of diggers. However, there really *is* a walled-up entrance to an underground passageway in the basement of another popular eating spot: The Keg Mansion (*515 Jarvis St.*). Home of the illustrious Massey family, it used to be connected to the nearby Wellesley Hospital, so that the Masseys' chronically ill son would not have to travel above ground for treatments.

Stream" still runs high enough to sustain stands of bullrushes a few dozen metres away. For another, the Central Prison was notoriously punitive. Its operating philosophy was that "criminal" tendencies (such as vagrancy, alcoholism, and petty theft) could be "cured" by a firm hand – sometimes grasping a whip – and by very hard work. To that end the prison incorporated factory shops, a bakery, and a smithy. There may well have been an orchard too, because until recently several varieties of apples still blossomed around the site every spring. But anything that hasn't been bulldozed lies in the path of the planned Front Street Extension. Soon the only reminder of the Central Prison may be Liberty Street itself, named (it's said) because when a prisoner stepped outside the walls, he had his first taste of Liberty.

GHOST TUNNELS

With a basement morgue and network of buried passages, is it any wonder that the grounds of Lakeshore Psychiatric Hospital are the site of multiple reports of paranormal activity? Now redeveloped as part of Humber College, the hospital used to consist of a central building where meetings and treatments took place, connected by half-buried, brick-vaulted walkways to the buildings where the patients lived. About five feet wide, with limestone foundations, these rather extensive tunnels were used to transport food, medicine, and other supplies between the various sections of the institution. Today they contain nothing but utility connections; however, frequent stories have surfaced from builders and other workers, who reported experiencing everything from abnormal sensations of dread to the unnerving apparition of a faceless nurse.

Jumping to Conclusions

Photo: Sarah B. Hood

The Prince Edward Viaduct (known locally as the Bloor Street Viaduct) is the most bittersweet spot in town. Built 40 metres above the Don Valley, the Viaduct offers a gorgeous view and dangerous opportunity. Since opening in 1919, an estimated 500 people have jumped to their deaths from here, making it North America's second-biggest "suicide magnet," after the Golden Gate Bridge. Something had to be done. So, in 1998, architect Dereck Revington designed "The Luminous Veil," a barrier of 9,500 stainless steel rods that is transparent enough to maintain the view, but sturdy enough to impede the act of jumping. But city council balked at the $3.6 million price tag, saying the barrier would only drive would-be jumpers to another bridge. Mental health advocates, including the Schizophrenia Society of Ontario, offered loads of evidence to the contrary, and the barrier was finally finished in spring 2003. Unfortunately, in the six years of fussing, financing, and fitting, another 60 people jumped to their deaths.

Photo: Ontario Tourism, 10289

Since before the Canadian National Exhibition was established in 1879, the exhibition buildings have been an evolving reflection of Toronto and its preoccupations. From 1846 to 1878, Ontario's Provincial Agricultural Association held an annual fair, but it moved around to other towns in southern Ontario. Early on, Toronto wanted to keep the fair on home turf so in 1858 we built the first permanent exhibition building. The now-vanished Palace of Industry, which was quickly nicknamed the Crystal Palace, was first erected on King, but soon moved to the present Ex grounds.

By 1879 there were already 23 buildings on the site (these days there are only 17), but the roster has never stopped changing. There have been three editions of the Dufferin Gate, for example; the first was erected in 1895. It was replaced in 1910, and the present structure dates from 1960. There've been four versions of the CNE Grandstand, the most recent of which – built in 1947 – was dynamited at dawn on January 31, 1999, after a noble career hosting not only the Blue Jays, the Toronto Argonauts, and the extinct Blizzard soccer team, but music icons from Frank Sinatra to Nine Inch Nails. The Coliseum – now being expanded as a home for the American Hockey League's Toronto Roadrunners under the name "Ricoh Coliseum" – went up in full Beaux-Arts splendour in 1922. At the time, it was the world's biggest display venue, and housed the R.C.A.F. during the Second World War.

Among the lesser-known structures is the Shriner's Peace Monument, a tall sculpture overlooking the Rose Garden. It was erected in June 1930 with 10 cents collected from every Shriner in North America, and faces the mouth of the Niagara River as a symbol of peace between Canada and the U.S. Also, there's a bell tower that chimes the hours (on the grassy area in front of the Bandshell), but what a waste! It's a full 50-bell carillon, a quarter-million-dollar gift in 1974 from

BRINGING HOME THE BACON

Toronto came by its nickname of Hogtown honestly. In the late 1890s and early 1900s, the bacon trade with England was booming and Toronto had over a dozen meat packing houses vying for the business. These days, there are less than half that number. Most notable is Quality Meat Packers, on downtown Tecumseth Street. The abattoir's barn holds up to 3,000 hogs at a time; good for production, but bad for the chi-chi condo owners on nearby Niagara Street, who resent the frequent whiff of pig poop and the odd rotting carcass. For its part, Quality Meat Packers meets regularly with neighbourhood groups to monitor complaints. The plant uses fans to push the stink towards the railway, but considering the area is zoned for both industrial and residential use, it's unlikely the issue will blow over any time soon.

Other abattoirs have already vanished. As recently as the 1980s, feathers commonly used to drift through the air above Queen and John Streets from the poultry plant at St. Patrick Square. New York Pork, which opened in the 1930s, was forced to move out of the St. Clair and Keele area (longtime slaughterhouse central) in 2001, after new condo owners objected to the stench and squeals of doomed pigs. (They actually resorted to blocking delivery trucks.) To the amusement of some, a McDonald's has sprung up on the site of a former stockyard in The Junction.

Rothman's and Carling-O'Keefe, but it's virtually never played (sort of the equivalent of storing half-a-dozen of the finest grand pianos in your basement).

One of the most common misconceptions about Exhibition Place is the name of its most visible structure, the triumphal arch at Strachan. Many a Torontonian refers to it as "the Princess Gate" or "Prince's Gate." However, it was named neither for a princess nor a single prince, but for a pair of princes, the brothers Edward and George, who officially opened the structure when they visited in 1927. At the time, Edward was Prince of Wales. He went on to become the Edward VIII who abdicated, leaving the throne open for George, the father of Queen Elizabeth. Remember this next time you pass through the *Princes' Gate* on your way to the Ex.

Bells Are Ringing

Photo: Sarah B. Hood

The first fire halls all had high towers so hoses could be hung up to dry. If you look west from the corner of Yonge and Carlton, you can see two of the oldest in Toronto. Station 8 is visible in the western distance along College Street. Built in 1878, its tower was consumed in a fire in 1972 and the bells plunged to the bottom. So the well-known local landmark, with its clock and chimes, is actually a replica, rebuilt in 1973. (But it is still used to hang damp hoses.) The second tower is much closer: the 1872 vintage Fire Hall No. 3 at 488 Yonge. The fire hall itself burned in 1939 and the new building became famous – or notorious – as the St. Charles Homestead Restaurant (later the St. Charles Tavern), a music venue and beacon for the gay community. Recently a developer has acquired the now-decaying building and is refurbishing the clock tower, which will once more ring the hours – at least from 9 to 5. (Incidentally, the oldest operating fire hall is Station 10 at 34 Yorkville. Built in 1876, it still receives over 2,500 calls a year.)

Water, Water Everywhere

Photo: Howard Akler

The topography of Toronto is defined by absence. Over 12,000 years ago, the post-glacial waters of Lake Iroquois receded to their current levels and left a deeply-scarred land of creeks and ravines. Today, almost 12% of Toronto is parkland, more than double the average of other major North American cities.

Walk west on Davenport Road and you're following the bluff line of old Lake Iroquois. You'll also hit the source for a lost waterway called Garrison Creek. Two small streams converge at Davenport and Mount Royal Avenue, then head southwest through 120 hectares of parkland. Christie Pits. Bickford Park. Trinity-Bellwoods Park, before entering the lake east of Fort York.

Buried in the early 1930s, Garrison Creek has nonetheless left several "clues" behind. Take the odd curve of Crawford Street, north of College. This is the only stretch of road that follows the natural course of the creek; all other streets are on a right angle grid. Further up is the Harbord Street Bridge, built in 1905 and rendered invisible when the land underneath was filled in. Still, you can see the bridge's north balustrade at Bickford Park. And then there are the handful of houses at Barton Avenue and Shaw Street that tilt ridiculously on poorly-filled, shifting ground.

The Garrison Creek Community Project, formed in 1995, has two goals: to raise awareness of the creek, then raise the creek itself. Two of the driving forces behind the Project, architects James Brown and Kim Storey, say a revived creek will provide natural water purifiers, saving millions on the costly chemical holding tanks the city now uses.

At the northwest corner of Walnut and Wellington, beside Stanley Park, there's a monument to the buried creek, including a map of the former watercourse, inlaid animal forms, and the word for water in many languages.

READING THE FINE PRINT

The Mississagua Indians once occupied most of the land that is modern-day Toronto. Then the British came buying. The 1787 Toronto Purchase and amended deal of 1805 gave the Crown ownership of everything from Ashbridge's Bay in the east to Etobicoke Creek in the west. The cost? £1,700, plus an assortment of goods that included 24 brass kettles, 10 dozen mirrors, and two dozen lace hats.

Today, many of the Mississauga's 1,600 descendants live on the New Credit Reserve, near the town of Hagersville. During the Annual Powwow in August 2002, it was announced that the Canadian government had agreed at last to discuss the band's compensation claim.

A LITTLE FRENCH RETREAT

Can you name the oldest European military fortress in Toronto? Here's a hint: it's close to the CNE. Nope, it's not Fort York. In 1750, 43 years before Simcoe started work on his own fortifications, the French had already armed Fort Rouillé to defend their fur trading interests. Its outlines are marked out in concrete at Exhibition Place, just west of the Rose Garden. (Actually, it was one of three French forts in Toronto, but it's the only one you can still visit.)

The British captured the fort in 1759, so the French burned it and decamped for Kingston. In 1878, the ruins were cleared for the construction of Exhibition Place. As a sesquicentennial project in 1984, the City of Toronto arranged for a student excavation of the site and it was rededicated in October 2000 for the millennium. If you do visit it you'll likely feel that it was a rather small home for the 15 or so soldiers who manned it. Perhaps those fellows were just as glad to head back east for some fresh St. Lawrence air.

How the White House Got Its Name

Canada and the U.S. have occasional differences, but most citizens of both countries are proud of sharing the longest undefended border in the world. It wasn't so in the early 19th century, however, when we Canadians were allied with the British in a war against the Americans. Thus it came to pass that on April 27, 1813, a force of 13 U.S. ships descended upon Toronto (then known as York).

Their objective was to knock out the British garrison at Fort York and capture the partly built warship *Sir Isaac Brock* at the foot of York Street. They landed near what is now Sunnyside and overwhelmed the first wave of defenders, made up of Mississauga and Chippawa Indians alongside British soldiers. As the retreating force fell back towards Fort York, the magazine inside the Battery near the present-day Princes' Gate was accidentally blown up, causing grievous injuries among the defenders.

At this stage, commanding officer General Schaeffe did the most sensible thing he could have done under the circumstances: he blew up the main magazine and torched the *Sir Isaac Brock* before marching east to Kingston. (Why did you suppose we had a "Kingston Road"?) The Americans, or those who weren't casualties of the massive second explosion, marched on York. They only held the town for a few days, but just before they left, they set fire to the provincial Parliament at what is now Front and Berkeley, and stole the ceremonial Parliamentary mace. (They didn't return it until 1934.)

The following year, the British, peeved by the whole proceeding, set fire to the American Capitol building and the president's own home in Washington, which had to be whitewashed to cover the singe marks. And that's how the White House got its name.

On the Naming of Streets

Most Toronto streets are rather prosaically named after notable early inhabitants and builders of the city, or their estates, or their female relations. (Actually, it's one of the few areas where women are immortalized as often as men.) A handful of thoroughfares have quirkier origins, however.

Bay Street is the oddest. In the late 1700s, legend has it one Mr. Justice Boulton's horses chased a wild bear into the harbour. It started as "Bear" street, later corrupted to "Bay." (Now, of course, it's bears again, with bulls instead of horses.)

Elm Street enshrines the memory of an ancient lone elm tree at Yonge Street.

Niagara Street was originally a path along the east bank of the now-buried Garrison Creek, made by troops from Fort York as they began the long march around the head of the lake to Niagara.

Parliament Street, you'd think, should be somewhere near the Legislature, yes? Well it was, once. In fact, Berkeley Street was first called Parliament, and it ran past the original Parliament of Upper Canada. Later on the names were modified and Parliament Street moved one block east. (In 2001, when remnants of the original 1798 building were discovered, there was a feeling of joy and disgust: joy because the city had a chance to commemorate an important piece of our past; disgust because the site was owned by Downtown Fine Cars, which had plans to build a Porsche showcase. At the time of writing, both the city and the province have tried unsuccessfully to buy the land back.)

Rebecca Street has a convoluted history. In the book of *Genesis* (24:60) there's a reference to Rebecca: "let thy seed possess the gate of they that hate them." Therefore, when in 1843 a group of disaffected South Wales rebels destroyed the local toll gates, they took the name "Rebeccaites." In Toronto, Rebecca Street began as a lane that allowed travellers to avoid the toll gate at Queen and Ossington.

Temperance Street was named by Jesse Ketchum. A great opponent of liquor (alcoholism really was a desperate social problem in 19th-century Toronto), Ketchum instituted his Temperance Hall there and donated the land to the city on the condition that a

Concrete Poetry

Your granny may have told you not to stare at the ground, but if you follow her advice, you'll miss out on many interesting details!

• In the sidewalk at the northwest corner of Queen and Parliament is a plaque commemorating the deaths of ten people on December 23, 1989, in the fire that destroyed the Rupert Hotel on that site. The tragedy brought about the creation of the Rupert Hotel Coalition, dedicated to improving the living conditions in Toronto rooming houses.

• At least three different types of local fish — a school of 41 in all — "swim" in the pavement outside the Second Cup at Queen's Quay near the foot of York Street, in the form of sculpted metal bas-reliefs.

Photo: Sarah B. Hood

portion of it remain "dry" forever. The condition was honoured for many years, but in 1907 the disreputable Star Theatre – a burlesque hall – opened on Temperance, providing an opportunity for all kinds of mischief to the street youth of the day. In more recent years, ironically, it's been the home of the bike courier bar of many names, which may very well sell more beer per square foot (it's tiny) than any establishment in the city.

• The northwest corner of Queen and Spadina commemorates the winners of the annual Toronto Book Award – at least for the first few years. The award was inaugurated back in 1974, but the plaques miss out on the winners since about 1980, including essential classics like Michael Ondaatje's *In the Skin of a Lion*; historian J.M.S. Careless's *Toronto to 1918*; Michael Bliss's *The Discovery of Insulin*, and William Dendy and William Kilbourn's *Toronto Observed*.

The Yonge and the Restless

It's a chicken-and-egg situation: are we fascinated with the intersection of Yonge and Dundas because it's our oldest intersection, or did John Graves Simcoe choose to demarcate these two routes first because of some inherent magnetism about the location? Yonge Street itself reaches from its roots at Lake Ontario right up to Rainy River on the Minnesota border. It was officially opened by Simcoe in February of 1796, and its bicentennial in 1996 sparked celebrations across the province. It was the route of Toronto's first horse-drawn omnibus in 1849 and the first place in the city where electric light was installed in 1879. In 1933, Eaton's on Yonge demonstrated Canada's first television signal.

Yonge is also the place people spontaneously go to celebrate. They did it as early as 1902 for the end of the Boer War; again in 1945 when the Second World War ended, and then in 1992 and 1993 when the Blue Jays won the World Series. In the early '70s, three blocks of Yonge were opened into a pedestrian mall; the action got so hot that the idea was discontinued in 1974.

But our favourite spontaneous tribute to the street that is the backbone of Toronto is the tradition of one group of local cycle racers. These hardy bikers meet at the foot of Yonge at dawn each year on the summer solstice to see how far they can ride up the longest street in the world on the longest day of the year.

Cast List

The people who've been honoured with public statues in this city make up a peculiar roster. Apart from Timothy Eaton, there's quite a bevy of monarchs and ministers around Queen's Park: Queen Victoria, of course, and King Edward VII as Prince of Wales, mounted on that unfortunate horse whose genitals have been gleefully defaced by generations of engineering students. Then there are Governor Simcoe, Sir John A. Macdonald, Ontario Premiers J.S. Macdonald, Oliver Mowat, and James Whitney; George Brown; William Lyon Mackenzie – who for some reason ranks only a bust – and Sunday School founder Robert Raikes.

In other parts of town you'll spot some politicians, but more artists and figures of importance among Toronto's ethnic communities. Sir Winston Churchill glowers over

Photo: Sarah B. Hood

the speakers' corner on Queen Street at Nathan Phillips Square. Hydro founder Sir Adam Beck towers over the nearby intersection of Queen and University. The muscular torso of Alexander the Great dominates a parkette at Danforth and Logan; a dignified Dr. Sun Yat-Sen peers out at Riverdale Park, and actor Al Waxman lounges casually at Bellevue Square Park in his kingdom of Kensington Market. A be-mittened Glenn Gould slouches on a park bench on Front, outside the CBC auditorium that bears his name. Rower Ned Hanlan stands proudly at Exhibition Place (but he may soon be on the move, to – where else? – Hanlan's Point). Poet Robbie Burns inhabits Allan Gardens; educator Egerton Ryerson stands

Photo: Sarah B. Hood

on Gould Street at Ryerson College; Sir John Colborne is enshrined at Upper Canada College, and Sir Casimir Gzowski is on Lakeshore Boulevard. Other truncated types – shown as busts only, we mean – are Simon Bolivar in the north end of Trinity Bellwoods Park and composer Jean Sibelius in his own park at Brunswick and Bernard.

But what do you have to do to become a statue if you're a woman? Apart from Queen Vic, the few females who *are* represented are heads only. These include local sculptors Florence Wyle and Frances Loring at St. Clair and Mount Pleasant; anthropologist and critic Margaret Fairley in her eponymous parkette at Brunswick & Ulster, and Mary Pickford at her birthplace on University Avenue. The sole exception? In High Park there is a full body sculpture of Lesya Ukrainka – the greatest Ukrainian poetess.

IF YOU PAINT IT ...

To some a fence is a barrier; to others, an opportunity. Take Christine Kowal, for instance. When the artist moved to a place on east-end Craven Road, reputed to have the longest continuous backyard fence in the world, she just couldn't resist. Soon the greying wooden expanse – running for blocks and blocks from Queen Street north to Danforth – sported Kowal's original work. She paints the images (often animals) on canvas first, then affixes them to the boards. The neighbourhood loves the impromptu outdoor exhibition; a few other residents of the street have added their own paintings – and some connoisseurs have paid Kowal the questionable compliment of stealing her work right off the walls.

Photo: Sarah B. Hood

Tracking Timothy

Generations of Torontonians used to assure themselves of prosperity by rubbing the toe of the statue of retail magnate Timothy Eaton in his department store. When Eaton's closed, the statue was moved – appropriately enough – to Eaton Court on the ground floor of the Royal Ontario Museum. First unveiled in 1919, the benevolent seated figure was modeled by Ivor Lewis and partly paid for with $15,000 collected from Eaton's employees. If you'd like to rub his toe to improve your financial fortunes, you're still welcome to do so, but you might want to go on one of the ROM's weekly Free Friday Nights.

Photo: Courtesy Royal Ontario Museum

monumental endeavours

What's more controversial than public art? Toronto has some of the most admirable, risible, and just plain puzzling examples. We're inclined to point out, however, that, over time, the worst conceived of notions become familiar and – eventually – even loved.

Photo: Sarah B. Hood

Gumby Goes to Heaven

Perhaps no public work in Toronto has had more scorn attached to it than British artist Oscar Nemon's 1984 *Canadian Airmen's Memorial*. The poor thing. Among other critics, Robert Fulford has called it "bumptiously, laughably, insistently bad." Maybe it's because it towers so very noticeably over University Avenue. Or maybe it's because it really does look a little bit like the bendable cartoon character after whom public opinion has renamed it.

The Italian Bird Man

Another work that has been unofficially renamed is Francesco Pirelli's *Monument to Multiculturalism*, just outside Union Station. The practical-minded wonder why it was positioned so close to the antique clock, because you can't take a picture of one without the

Photo: Ontario Tourism, 11170

other. Artist Charles Pachter has stated that he thought it should have gone on Centre Island, "dappled by sunlight and water." When it was installed, there was a surprisingly large outcry against it; people even wanted it removed. But a couple of decades have softened

HIDDEN IN PLAIN VIEW

One of the best urban mysteries of Toronto in the '80s was summed up in the question: Who does those books? An unknown artist in town (with considerable technical skills) was creating a series of peculiar, lovely ornamented books. Thing is, they weren't turning up in galleries or bookstores or even cafés. Instead, they could be found bolted to fences and posts and buildings in the oddest places, all over the city. Sometimes they were signed by "Darryl." Occasionally a journalist would attempt to locate the artist, but to no avail. More recently, from the same hand has come a series of engraved metal plates with decorative imagery and words. Several present memorial texts like "Ronald Born 1959 Died 1978."

Finally in 2002, after 25 years of producing anonymous street art, the artist, whose real name, it turns out, is Rocky Darrel Dobey, finally emerged into the light of celebrity with a show at A Space Gallery. His guerrilla work (some of which has endured for a decade or more) continues to delight observant pedestrians in spots like the northeast corner of College and Bathurst; several are around the Kensington Market neighbourhood.

resistance and it's even played a prominent role in several TV commercials.

The Donkey-Dogs

Photo: Sarah B. Hood

New York artist Cynthia Short designed the herd of peculiar long-eared animals installed in 1992 on Wellington Street at John, south of Metro Hall. Turns out they're not really meant to be any particular type of beast; they're just supposed to celebrate childhood innocence. Entitled *Remembered Sustenance*, the work delineates the transition between Metro Hall's day care and the wicked world without. The metal curtain and the live cedar hedge are also part of the work.

Iroquois Furrow Survey

Photo: Howard Aller

In the "puzzling" category is Brad Golden and Norman Richards' 1991 site-specific installation *Spadina Line*. It begins at the "Baldwin Steps" that lead up from Davenport Road to Casa Loma and continues along Spadina towards Dupont. Metal words are inlaid into the sidewalk on both sides of the street, illuminated by fancy light fixtures (unless it's been snowing). They all refer to the layers of history that have accrued in the neighbourhood. In order, they are: "Iroquois" (for the escarpment that is the ancient shore of Lake Iroquois), "Furrow" (for market gardens), "Survey," "Avenue," "Power" (for Hydro lines and public utility buildings in the area), "Dairy," and "Archive" (for the new Toronto Archive building). Under the adjoining railway underpass you'll find more bits of it: a stainless steel time capsule, a digital clock, and strips of iron, nickel, and copper that are picked out by the sun on the winter and

---

DESCENT TO THE UNDERWORLD

The biggest manhole cover in Toronto — and it's a doozy — is located on King's College Road on the University of Toronto campus, next to the laneway that separates the Mechanical Engineering Building at 5 King's College and the Medical Sciences Building at 1 King's College. Inscribed "Reid & Brown Structural Steel and Iron Works Toronto 1911," it's made in two parts, to allow sufficient access for a human being through the centre opening, or to create a larger passageway for equipment.

summer solstices and the vernal equinox. Taken altogether, it comments on "time's various rhythmic perspectives." We kind of like it because it makes us think. (We would even say that the "Aquarian Conspiracy" graffiti adds to the concept, but we think they should reset the clock to the right time.)

P r o g r e s s   o f   T i m e

Photo: Sarah B. Hood

An even more spread-out statement is that made by Eldon Garnet's *TIME: And a Clock*, which unfolds over several blocks of Queen Street. It begins with the curvy banner and inscription "This river I step in is not the river I stand in," and the clock, retrofitted to the existing Queen Street bridge over the Don Valley. (The clock's wrong on this one too; what's with that?) It's a bit of a brain-stretcher, but it apparently refers both to the actual Don River below and to the conceptual River of Time, in which we all stand. But that's not all. Further east, the sidewalks around the intersection of Queen and Broadview are inscribed with four more timely messages: "Distance equals velocity x time," "Better late than never," "Too soon free from time," and "Time is money: money is time." To get the full impact, you have to drift even further, past the railway underpass to the park at Queen Street and Empire Avenue, where seemingly swirling metal banners atop four flagpoles bear the words "Coursing," "Disappearing," "Trembling," "Returning." Maybe these are things time does, or that rivers do, or that we do when confronted by time and rivers. We thought "Flowing" would have been nice too, but perhaps Garnet was content to stick with just four flags.

Ghost Signs

Long before the advent of electronic media, local companies advertised in the simplest way possible: they painted signs directly on the walls of their buildings. Some of these ads, because of durable lead-based paint and protection from the elements, endure to this day. However, many of them are slowly fading off the walls, one flake at a time. Here's a sampling of some of the best. Others can be seen at *davetill.com/torontoghostsigns/*

• **Eno's Fruit Salt**, 296 Richmond Street West. This bubbly laxative was J.C. Eno Company's number one product from the late 1920s to the early 1950s.

Photo: Howard Akler

Squiggly Maps

On both sides of the railway underpass on Gerrard Street at Carlaw, there are irregular blue cutouts with some kind of writing on them. They look like map views of lakes. Titled *Blue Fire*, they were installed in 1996 by artist Dereck Revington, who describes them as "paired aluminum fragments etched with traces of a poem by Robin Blaser." They are designed to "lift the spirits of the underpass." (We think that scraping the pigeon poop off the underpass would also go a fair way towards lifting its spirits, but never mind.)

• **Lovable** brassieres and corsets were made at this 471 Adelaide Street West building during the 1950s and 1960s.

• **Reliance Engravers** set themselves in your memory at 104 Bond Street, just south of Ryerson Polytechnic University.

• **Robertson's Chocolates** were a sweet deal for anyone passing by the Queen and Jarvis intersection beginning in 1873.

Another Mystery Solved

In front of the eastern end of Hart House on the University of Toronto campus there's a progression of angular installations on the lawn. Their purpose and position becomes clear if you view them from a spot that allows you to line up all the top points. *Voilà!* They match up exactly with the top of the CN Tower across town! (We suspect that they're also oriented north-south, but we didn't have a compass handy when we checked them out.)

Placid Cows

There's no particular controversy about Joe Fafard's big happy cows at the TD Centre. Everybody loves 'em and so do we. We just thought we'd like to say so.

A much anticipated reopening was that of the long-locked top floor of College Park, including the Eaton Auditorium, preferred recording hall of Glenn Gould. As first imagined, College Park was supposed to cover four times its present area and soar to 38 stories high. (If you examine the exterior detailing, you can see that it's lopsided, and awaiting an addition.) The first home of Eaton's, the building was seen as a relative of Manhattan's Rockefeller Center and its concert hall as a sister to Carnegie Hall. It would have been the largest building in North America, but as the Depression encroached, the plans were never completed. However, the seventh floor, which opened in 1931, was the special delight of Lady Flora McCrea Eaton (wife of Timothy). She envisioned recreating the atmosphere of her favourite ocean liner – the Jacques Carlu-designed *Ile de France* – in its Round Room, a society luncheon spot. She recruited Carlu himself to conceive it (in the style of Art Moderne), and he installed Lalique light fixtures and a black vitrolite fountain, which have been faithfully restored in the venue's new incarnation as a special-events venue known as "Carlu." To this day, they say Lady Eaton's ghost is active around College Park, especially on the stairways: a benign spirit, in any case, who may simply hate to part company with another elegant old lady.
444 Yonge St., 410-8727, thecarlu.com

HOW LOW CAN YOU GO?
The lowest publicly accessible point in the city is the fifth underground level at the Royal Bank Plaza. It's 70 feet below the sidewalk, or 43 feet below the level of Lake Ontario.

TOP FLOORS, CLOSED DOORS

College Park has reopened its top floor, but others around town remain locked. The Winchester Hotel (*537 Parliament St.*) is an old Cabbagetown landmark that's seen some rough, tough times since it was built in 1888 (one of its nicknames was "Bucket o' Blood"). Whereas the downstairs section has been recently refurbished, the formerly tonier **Laurentian Bar** — an ample second-story room with a long Art Deco wooden bar — has been closed since the early 1990s. Similarly, the King Edward Hotel (*37 King St. E.*) was built in 1903 by George Gooderham and designed by E.J. Lennox, who also built Old City Hall. In 1921 an addition was made that included the opulent and now legendary **Crystal Ballroom** on the top floor of the east wing. It's been closed since the late 1950s, except to the occasional video shoot.

Expand and Contract

In this era of superstar architects and eye-popping design, Toronto zealously approved three big projects in the years 2000 to 2002.

• The **Royal Ontario Museum** was thrilled with architect Daniel Libeskind's radical $200 million design, which calls for a giant crystal addition to the ROM's more conservative exterior. But engineers realized that the crystal, constructed mostly of transparent glass, would not withstand a typical Canadian winter. In the revised plan, 80 percent of the "crystal" roof will be clad in stainless steel.

• Architect Will Alsop wants his brightly-coloured rectangular addition to hover nine stories above the existing **Ontario College of Art and Design** building. No problem; 12 steel legs and a large concrete core will keep his baby aloft. But pricey building materials means the cost of the project has increased from $38 million to $42 million while the size has shrunk from 115,000 square feet to 90,000 for the projected opening in early 2004.

• Architect Frank Gehry used to play in Grange Park as a boy. Now he'll get to play again, albeit with $178 million — the price tag for the **Art Gallery of Ontario** expansion. Gehry, arguably the biz's biggest name because of his Museo Guggenheim Bilbao, hadn't unveiled a plan at the time of writing. But one thing is certain: his design will replace architect Barton Myers' old version, built to much fanfare only ten years earlier.

Photo: Sarah B. Hood

You may hear several spurious interpretations of the significance of the Canada Life Beacon, but here's the straight dope. The tapering tower that tops the gracious Canada Life Assurance Building (*330 University Ave.*) is in fact a weather forecasting device. The horizontal white bars along its shaft run up or down or remain stable according to the temperature (warming, cooling, steady). If the cube at the top is green, the weather will be clear; if red, it'll be cloudy; if it's flashing, there'll be precipitation (red stands for rain, white for snow). During the daytime, the beacon forecasts the weather for the balance of that day; at night, it predicts the following day's weather. Canada Life gives out handy little laminated wallet cards with all the info (and a handsome photo of the beacon itself) in the lobby at 330 University or its adjoining offices at 180 and 190 Simcoe. (Another reason to visit the building – apart from its elegant doors – is the grapevine tangle along the iron fence on the southern perimeter, from which knowledgeable passersby pluck fresh fruit in season.)

LET'S GET LOST

What does PATH stand for? Nothing. Where does it take you? Nowhere. Okay, it does take you somewhere, but not always the place you want to go. Tourist guides may effuse over PATH's 10 km of underground shopping (over 1,100 stores and restaurants), but locals often have a more jaded view. As in: getting lost in PATH is the resident's rite of passage. Looking for First Canadian Place but end up in some food court? Missed the turn for Sheraton Centre? No worry. Now you're one of us. And for the next time, try *MAZE* magazine. Started in late 1999 by Ross Skoggard after he got lost one time too many, *MAZE* is printed on a PATH map so you can casually peruse articles while secretly searching for the nearest exit.

Free Gold

Photo: Ontario Tourism, 10123

TIME FLIES

No, you're not losing your mind: the sculptural clock outside 2 Bloor Street West at Yonge used to stand on the Bloor side of the building. Building owners Oxford Properties moved it around the corner to Bay when they extended the front lobby in the summer of 2002.

How much does a million dollars' worth of gold cost? It may sound like a stupid question, but sometimes the answer can be nothing at all. Skeptical? Allow us to demonstrate. The Royal Bank Plaza (*200 Bay St.*) opened on March 10, 1977. Its windows are covered with a very thin film of gold: about 2,500 ounces in all, which, by today's prices, could well cost close to $1 million. But it was built just at the time when the U.S. stopped guaranteeing an international standard price of $35 an ounce and, over the next four years, the price of an ounce of gold climbed to about $850. So, the story goes, when the leftover gold from the Royal Bank Plaza windows was sold, it paid for all the metal that had been used to coat the windows! After all this time, the glass fabricators could neither confirm nor deny the truth of the rumour, but when we spoke with Fedor Tisch, a partner with ZMH Architects, the company that designed the building, he said it would be normal to overbuy a commodity like gold by about 10 percent. We did the math, and – even if the gold had been bought at $50 per ounce – within a couple of years (a little after the date the building opened), the sale of 250 ounces could easily have paid back the total purchase price. So, in effect, the cost of a million dollars' worth of gold was … nothing!

Good Idea, Bad Timing

In 1929, the city was thinking big. Really big. Plans were made to transform University Avenue into a Beaux Arts boulevard. The Beaux Arts style, which espoused architecture on a massive scale, was really a paean to prosperity. So University was extended south to Front Street, linking the monumental colonnade of Union Station to the grand vista of Queen's Park. Some were talking up Vimy Circle, a proposed war memorial roundabout between Simcoe and York Streets. And just north of Queen Street, construction began on the Canada Life Assurance Building. Rising high above street level, Canada Life's HQ was the first building in the Beaux Arts plan. And the last. When the stock market crashed in October 1929, all hopes of civic grandeur went with it.

Eat Your Veggies

One building that did open during the late 1920s is the Royal York Hotel (now called the Fairmont Royal York). Because of its size and grandeur, the hotel was immediately described as a "city within a city." This isn't just hyperbole. The kitchen, for example, is the biggest in Canada and can hold seven Boeing 747 airplanes. More impressive, however, is the storage of vegetables. Hotel guests consume 188,123 kg of veggies each year. That breaks down to 30,210 kg of onions, 17,898 kg of tomatoes, and 17,690 kg of carrots. At the low end of things is broccoli, with only 2,352 kg being eaten.

RAY WAS HERE

If you happen to be flying over the Valley Building of the Ontario Science Centre, check out architect Raymond Moriyama's signature – in Japanese – on the roof.

No Wonder the TV Reception is Bad

In February 1959, Mayor Nathan Phillips met with Russian ambassador Amasaps Aroutounian. His Honour's tongue tripped all over that name, calling his guest Mr. Rootin' Tootin'. While the Cold War appellation might sound fitting, Mayor Phillips wasn't about to sweat any fallout over the mishap. The city had a top-secret bomb shelter, where the Mayor and his cronies could hide when the Big One hit. Hidden under a Victorian-era farmhouse at 220 Old Yonge Street north of the city in Aurora, the 10.6 x 18.3 metre bunker contained canned goods, sleeping cots, and a large illuminated city map, so our esteemed leaders could chart casualty reports and radiation levels.

BUT IT'S NOT BUILT OF MASONITE

The concert venue-cum-TV studio at Yonge and Davenport isn't called the Masonic Temple just for fun. It's an honest-to-goodness Masonic Temple, and if you doubt our word, just glance up at the corner of the building next time you're passing by to see the compass-and-square-rule Masonic symbol plainly visible in the upper level.

Having Faith

During the 1920s, Kensington Market was primarily a Jewish neighbourhood, and an estimated 30 places of worship were packed into the small area. The First Narayever Congregation was established in 1914 by the former citizens of Naraiev, Galacia, who raced their fellow townspeople in New York City for the rights to set up their first North American synagogue. In 1940, they moved from Huron and Dundas Streets to their current location, nestled in a residential neighbourhood, at 187 Brunswick Avenue. Over the years, a new generation of worshippers has turned Narayever into the only traditional, gender-egalitarian congregation in the city.

Construction on the Anshei Minsk Congregation at 10 St. Andrew Street started in 1922 and finished eight years later. Sadly, it is currently undergoing more work; early in the morning of March 11, 2002, a homeless man broke into the synagogue. Wanting to keep warm, he started a small fire on the upper balcony. The flames burned out of control. Damage was estimated at $200,000, but the real worry was the destruction of thousands of prayer books and historical texts, some of which dated back to the 19th century. Workers sifted through the charred remains and, with the financial help of Heritage Canada, will attempt to restore some of the salvaged pages and books.

Fine and Private Places

The dead are still with us; especially in Toronto's many old and hidden cemeteries.

• One of the very oldest is in the park to the west of Fort York, accessible by a pedestrian staircase from Strachan. The gravestones have been taken up and installed into a memorial wall, and though moving they are very difficult to read. They include that of Katherine Simcoe, who died on April 17, 1794 at the age of one year and three months, the infant daughter of Sir John Graves Simcoe and his wife Elizabeth.

• Over time the burial ground in Portland Park, at Portland south of King Street, has been called Garrison Cemetery, Military Memorial Park, St. John the Evangelist Cemetery, and St. John's Square. Established around 1794, its last known burial took place in 1862, by which time it had received 400 people, as well as 20 horses, who were left behind by departing British soldiers after the War of 1812. (They preferred to kill their animals rather than abandon them to possible mistreatment.) A memorial to the war dead marks the spot; from time to time a fragment of bone pokes through the grass.

• Of the thousands who pass the corner of Yonge and St. Clair each week, few know about the surprisingly large St. Michael's Roman Catholic Cemetery behind the buildings on the southwest corner. The gate is set back from the west side of Yonge Street, down a drive a dozen or so doors south of the intersection. Containing about 29,000 graves, it opened in 1855 to replace St. Paul's Parish Cemetery – now built over – at Toronto's oldest Catholic Church on Queen just east of Parliament.

• The oldest Jewish cemetery is Pape Avenue Cemetery, south of Gerrard Street. Also known as Holy Blossom Cemetery or Jews Cemetery, it was established in 1849 by British optician and jeweler Judah G. Joseph and Bavarian piano maker Abraham Nordheimer. The burial of Joseph's son Samuel in 1850 is believed to be the first Jewish burial in Toronto, although – like many of the earliest burials – it's unmarked. Pape Avenue Cemetery has been closed since 1930.

• Even a well-known graveyard has its secrets. For example, Mount Pleasant, the largest and best-known cemetery in the city, is the resting-place of four unknown

souls, the unidentified dead of the terrible *Noronic* disaster. Some have speculated that they may have been visiting the ship for shady purposes; others suggest that they were simply tourists who were never connected with their families after the excursion steamer burned at the docks on the evening of September 16, 1949, leaving 104 dead and 14 missing.

PLUMBING THE PAST

The first public loo was located in the old financial district at Adelaide and Toronto Streets. Built in 1897, a more genteel time, the potty was placed underground and was an immediate success because six more were set up beneath the surface of the city. The most popular, at Queen Street and Spadina Avenue, averaged over 50,000 ablutions per month in the early 1930s before mounting costs and dwindling use closed the doors in 1937.

Another toilet, built above ground on the southwest side of the Prince Edward Viaduct in 1920, still stands. But it's easy to miss. With a front porch and bay windows, the Prince Eddie was designed like a house so it fits in with the rest of the 'hood. Shut down in 1988, its sinks were salvaged and installed in the basement of the blue barracks at Fort York.

A Soldier Comes Home

Photo: Sarah B. Hood

The wind whistles around the wide expanse of Parliament Street at Danforth, but there's a quiet resting-place nearby for a mother and her boy. Anna Peel Durie was the wife of Lt.-Col. William Smith Durie, founder of the Queen's Own Rifles. Naturally their son, William Arthur Durie, answered the call when the First World War was declared. He joined the Canadian 58th Battalion and died, at the age of 36, fighting in the front-line trenches of France on December 29, 1917. In those days, it was decided that all the war dead, whatever their national origin, would be buried together in France, so William Durie's remains were interred in Corkscrew British Cemetery, near Lens. His grieving mother Anna requested the return of his body, but the request was denied. She waited patiently, until 1925, when the bodies in Corkscrew were exhumed for reburial at Loos British Cemetery, at which point she travelled to France and – in the dark of night – retrieved her son's body from its new grave and reburied an empty coffin. On August 22, 1925, Captain William Durie was buried with full military honours in St. James Cemetery at 635 Parliament Street. When Anna Durie died in 1933, she was, of course, buried beside her son.

Photo: Ontario Tourism, 10746

Yes, that's a functional lighthouse on the Toronto Islands. Built in 1808 when the Town of York was still a modest settlement of 400 souls, it's the oldest remaining building in Toronto, and after Sambro Island Lighthouse in Halifax, it's the oldest lighthouse in Canada. Gibraltar Point Lighthouse burned sperm whale oil at first, but has been electric since 1916. Its original purpose was to attract vessels to the city while keeping them off the sandbars that are the present Islands. However, its usefulness has been eroded by the glare of city lights and the trees that now obscure its beam.

It is said that in 1815 the lighthouse keeper, J.P. Radan Muller, was murdered in the tower by soldiers from Fort York – possibly bludgeoned to death on the 13th step – and that his ghost still haunts the lighthouse. Some say he was involved in smuggling, and that that was the cause of his demise. His body was never found (although in 1893 some body parts were theoretically unearthed nearby). Present-day lighthouse keeper Manuel Cappel is skeptical. "All that's really known is that he disappeared – fast – on January 2, 1815," he says. Cappel, a lifelong Islander, offers occasional tours of the lighthouse. Call 416-203-7717 for more information.

DOWN MEMORY LANE

Apart from its unforgettable name, Memory Lane in Leslieville has a special place in Canadian history. To this day at the corner of Memory Lane and Laing Street there stands the very maple tree whose falling leaves inspired Alexander Muir to pen our most nationalistic anthem, "The Maple Leaf Forever," in 1867. Its Britophile lyrics make the song seem dated, but you can gauge its enduring impact by the fact that it was chosen to be sung by Anne Murray at the 1999 closing ceremony for Maple Leaf Gardens, albeit with new words by Vladimir Radian.

Labour of Love ... and 200,000 Screws

Photo: Howard Akler

DOORWAYS FROM THE PAST

When you see a lone lilac in an Ontario field, chances are you're looking at the doorway of a vanished farmhouse. The presence of popular domestic plants like day lilies — and occasional traces of stone and brick — mark where the houses once stood. There are similar botanical giveaways along the north side of the Boardwalk on Ward's Island, which used to be lined with homes.

The house at 473 Clinton Street looks like a summer camp arts and crafts project that just wouldn't end. The entire house, porch, fence around the yard, and the small gazebo are covered with convoluted ornamentation. Made from wooden spools, sections of branches, or pool cues, each ornament is attached with a single screw. For extra effect, the spools are decorated with bugs, lucky charms, small toys, and other tiny plastic objects. The story goes that Albino Carreira, author of the project, was incapacitated for many months healing a broken back after a 1993 fall from a scaffold. To while away the time, he designed a new mailbox so he wouldn't be disturbed by the sound of the old one clanging shut when the mail was delivered. Since surgical screws had saved Carreira's life, he decided to do something else with them. It all followed from there. He has also decorated his van to match, with spools on the roof rack and an arrangement of plastic bugs and lizards on the front. The City has officially recognized the Carreira residence as having the "Best Eccentric Garden" ... an understatement at best. As you might expect, his Christmas display is also formidable; recently it featured a Spider-Man theme.

Home is Where the Art is

Photo: Sarah B. Hood

Victorian homes and post-First World War cottages crowd the east end, but one colourful exception is 157 Coxwell Avenue. Forsaking bland brick for squares of violet and green plywood, the house hues were inspired by the Group of Seven. Designer Rohan Walters (*spacesbyrohan.com*) saw the colour scheme as a natural part of the landscape. Landscape influenced other aspects of the design. Built on soft, marshy ground, the three-storey, two-bedroom house sits on stilts to prevent sinking. Walters loves such a challenge. "We're not growing land in this city," he says. "Solutions sometimes scream for something original."

Living Lightly

The home of Peter Duckworth-Pilkington and Suzanne Cheng, situated in a laneway that runs south from Sproat Street near Jones and Gerrard, is a pioneer of environmental design principles. When the couple built the home, they had to make special arrangements at their own cost to ensure services that most urbanites take for granted, like mail, garbage, sewage, and water. To reduce building materials, they left some of the structural elements visible on the inside. The materials that they did use were carefully chosen; for instance, they avoided certain substances like PVC piping in favour of concrete slabs and galvanized steel that can someday be recycled. They also bought reused material whenever they could, and they even managed to use a bicycle cart for most of their lumber and scrapyard shopping. The house is already extremely energy-efficient, but Duckworth-Pilkington and Cheng are taking one more step to improve its insulation: they're planting live greenery on the roof.

IT'S NOT THE SIZE THAT COUNTS

Like a little irony? While building Casa Loma, the biggest house in town, many labourers lived nearby in tiny temporary houses. Bricklayer Stephen F. Barter lived at 643 Davenport Road with his wife and daughter. The house, no longer standing, was eight feet wide and in 1913 had an assessment value of $50.

Currently, the narrowest house in town stands at 383 Shuter Street. The lot is barely eight feet across and the house itself is not even that wide. The tiny east-end residence has been extended upwards to match the height of the more substantial red brick Victorian home next door. The exterior is clad in idiosyncratic weathered wood and the Hydro meter is whimsically enclosed behind a porthole.

Photo: Sarah B. Hood

Photo: Sarah B. Hood

Want to take a perfect souvenir-type snap of the city? We recommend the following vantage points:

- From the west: Descend the little-known wooden staircase into Fort York from the east side of Strachan, midway over the railway overpass. Continue walking east into the park, but not quite as far as the memorial wall. There's a perfect point where you get a stretch of grass, a wall of trees and, behind them, the downtown skyscrapers and the CN Tower. This location is best in midsummer when the trees are at their fullest. (You can also drive into Fort York and walk from its parking area to the same location.)

- From the east: Stand on the west side of Broadview between Danforth and Gerrard, at about the mid-point of the park where the ground is highest. You'll have a great vista that includes the park, the greenery of the Don Valley, and a wide swath of the downtown core. If you have the right equipment, this one's especially effective just after dusk with the vestiges of an ominous late fall sunset and the buildings lit from within. (At one time, this view was obstructed by a house-sized boulder, which was eventually broken up and removed as a Depression-era employment project.)

- From the waterfront: Take the ferry to Ward's Island and walk or cycle west for a few minutes (towards Centre Island). About 50 metres after you pass the arching bridge to Algonquin Island on your right, you'll spot the break between Algonquin and Snake Island. The placid waters of the lagoon and the foliage of the two neighbour islets perfectly frame a view of the city that includes the CN Tower and the SkyDome. An alternate: make your way to the end of the Leslie Spit (a.k.a. Tommy Thompson Park) for a less romantically framed but nonetheless impressive image of the waterfront.

IN THE STARS

The good folks at the Royal Astronomical Society inform us that Toronto is well represented in space: there are quite a few asteroids named for local celebs. First of all, there's one called "Toronto," discovered at the David Dunlap Observatory in 1963, which is 12 miles wide and orbits between Jupiter and Mars. As you might expect, most of the others are named after Toronto astronomers, but as of 1998 there's also an asteroid named in honour of Czech Canadian writer and University of Toronto professor Josef Skvorecky.

Transportation

We're a city on the move: we walk, bike, scoot, skate, taxi, TTC, and drive. A few of us regularly travel across the waters of Lake Ontario. Trains zoom in and out of Union Station all day, while airplanes and helicopters arrive and take off from three local airports. The life of this city has shaped and is shaped by our rivers, our roads, our train and trolley tracks, our bridges and tunnels, our parking lots, alleys, lanes, docks, driveways, stations, and terminals.

Photo: Courtesy Tourism Toronto

Lost Stations

The Bay subway station was originally conceived as a double-decker station like St. George, where two lines could intersect, so below the existing station there lies a complete second platform. Because Lower Bay Station was very briefly active when the Bloor line opened in 1966, it's completely equipped with signs, lights, tiled walls, and tracking. It's used all the time for movie shoots like *Johnny Mnemonic* and *Bulletproof Monk*, and television commercials like the one where the super heroine fights off the bad breath monster. The tracks through Lower Bay still link to the main line, and if you look out the front window of a subway train as it passes west out of the Bloor/Yonge station, you'll catch a glimpse of the unused station.

There's also an unfinished second level at the Queen station, where, it was once thought, Queen streetcars would connect underground with the subway system (something like the present arrangements at St. Clair West and Spadina). The idea of building a full-fledged Queen subway line that would intersect with the Yonge line has been aired from time to time, but not within the past 20 years, so Lower Queen waits, with bare concrete walls and no fixtures, unused.

Get It On Paper

City explorers don't have to chart any of this terrain; it's already been done.

• If it's public transit routes you're after, the TTC's **Ride Guide** is available at every subway station.

• The map of **Toronto Regional Parks and Trails** (that is, the Toronto Islands and the ravine systems) may be had from any community or civic centre.

• For **Toronto, Our City Our Park**, which shows urban parks, inquire at 416-392-1111.

• The Toronto City Cycling Committee (*416-392-7592, toronto.ca/cycling*) publishes a comprehensive **Toronto Cycling Map** listing trails and bike programs, available at bike shops, community centres, and civic centres.

• Mississauga's **Trails in Mississauga**, for hikers and cyclists, is available through *905-896-5042* or *city.mississauga.on.ca.*

• The map of all maps is probably **The Other Map of Toronto**, produced by the Green Tourism Association (*416-392-1288, greentourism.on.ca*). It lists a plethora of engaging activities, attractions, and resources – like arts and cultural events, heritage sites, and bike repair locations – all included because they tie in with the theme of urban green tourism.

GOING PLACES

More than 160,000 people commute into Toronto for work every day. For every thousand people who work in town, 650 drive to work (second lowest figure for any Canadian city, after Ottawa), 224 take public transit (more than any other Canadian city), 46 walk, and eight bike.

Photo: Courtesy Tourism Toronto

Photo: Courtesy Tourism Toronto

TUNNEL VISION

In 1911, city controller (later Mayor) Horatio Hocken stood up before the Board of Trade and advocated for a subway under Bay Street. "Toronto is notorious for postponing necessary improvements until the cost has doubled or tripled," he said. "A transit system must be built eventually." On election day, January 1, 1912, a public referendum voted against the proposed $5 million project. In 1954, the Yonge subway opened — at a cost of $67 million.

It's hard enough to understand the TTC public address system anyway, but what's up with those code numbers you hear all the time, as in "99 Bathurst, 99 Bathurst"? Here's an inquisitive commuter's guide to the most common calls:

40: Line Supervisor
42: Tower Supervisor
99: Subway Mechanic
199: 99's Supervisor
506: Janitors
520: Painters
606: Radio Crew
632: Signal Maintainers
653: Electrical Crew
721: Track Patrol
722: Track Lubricator
RT10: Garbage Car

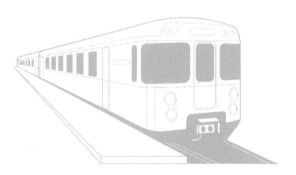

The TTC may be "The Better Way" to get around, but some of its routes don't go anywhere at all. At one time, Woodbine and Keele were the eastern and western terminals of the Bloor subway line. Passengers who wished to travel further connected with streetcars via long pedestrian tunnels in each station. When the Bloor line was extended, the tunnels were closed to the public, but they're still there. In Keele, there's still a doorway to the left of the staircase at the Indian Grove/Indian Road automatic entrance. Beyond the locked door is a people-moving ramp – turned off, naturally – that leads up to the walled-off area that was once the access to the streetcar platform. At Woodbine, part of the tunnel has become a staff room, and the rest is used for storage, although it still contains a staircase and phoneless telephone booths. The tiles have been torn out, and – as at Keele – the former access to the streetcar level is walled up.

BUSIEST TRANSIT ROUTES

According to the TTC's 2002 Service Reports, the top ten busiest buses and streetcars are:

1. 504 King/508 Lakeshore streetcars, with an average of 51,800 riders per weekday
2. 501 Queen streetcar (45,100)
3. 510 Spadina/509 Harbourfront streetcars (42,700)
4. 29 Dufferin bus (41,400)
5. 506 Carlton streetcar (41,200)
6. 36 Finch West bus (38,300)
7. 32 Eglinton West bus (37,400)
8. 25 Don Mills bus (36,700)
9. 505 Dundas streetcar (36,600)
10. 85 Sheppard East bus (36,500)

Belt Loops

Between 1884 and 1889, Toronto annexed the formerly independent villages of Rosedale, The Annex, Sunnyside, and Parkdale and, in the new metropolitan spirit, a rail line was launched to connect the city with the suburbs and the countryside. The bigger, eastern loop travelled from Union Station up the Don Valley to Winchester Street, northwest to Mount Pleasant Cemetery, then west along the south side of Merton Street. There it crossed Yonge via a wooden bridge, continuing northwest to Eglinton near Spadina Road, then west again before returning to Union Station on the tracks through Parkdale that are still in use. There was a smaller, western loop that left Union Station through Swansea, turning north in a ravine east of the Humber River, east at St. Clair, and back south again through Parkdale to Union Station.

In its day, the Belt Line charged five cents per station. It was a financial disaster, and closed in the fall of 1894, only two years and four months after it had opened. Its legacy to the city includes a nice recreational trail on the northeast leg of the route from Yonge to the Allen Road, the bridge at Yonge Street, and a station that still stands at Todmorden Mills. There's also some fun to be had by urban archaeologists who follow the missing section of track west from the end of the existing Beltline Trail. Although some parts have been completely swallowed by high-rise parking lots and suchlike, in many places you can still trace the route of this vanished urban railway.

EMPTIEST BUS

You can pretty much be sure of getting a seat on the 120 Calvington, which carries only 330 people a day — fewer than any other bus or streetcar.

Off Track, Part One

Union Station is many things: a transportation hub serving 35 million rail passengers a year; a marvel of Beaux Arts architecture; and a really expensive piece of real estate. All three factors can make for a very confusing future. Take the recent hullabaloo: in late 2001, the city received two proposals to redevelop Union on a 50-year lease with an additional 50-year option. After a secret review by city and federal bureaucrats, Union Pearson Group, an assemblage of money and planners with close ties to the Mayor's office, won the bid. In second place was LP Heritage + Union Station Consortium, which was said to have more vision but less cash. Critics cried foul and an independent review said the process, while not corrupt, should have been open to the public.

This isn't the first time the public has battled politicians over the fate of the station. In the early 1970s, city council deemed rail use to be on the way out and wanted to demolish Union to make way for new real estate deals. Folks kicked up such a fuss that the city trashed the plan, not the station.

BEGINNER'S LUCK

Toronto's first recorded automobile accident was a very close call indeed. A 1912 skid on a snowy road left a car with its front wheel hanging precariously over the edge of a 60-foot drop from the Rosedale Bridge. Luckily — and somewhat surprisingly — no one was hurt.

Photo: City of Toronto Archives, Fonds 1244, 62A

To the untrained eye, Union Station is a building both massive and stable. To the trained eye, however, it is anything but. Peter Duckworth-Pilkington has just such an eye and it has seen the station in ways most of us never will. As XAS Architects' project manager on the renovation of VIA Rail at Union, Duckworth-Pilkington has been exploring the station since October 2000. What he has seen is a place always in flux, a place where even large changes can get lost because of the sheer size of the building.

Take the pneumatic tubes that were part of the original station. Located behind the south side ticket counter where the baggage check used to be, the tubes haven't been used for decades, but the suction that made them work still operates because no one can locate the pump to turn it off. And then there's the sub-basement room with over 80 old-fashioned toilets and urinals. These curios were probably stashed away and forgotten when the station installed new ones. "It's like living with the worst pack rat in the world," says Duckworth-Pilkington.

How did all this happen? The explanation lies in ownership. Before the city took charge of the station, Union was co-owned by Canadian National and Canadian Pacific Railway. Neither company was big on communication, so layer upon layer was added without any cohesion. There's a room on the sixth floor, pitch black save for a single light bulb, that holds countless folders of uncatalogued architectural drawings.

ONLY THE NAMES HAVE BEEN CHANGED

While the subway system was being built, the TTC applied working names to each station, of which most were kept once the lines were opened to the public. A few never made it to ribbon-cutting day, however. Dundas West Station was originally conceived as "Vincent Station," Bay was "Yorkville," and Islington was "Montgomery." The Spadina line portion of the Spadina station was to be called "Lowther," while the portion on the Bloor line was to be "Walmer." Most recently, the Yonge stop on the new Sheppard line was referred to as "Princess" — for the late Princess Diana — during the building period, but when it opened officially it was christened with just the intersection name.

Expressing Stupidity, Part One

Take a walk through Forest Hill. Or the Annex. Or Chinatown. Three unique neighbourhoods, all nearly amputated by the proposed Spadina Expressway. Designed during the heyday of 1950s car culture, Spadina was one route in a planned system that would have carved up huge swaths of the city. The Cross Town, from the eastern curve of Davenport Road to the CPR tracks in the west, was one plan. So was the Christie-Grace extension, which was supposed to hook up with Highway 400.

Construction on the Spadina Expressway got as far south as Eglinton before grassroots opposition, led by urban planning's grande dame Jane Jacobs, grew too loud. On June 3, 1971, the Spadina Expressway was officially killed, much to the chagrin of Metro traffic commissioner Sam Cass, who had dreamed of transforming Toronto into a subway-free city like Detroit. Really.

Dangerous Crossings

Here are the ten most common sites of serious car crashes from the years 1999 to 2001, according to the Department of Works and Emergency Services.
1. Black Creek Dr. at Lawrence Avenue W., with 71 crashes from 1999 to 2001
2. Eglinton Ave. at Warden Ave. (61)
3. Kennedy Rd. at Sheppard Ave. E. (60)
4. Lawrence Ave. E. at Warden Ave. (59)
5. Ellesmere Rd. at Warden Ave. (58)
6. Lawrence Ave E. at McCowan Rd. (57)
7. Finch Ave.W. at Jane St. (55)
8. Lawrence Ave E. at Victoria Park Ave. (55)
9. Dufferin St. at Finch Ave.W. (55)
10. Markham Rd. at Progress Ave. (55)

TORONTO THE GOOD

Jacques Bergeron, a University of Montreal psychologist, studied pedestrian behaviour in Toronto and Montreal. He found that 90% of Toronto pedestrians obey traffic lights, compared to just 76% in Montreal. He also found that 86% use the crosswalks here, while only 65% of Montrealers follow suit.

Photo: Sarah B. Hood

Expressing Stupidity, Part Two

When the Expressway died, what was the fate of all that land? In the 1960s and 1970s, the city expropriated 112 properties to make way for the big road. Most of these were single-family homes, and the owners received fair market value. Jerome and Elaine Cooper, for example, were paid $50,000 for their Heathdale Road home in 1967. Several times they tried to buy it back, but the government adamantly said no sale. Until 1997, when all the properties went on the block. Asking price for Cooper's old home: $440,000.

CITY OF LIGHTS

The city's first traffic light was installed at the intersection of Yonge and Bloor Streets on August 8, 1925. Prior to this, police officers controlled traffic with hand-held stop signs. By 1928, 71 intersections had automatic traffic signals.

A Ride in the Country

Just west of Toronto lies a surprising sanctuary where the relics of a more gracious and gentle time are preserved and cared for. The Halton County Radial Railway, also known as Ontario's Operating Streetcar and Electric Railway Museum, is the retirement home for old trolley cars, including many from Toronto, along with rolling stock that ran through the streets of Hamilton, London, Oshawa, Cleveland, and Chicago. True to its name, the Radial Railway operates its collection on an oval track through its rural acreage. Visitors can board meticulously restored trains that date as far back as 1901 and ride sedately about the grounds, learning a proper appreciation of the particular voice of each car and the lustre of leather upholstery, brass fittings, and fine wood detailing. Special celebrations abound, including the annual Wildflower Weekend and December's Holly Trolley Rides.
13629 Guelph Line, Milton, 519-856-9802, hcry.org

Photo: Sarah B. Hood

When somebody needs an extra bike, but just
once in a while, **Bikeshare** (*101-761 Queen St. W.,
416-504-2918, bikeshare.org*) comes to the rescue.
An annual membership fee of $25 lets members have
their pick of the sunny yellow fleet of 150 basket-toting
cruisers, available at hubs around the downtown core.
When they're done, they just drop their temporary
steed off again. Each bike has its own distinctive,
hand-painted name – like Lemon Drop, Ganesh,
Froggi Eyes, Paris-Roubaix, The Winona Ryder, and
King of Kensington.

A similar (though unrelated) service exists for
cars. **Autoshare** (*24 Mercer St., 416-340-7888,
autoshare.com*) deploys 39 cars around town that
can be reserved for as little as an hour or as much as
several days. It's far cheaper than owning your own or
even renting. (A few years ago the TTC estimated that
it costs $4,022.51 to run a car for a year in Toronto.)
Autoshare requires a refundable deposit of $500. After
that, users are billed monthly for membership plus usage.
(One-day rental with less than 300 kilometres of driving
runs around $30, gas included.) Drivers can even pick
up a car in the middle of the night.

RIDE RUSTLERS

Toronto is informally known as the
Bike Theft Capital of North America.
The largest number of disappearances
are from porches and garages.

Photo: Sarah B. Hood

Sassy Mass

Photo: Pete Gray

BEST BIKE LANE FOR COASTING

Russell Hill Road, south of St. Clair. It's not only long and steep, but it's also really curvy!

Since May 1994, Toronto has had its own version of the global phenomenon called Critical Mass. It's a movement (or a party) that first started when a big group of San Francisco bike couriers decided to go somewhere together, all at the same time. They liked the feeling so much that they arranged to do it every month. First named Commuter Clot, it soon took on the more mellifluous moniker of Critical Mass and spread to dozens of cities around the world.

Essentially, Critical Mass is just a regular appointment for a bunch of cyclists – as many as 350 – to get together and ride around. There's no set route, although the group is usually willing to take suggestions. The reason? Well, that's pretty much summed up by the rallying cry "We're not stopping traffic; we *are* traffic!" Toronto cyclists can attend Mass at 6 p.m. on the last Friday of every month. The meeting place is Temperance Street, two blocks south of Queen between Yonge and Bay – coincidentally right outside the bar where the bike couriers like to stop off after work.

Bike messengers are the wheel heroes of urban commerce, and Toronto stands proudly in the active and tightly-knit international courier community. Some tidbits of messenger lore:

• Many of this city's 200 to 300 bike messengers have been riding for 8 to 12 years. It's normal for a rider to cover at least 100 kilometres on an average day. Most have no health insurance and are not paid for holidays or time between calls.

• The Toronto Environmental Alliance estimates that each full-time bike courier annually prevents 9.2 tonnes of carbon monoxide emissions, 322.8 kilograms of carbon monoxide, and 2.6 kilograms of sulphur dioxide.

• In courier slang, "The Dungeon" (a.k.a. "The Pit") is the shipping area at BCE Place, "road rash" is the result of skin sliding on asphalt, and a "door prize" is what you get when someone opens their car door without looking.

• The phenomenon of the "Alleycat" race began in Toronto and has spread all over the world. It can take many forms, but in its purest incarnation it consists of an after-dark race through the urban landscape, with the goal of being the fastest to complete an itinerary of checkpoints. Sometimes there are tasks to be accomplished, like swallowing an oyster at Rodney's, downing a beer on the patio of the Amsterdam, or collecting a specific bus transfer or shopping receipt.

EARLIEST BIKE LANES
By 1896, Toronto already had three-foot bike lanes on many streets, including Spadina, Arthur, Winchester, and Harbord.

• In 1995, Toronto was the first North American city to host the Cycle Messenger World Championships (after Berlin and London). Some 500 messengers from 15 countries competed on an urban racecourse created in the Liberty Village neighbourhood. (Some non-couriers may recall sighting a congenial Boston custom: a nude recreational ride of about two dozen bikers through the downtown core.) Toronto went on to host the 2nd North American Cycle Courier Championships in 1998.

• October 9 is Bike Messenger Appreciation Day in North America, and it's generally celebrated in Toronto with an official mayoral proclamation and a party. Some businesses augment the usual bowl of candy at the reception desk with treats like free whistles, muffins, tire patches, or water bottles. The date was chosen because, in radio jargon, "10-9" means "Huh?"

• Within the first ten years of its existence, two of our local messengers (Joe Hendry and Derek Chadbourne) have been honoured by the international community with the Marcus Cook Award for outstanding community service.

• Over seven years, messengers raised more than $20,000 for downtown social service agency St. Stephen's Community House with a competition pitting couriers against police and firefighters. Held behind College Park, the Courier Classic course included gravel paths, sections of the underground parking garage, and a terrifying finish down a flight of concrete steps.

FREE ENTERPRISE

Thornton Blackburn owned the first taxi in Toronto. He and his wife, Lucie, were escaped slaves from Kentucky who settled in Toronto in 1833. While working as a waiter at Osgoode Hall, Blackburn learned about a Hansom cab that was in use in Montreal. He acquired the building pattern and, in 1837, started up The City. The red-and-yellow, horse-drawn cab held four passengers.

Here are some devoted volunteer advocates of walking, biking, and public transit in Toronto. (Sadly, we don't know of any local support groups for motorists.)

• **Rocket Riders Transit Users Group** – named for the Red Rocket streetcars, of course – support more, better, cheaper public transit. Recently, with the help of the Rocket Riders, university and college student unions lobbied successfully for new, discounted transit passes for students. Their website includes songs by Stompin' Tom Connors and the Shuffle Demons inspired by the TTC. *201-30 Duncan St., 416-596-0660, rocketriders.org*

• **Advocacy for Respect for Cyclists (ARC)** speaks out for cyclists in Toronto. Iconoclastic, ironic, irreverent, and idiosyncratic, they're the folks who created parking meter parties (put the loonie in the meter to rent your party space and roll out the lawn chairs and canapes). They also stand up for cyclists who've been injured or unfairly charged, and their website is a treasure trove of useful resources.
101-761 Queen St. W., 416-504-2918 ext.1, respect.to

• Tireless former Public School Trustee Joan Doiron is the driving force behind **Feet on the Street** (*229 Brunswick Ave., 416-929-5483*), an advocacy group for pedestrians. One of the group's special interests is making the streets safe enough (from cars) for children to walk to school instead of being driven.

• The **Toronto Public Space Committee** (*416-838-9331, publicspace.ca*) isn't your average transportation lobby group. They focus on getting cars and corporate advertising out of public places, in favour of more freedom of passage and expression. They initiated a "TV Free Taxis" campaign, they fought the proposed ban on street postering, they superimposed hand-drawn art posters over streetside advertising, and they support guerrilla gardening initiatives, cargo bike delivery, and general fun in the streets.

I TOLL YOU SO

Lately, there's been some loose political talk of toll roads. Put one at the northern Don Valley Parkway and another at the western Gardiner Expressway so the out-of-towners can contribute a little coin to our fair city. This idea is nothing new. In the 19th century, tolls were all over town: Queen and Broadview; Avenue Road in the (then) town of Yorkville. Trouble ensued in 1890 when a group of farmers from nearby towns, upset with having to pay to bring their produce into town, attacked a tollhouse at Islington Avenue and Clarence Street, just north of the city. The tollkeeper returned fire, wounding several farmers and a handful of vegetables.

• The Toronto City **Cycling Committee** (*416-392-7592, city.toronto.on.ca/cycling*) was founded back in 1975; the **Pedestrian Committee** – which also addresses the needs of people with mobility devices, for example – is a much more recent fixture (*416-392-5230, city.toronto.on.ca/tpc*). The Cycling Committee co-ordinates the annual Bike Week; one of its many victories was getting the dangerous "tire-eater" style of sewer gratings replaced throughout the city. As for those on foot, in October 2002 no less a personage than renowned city planning visionary Jane Jacobs unveiled Toronto's Pedestrian Charter, founded on principles like Accessibility, Equity, and Environmental Sustainability. Vacancies on both committees are publicly advertised, and non-members are welcome to audit meetings or to request that a certain item be included in the agenda.

CLOSE CALL FOR ASHBRIDGE'S BAY

In April of 1957, the federal government received five recommendations for potential locations of Toronto's new international airport, including Hanlan's Point, Ashbridge's Bay, the Eastern Gap, and the Dufferin/Wilson neighbourhood. Luckily for fans of the waterfront, the feds picked the fifth suggestion, its present site in Malton, for the home of Lester B. Pearson International.

Photo: Ontario Tourism, 12217

Ask What Your City Can Do for You

It's hard enough just getting around town without getting tripped up by the roads themselves. So ...

• If your street needs cleaning, you can call the City of Toronto Street Cleaning hotline at 416-39-CLEAN.

• When a yawning pothole appears on your morning commute route, you can get it fixed by reporting it to 416-392-7737.

• If the snowplows have forgotten your street, contact 416-338-SNOW (or 416-392-7737 for bike lanes), but don't make the call until at least 12 hours after the snowfall has ended or you won't get much attention.

• Do you think the City should install one of those post-and-ring bike parking stands? You have but to ask. (About 300 new ones are installed each summer.) Download a form to request one at *city.toronto.on.ca/cycling/postandring.htm*. For more information, or to report a damaged post-and-ring, call 416-39-CYCLE.

Waterworld

There's a surprisingly large choice of ways to ply the waters of Toronto Bay.

• Most people don't realize that they're not bound by the ferry schedule if they're willing to pay a bit more for water taxi service between the mainland and the islands. You call 416-203-TAXI to meet a small boat at a location like Harbourfront, The Docks nightclub, Ontario Place, or one of the island yacht club docks. It's a $24 flat fee for up to four people, or $6 per person for larger groups.

• Several competing services run short harbour tours. They cater to tourists, so the first quoted price may sound a little high. Comparison shopping is recommended, and bargaining is allowed, especially if it's a quiet day and you're with a few other people. To find the boats, simply walk along the shoreline near Harbourfront.

• **Hippo Tours** (*416-703-4476, torontohippotours.com*) runs the amphibious Hippo Boat. It tours the streets, then drives right into the water to tour the harbour. And it looks like a hippo. You've gotta love that.

• The charter companies operate longer cruises with dining and dancing. Many are booked by groups, but **Toronto Dinner Cruises** (*416-777-5777, torontodinnercruises.com*) runs special events like Mother's Day brunch tours and Air Show dinner cruises in the $50 to $100 per person range. **Great Lakes Schooner Company** (*416-260-6355, greatlakesschooner.com*)

FLYING LOW

The Toronto Island Airport has always had an uneasy relationship with its neighbours. In 1938, a small residential community was razed to make way for the federally-operated terminal and ever since there have been disputes over noise and air pollution. In 1982, the city and the feds signed a 50-year deal to lessen the impact on locals, banning commuter bridges and big commercial jets. Those limits were good for the people, but bad for the airport, which has lost millions annually. So the feds put the pressure on and, in fall 2002, city council approved construction of a bridge and new terminal, called Toronto City Centre Airport.

Now, a local group called CommunityAIR is involved. They say expansion, which will mean jets buzzing overhead every three minutes, will ruin waterfront revitalization and diminish prospects for the thousands of apartments ready to spring up in the area. Things got even more confusing in spring 2003, when the airport's biggest commercial tenant, Air Canada Jazz, cancelled all service to Montreal and London, Ontario. Seems some ideas were never meant to fly.

Photo: City of Toronto Archives, Fonds 1244, 261

FLYING LOWER

It was a joyous act of synergy. Roots Canada, the hip clothing company, got into bed with Skyservice Investments, and ba-boom, Roots Air was born. The plans called for Skyservice to operate the new airline while Roots would add a little style to their substantial investment. The food would be good, the leg room generous, and the Roots beaver would adorn every seat. "This is the perfect time to take Roots Canada's style to national and international skies," said Roots cofounder Michael Budman. Alas, their timing was off. Skyservice got involved with Air Canada and Roots Air was officially grounded in early May, 2001. Total flying time? One month.

has some of the best boats, including the three-masted schooners *Kajama* and *Challenge*, and the original *Trillium*. (Built in 1910 as an island ferry, the *Trillium* is the only real steam-powered, side-paddled ferry still working in North America. From 1956 to 1976 it was left to rot, but it's been beautifully restored, largely thanks to the efforts of historian Mike Filey.)

• In the '20s, you could run by steam to Kingston or Montreal, but these days there's only one option for water travelers: **Seaflight Hydrofoils** (*416-504-8825, seaflights.com*), which zips over to Niagara Falls via Port Dalhousie. Their ticket office is at 109-249 Queen's Quay West, and boarding is at 339 Queen's Quay West, behind Fire Station No. 9. (They take bikes, so it's a great way to start a cycling holiday.)

Go Leafs go. There. We said it. But even though Toronto is a hockey town, that doesn't mean we're without any other contenders. Take a gander at our kick-ass lacrosse team or our own honest-to-goodness Rock Paper Scissors champion. And if you prefer the great outdoors, well, we have more green space than you can shake a stick at.

The Name Game

Photo: Ontario Tourism, 10155

Eddie Livingstone is the forgotten man in hockey history. He single-handedly established a puck presence in this town before being shunted aside by a group of Montreal-based hockey magnates. In 1912, the National Hockey Association included the Montreal Canadiens, Montreal Wanderers, Ottawa Senators, and Quebec Bulldogs. Then came the Toronto Blueshirts and Toronto Tecumsehs. The Tecumsehs changed names (to Ontarios) and owners the following season and again in 1914, when Livingstone bought them and called them the Shamrocks. But he didn't stop there; prior to the 1915-16 season, he also bought the Blueshirts. The other owners cried foul, so Livingstone folded the Shamrocks and sent the best players to his Blueshirts. Again, the other owners cried foul, and found a creative form of revenge. Resigning from the NHA, they regrouped, minus Livingstone, as the National Hockey League. A Toronto team, stocked with out-of-work Blueshirt players, was established in the old Mutual Street Arena. The "Arenas," as they were called, actually won the Stanley Cup that year. In 1919 they became the St. Patricks and finally, in 1926, the now-familar Maple Leafs.

And Livingstone? He bounced around a number of lesser leagues before his death on September 11, 1945. Buried in Mount Pleasant Cemetery, he left no wife, no children, and a bank balance of $32.49.

A Tale of Two Sites

It's a short walk from Carlton Street to Bay Street. But it's a long way. In February 1999, Maple Leaf Gardens made way for the Air Canada Centre, ending a 68-year-old local love affair. The Gardens was built in a miraculous five-and-a-half months during the Great Depression (one of the row houses razed for construction, 52 Carlton, used to be a brothel) and, after 2,533 hockey games, it has been called the city's truest shrine. Sadly, not much is up there these days except a million-dollar-a-year property tax bill. The Gardens is, however, unofficially up for sale, with the stipulation that the lovely Art Deco exterior be maintained.

One of the charms of the Air Canada Centre is its connection to the past. Built on the site of the old Canada Post Delivery Building, the ACC retained the east and south walls of the original façade and built the new arena around them. During construction, workers were surprised to find a narrow, hidden hallway around the perimeter of the building. There were even eyeholes in the walls (and outside the ladies' washroom), leading some to suspect management used the secret route to spy on employees. More traditional sightlines come from the 20,000-seat arena. And even though the ACC hasn't recorded as many hockey games as the Gardens, there is one statistic that won't (we hope) be broken: 200 pounds of nacho cheese "sauce" are used during every game.

LAST DOWN

When Dick Shatto died of lung cancer on February 4, 2003, he had one last request. The former Argo running back, who retired in 1965 with a team-record 91 touchdowns, wanted to be cremated and have his ashes scattered on the grounds of old Exhibition Stadium. Even though the stadium had been torn down years earlier, Shatto drew a map and marked his final resting place with an X.

Don't be surprised if you hear the echo of a ghostly cheer rise up some day as you stroll along Mutual Street. That was the site of the old Mutual Street Arena, a vanished beacon of Canadian culture. Open from 1912 to 1989, it stood on the site of 60 Mutual, at Shuter Street, and could seat 8,000. It was home ice for a series of Toronto hockey teams from 1917 to 1931. The legendary Foster Hewitt broadcast his first game from the arena by telephone on March 22, 1923, and in 1925, the inaugural service of the United Church of Canada was held there. When Glenn Miller made his first visit to Toronto in 1942, he sold the space out. However, its era eventually passed away; it was kept in use as a roller rink until the '70s and is now mostly forgotten, although a brick from the now-demolished building is on display at the Esso Maple Leaf Memories and Dreams Room at the Air Canada Centre.

MUSH, MUSH

Long before the Raptors came to town, local hoops fans had to make do with the Huskies. An inaugural member of the Basketball Association of America (forerunner to today's National Basketball Association), the Toronto team took to the court against the New York Knickerbockers on November 1, 1946, which they lost, 68-66. A close game and an encouraging start, but the Huskies would often be on the losing side of the scoreboard during those first few games. Things got even worse ten games into the season, when player-coach Ed Sadowski missed a game. Then another. The sports pages said it was just an injury, but it seems the 6'5" Sadowski had already seen enough. He had walked away from the team in frustration. But what Big Ed lacked in commitment, he more than made up for with foresight: the Huskies went through three more coaches and several losing streaks, finishing the season tied for last place with a record of 22 wins and 38 losses. The team folded after that year.

A Good Sport

Photo: Courtesy Canada's Sports Hall of Fame

Lionel Conacher may have been the best athlete this city has ever seen. The "Big Train" played baseball with the Maple Leafs, lacrosse with the Maitlands, and hockey with the Montreal Maroons. He won the Canadian light heavyweight boxing championship in 1920 and scored three touchdowns for the Argos in the 1921 Grey Cup game.

Later, he moved into politics. As a Liberal MPP for Bracondale in the late 1930s, he was rumored to be the bagman for the big casino owners in town, collecting payoffs and distributing them to the higher-ups. In 1954, Conacher was a federal politician, playing in the annual softball game between MPs and the press. In the sixth inning, he hit a flyball to left field, legged out a triple, and collapsed from a fatal heart attack.

When Harold Ballard took control of the Maple Leafs in 1961, it was the beginning of the end. Penny-pinching ways, boorish behaviour, and an utter disregard for knowledgeable hockey people turned the once-proud franchise into a national joke. Still, as bad as the team was, the off-ice antics were even worse....

• After the death of his wife Dorothy in 1969, Ballard moved out of his Etobicoke home into a second-floor studio apartment in Maple Leaf Gardens. Now, he was free to harass employees around the clock and ride the Zamboni naked at all hours of the night.

• Gerry McNamara, Ballard's most fallible general manager, lost plenty of hockey games, but he was a winner in the courts. After a car accident left him with reduced cognitive abilities, Big Mac successfully sued the other driver in 1984. The next day's headlines read, "McNamara Proves He's Brain-Damaged." For many Leaf fans, this was not news.

• Ballard's girlfriend later in life was an ex-con named Yolanda MacMillan. She was often in the news in the 1980s, whether it was for assaulting a Gardens employee or hustling a dying Hal off to the Cayman Islands for a quickie wedding. One of the strangest moments in their long on-again, off-again relationship occurred near the end of Ballard's life: as he became more and more infirm, Yolanda began to lose her grip; claiming Ballard's son, Bill, was pumping poison into Maple Leaf Gardens, Yolanda was often seen around the arena in a gas mask.

THE SULTAN'S FIRST SWAT

Most people know that Babe Ruth hit a lot of home runs. In fact, he totalled 714 in his big-league career. But before he was a star, Ruth pitched for Providence of the International League. On September 5, 1914, Providence played Toronto at the old Maple Leaf Stadium at Hanlan's Point. The Babe tossed a one-hittter as his team beat Toronto 9-0. He also did his job with the bat, hitting a three-run homer off Ellis Johnson that landed in Lake Ontario. It was the Babe's first professional home run.

Grace Under Pressure

He may have been a flash in the pan, but his name still lingers in the memory. Of all the athletes in Hogtown history, none has the ring of Frank "Ulcers" McCool. When the Maple Leafs' regular goalie, Turk Broda, went off to war during the 1944-45 season, McCool stepped in. Despite his surname, poor Frank was often ill at ease; he'd sip milk in the dressing room to calm his nervous stomach, sometimes throwing up between periods. On the ice, though, he was cool as a McCucumber. After winning Rookie of the Year honours during the regular season, McCool led the Leafs to a Stanley Cup victory; he shut out the Detroit Red Wings in three consecutive games to establish a league record and quickly became the toast of the town. His success, however, was short-lived. Turk Broda returned the next season and McCool moved to the bench. When the 1945-46 season ended, McCool called it a career. He returned to his native Alberta and found work at the *Calgary Albertan*, eventually working his way up to publisher. McCool died May 20, 1973. Cause of death? Stomach ulcers, naturally.

She Shoots, She's Scorned

Considering the Hockey Hall of Fame is hallowed by history, it's a little surprising to learn the place is haunted. Equally surprising is who does the haunting. We're not talking the ghost of King Clancy here, but rather a young woman named Dorothy. See, the lovely Beaux Arts building at the northwest corner of Yonge and Front Streets has not always been home to the Hall of Fame. From 1847 to 1983, this was a branch of the Bank of Montreal. Dorothy, a teller at the turn of the last century, was lively and smiling; the most popular girl at the bank. She was especially popular with the bank manager, with whom she was having an affair. When word of their relationship leaked out, Dorothy became distraught. She came to work early one morning, locked herself in the second floor washroom, and shot herself in the head with the bank pistol.

Not long after, bank employees started to notice the lights flicking on and off. Locked doors were found to be mysteriously open. Dorothy was even seen on the second floor balcony. These sightings have continued over the years, even with the building's new inhabitants. We hope Dorothy is a hockey fan.

HIT MAN

Hall of Fame slugger Dave Winfield will always be remembered in these parts for helping the Blue Jays win the 1992 World Series. But his biggest hit came nine years earlier. Winfield, then a member of the New York Yankees, was warming up his arm in right field at old Exhibition Stadium. Just before the bottom of the fifth inning, he threw a one-hopper towards the Yankee bullpen, but the ball struck and killed a seagull. Constable Wayne Hartey was on hand to charge the big outfielder with animal cruelty. After posting $500 cash bail, Winfield said: "I'm just sorry the national bird of Canada no longer exists."

Field of Dreams

In 1985, city workers paved over a dead-end street called Baseball Place. The tiny laneway, on the southwest corner of Queen Street and Broadview Avenue, accommodated only six houses, but plenty of history: almost a century earlier, this was the entrance to the Toronto Baseball Grounds, the first ballpark in town. Built in 1886, the Grounds seated 2,250 people and charged 25 cents admission. A few years later, the name was changed to Sunlight Park, because of its proximity to the Sunlight Soap Works.

Hogtown's first baseball hero was Edward "Cannonball" Crane. In 1887, the 24-year-old won 33 games and hit .428. Then he pitched both ends of a championship doubleheader against Newark. Game One was an easy 15-5 victory; in Game Two, Cannonball blasted an 11th-inning homer to give Toronto a 5-4 win and the International League crown. This was the highlight of Cannonball's career. He bounced around a number of New York towns after that – Providence, Rochester, Springfield – before committing suicide in 1896, the same year Sunlight Park shut down.

And in This Corner ...

Boxing and Cabbagetown go way back. At the Canadian National Exhibition Coliseum on November 28, 1927, local boy Albert "Frenchy" Belanger beat Frankie Genaro to win the National Boxing Association's flyweight championship. Three weeks later, the 5'4" Frenchy returned to a sellout crowd at the CNE and beat British fighter Ernie Jarvis to become the undisputed world champ. Alas, his reign was a short one. Frenchy lost a rematch with Genaro the following February and was never a contender again.

History repeated itself in the next century, however, when Lisa "Bad News" Brown beat Leona Brown for the International Women's Boxing Federation bantamweight crown. "Bad News Brown," who lives in Scarborough but trains at the Cabbagetown Boxing Centre, has held title defences several times since and has threatened to retire if she can't find a worthy opponent.

BATS AND BALLS

Baseball at SkyDome has always been full of action. Like the game against Boston on May 12, 1996, when sharp-eyed fans caught a couple having sex in the window of SkyDome hotel room 43. Or a game against Seattle, five years earlier, when another amorous pair engaged in a very public display of affection. And six weeks before that, a lone man was seen masturbating, but got off (pardon the pun) after telling police he thought the window was one-way glass and no one would see him.

Photo: City of Toronto Archives, Fonds 1244, 8202

COME OUT FIGHTING

Boxing has a long history of strange moments. One of the strangest took place at the Royal York Hotel in January 1970. Welterweights Clyde Gray and Humberto Trottman were slugging it out in a close fight, with a lot of work in the clinches. Local referee Sammy Luftspring was constantly separating the two fighters. Trottman didn't like being pulled away and, just before the start of the sixth round, he threw a right hook at the ref's head. Luftspring, a 54-year-old former welterweight champion, slipped the punch and replied with a quick combination of his own. Both corners rushed into the ring, trying to restore order. When the dust finally cleared, Gray was declared the winner, Trottman was suspended, and Luftspring went down in history as the only referee to score a TKO.

Lacrosse has a longer history in these parts than any other sport, but it never seems to get much attention. Played by the Iroquois over 350 years ago, lacrosse is the game for those who think hockey is too soft. That little rubber ball is thrown at speeds topping 200 kilometres per hour, twice as fast as one of those piddly pucks. And whereas cross-checking will get you two minutes (minimum) in an NHL penalty box, lacrosse players view it as standard defensive procedure.

Despite their dalliances with speed and violence, players are just folks. With an average salary of US$15,000, most of them work full-time jobs as teachers or firefighters. And most important of all: our team wins. The Toronto Rock won four National Lacrosse League championships in five years, from 1999 to 2003.

Lords of the Ring, Part One

Toronto has had its share of heavyweights (literally and figuratively) in the larger-than-life world of pro wrestling. Born William Potts on June 25, 1915, Whipper Billy Watson was one of the greatest ever to step into the ring. Always a good guy who played by the rules, he was a constant crowd favourite who got his nickname from a move in which he would "whip" another wrestler up onto his powerful shoulder – simultaneously knocking the breath out of his opponent. One of his signal moments of glory came when he defeated the reviled Gorgeous George, forcing the dandified villain to shear his long blond locks. Out of the ring, Whipper Billy Watson was as much a hero as he was in it, using his fame to support charities serving people with disabilities. He was greatly mourned when a heart attack took him to that big ring in the sky in January 1990, and on February 4 of that year the Maple Leaf Gardens ring bell was sounded ten times in a solemn memorial during a WWF (now WWE) Hulkmania matinee.

Lords of the Ring, Part Two

If Whipper Billy Watson was loved by the fans, the mysterious Masked Marvel was hated in equal measure. Wearing his signature hood, which concealed all his features except his eyes, he won the American Wrestling Association Championship title in 1938 (the organization was a precursor to today's WWE). An object of particularly vitriolic dislike, he prevailed against many favourites. Always they would try to unmask him, but always he escaped from the ring with his identity still unknown. Speculation grew until some Toronto wrestling fans might not have been surprised if Hitler himself had been the figure beneath the mask. Finally, the fateful day came when the Marvel's mask was torn from his face and the momentous announcement was made that "Ladies and Gentlemen, the Masked Marvel is … *King Kong Cox*?" Somehow, despite the impressive nickname, Ted Cox just didn't command the same evil glamour without his mask.

A HANDY SPORT

Want to try your hand at a new sport? How about Rock, Paper, Scissors? In November 2002, the first-ever world championship was held in Toronto. Local boy Pete Lovering beat Moe Asem in the best-of-five final, with a winning combination of Paper, Rock, Rock.

The World Rock Paper Scissors Society (*worldrps.com*) promotes the game as both a competitive sport and an everyday decision-making tool. According to Doug Walker, managing director of World RPS, a successful strategy is based more on a fast mind than a fast hand. You need to know your opponents well enough to either predict the next throw or force them into a poor throw. "It's kind of like chess," he says. Beginners will often open with Rock, the most aggressive throw. More advanced players prefer the subtlety of Paper. Then there is the gambit, a series of three, pre-planned, successive moves that eliminate any need for last minute decision-making.

Lords of the Ring, Part Three

Toronto's still turning out pros. Among the facilities for those who see themselves as the next Bret Hart are **Sully's Gym** (*416-719-2337, wrestlingtraining.com*) and the **Squared Circle Pro Wrestling Gym** (*416-236-3980*).

CHECKMATE

For thirty years, local chess players always knew where the action was: the corner of Yonge and Gould Streets, right beside Sam the Record Man's flagship store. No matter the hour, hustlers were always ready for a game. That's how it's been since the early 1970s, when players used to set up folding tables to take on all comers. In 1979, the city installed ten permanent tables. The corner was eventually named Hacksel Place, in memory of regular player Al Hacksel, who died in 1994.

But in the spring of 2003, Sam the Record Man announced renovation plans, with the idea of adding an entrance off Gould Street. The city has offered to move the chess tables to the southwest corner of Nathan Phillips Square, but the players are not happy. Of course not: chess players never like to move before they're ready.

Bullseye!

To pub regulars throughout Britain, Holland, and Australia, John Part – a.k.a. "Darth Maple" – is a formidable character. The Toronto native and Oshawa resident is a champion darts player on the PDC (Professional Darts Corporation) circuit, and well-known as a top darts pundit on the BBC. A graduate of the posh Upper Canada College, Part has been making a living by throwing darts for nearly 10 years. In 2003, he beat Brit Phil Taylor to win the World Champion title (which Taylor had held for an eight-year run). It was a match-up that some aficionados consider the greatest darts final of all time. Part still plays around his home turf; you'll periodically catch him in tournament action at establishments like the Unicorn Pub (*175 Eglinton Ave. E.*) and The Sailor's Dickey (*3391 Yonge St.*).

We Are Champions!

Since local rooters represent over 100 different ethnic backgrounds, World Cup soccer time can make Toronto a confusing place. Spontaneous and not-so-spontaneous post-game celebrations always occur and it's a good idea to make certain you're in the right neighbourhood. The first big celebration came in 1982, when an estimated 200,000 crowded the Dufferin and St. Clair area to cheer Italy's big win. When France beat Brazil in 1998, cars honked up and down Yonge Street, flashing *le bleu, blanc, et rouge*. However, the Brazilians decided to party anyway, so their screaming fans packed the intersection at College Street and Ossington Avenue. Not to be outdone, South Korean fans filled the Bathurst and Bloor neighbourhood when their team went on its surprising run in 2002. Because the games were in another time zone, they cheered twice: once when the game was played live and again when the taped version was over.

Photo: Ontario Tourism 10172

Many a sound sailor and oarsman has learned their craft on the waters of Toronto Bay. The most famous of these, of course, is champion rower Ned Hanlan, who in 1880 was the subject of a $500,000 bet when he bested Australian world champion Edward Trickett on the Thames. (Nicolas Cage played Hanlan in a 1986 film called *The Boy in Blue*.)

Brothers Terry and Frank McLaughlin learned to race sailboats at the Royal Canadian Yacht Club on the Toronto Islands. In 1984, Terry won a silver medal at the L.A. Olympics competing in the Flying Dutchman class, and Frank won a bronze in the same class in Seoul in 1988. Another fellow who acquired his sailing chops at the RCYC is championship sailor Paul Henderson (not the hockey player). He competed in the Tokyo and Mexico City Olympics and won international championships; now he makes waves in the top echelons of international sport as an IOC member and president of the International Sailing Federation.

Another Islander, Tom Butscher, is a former Canadian champion speed skater, but he's better known these days as the man who likes to row across Lake Ontario, a feat he's accomplished five times. Butscher, who uses his excursions to raise money for various good causes, is the first person known to have done the 100-kilometre double crossing from Ward's Island to Port Dalhousie and back. It took him a total of 13 hours and 42 minutes, including a rest stop of about one hour. Using a 20-foot racing boat, he prefers to make the crossings at night when the lake is calm. Understandably; on his first attempt at the double crossing, he was overwhelmed by water and had to abandon his boat. (It was later retrieved by the coast guard. Butscher was retrieved by his escort boat.) The determined 60-year-old is now considering a 320-kilometre, five-day jaunt from Hamilton to Kingston.

STINK OR SWIM

It's a Toronto tradition. Every summer, thousands flock to the city beaches for fun, sun, and ... no swimming. Residents long raised on bacterial horror stories dare to dip only a toe in the water. And the lake's unpleasant aroma does nothing to dispel those myths. But the truth is the city has been working to improve water quality for almost thirty years. In 2002, engineers installed three huge, underground holding tanks that intercept and treat the contaminated pipe water. The cost? Only $100 million or so. The result? Mixed. While the eastern beaches were open for swimming most of that summer, ones on the west, such as Sunnyside and Gzowski Park, were closed. Let's see what another thirty years will do.

Photo: Ontario Tourism 10183

Peek-à-Boo

Nothing makes his heart beat faster than those three little words: Do Not Enter. For Ninjalicious, this means the start of another adventure. The self-proclaimed urban explorer has wandered through the back rooms and hidden corridors of many a local landmark: City Hall. Union Station. The abandoned subway station Lower Bay. One of his favourites is the Royal York Hotel because of "the tremendous distinctions between its ritzy outward appearance and its vast, dirty, and chaotic hidden spaces." As nattily-dressed as any other guest, Ninj (*nom de plume* for this unassuming, late 20-ish office worker) worked his way from two basement levels all the way up to the 26th level rooftop.

He records all his findings in his zine, *Infiltration* (*infiltration.org*), and provides a space for like-minded urban explorers. Circulation of the zine has gone from 200 in 1996 to 2,000 in 2003, making Ninjalicious a leader in the community. His advice to rookies? Don't steal, don't vandalize. Just look around. If you get caught, be honest and say you were just curious.

Or run like hell.

SICK SKATE SITES

Rippers seeking to work on their flips and grinds will likely find themselves checking out the small but well designed indoor skatepark **Shred Central**, co-owned by Jamer and former Dayglo Abortions member Jimbo (*19 St. Nicholas St., 416-923-9842, shredcentral.com*). Outdoors, there's the free **Cummer Skateboard Park** (*6000 Leslie St.*), which reportedly boasts decent stairs, railings, and curbs, but is not lit at night. Now under construction is a new skatepark at Lawrence and Port Union roads in Rouge Hill, designed by the revered Jim Barnum of Vancouver's Spectrum Park Creations.

Only Lion-Hearts Need Apply

Lacking a little adrenaline in your life? Well, there's plenty of ways to get those glands going. Try the **Parachute School of Toronto** (*800-361-5867, parachuteschool.com*), which, at the Baldwin Airport south of Lake Simcoe, is actually about 40 minutes north of Toronto. But don't let that distance worry you because the 2,800-foot jump out of a plane is the real doozy.

If you prefer something a little closer to the ground, how about trying the trapeze? (Okay, we didn't say all the way on the ground.) You can take a flying leap with the **Toronto School of Circus Arts** (*425 Wellington St. W., 416-935-0037, torontocircus.com*). Located in the old press hall at the *Globe and Mail* building, the school offers a flying trapeze drop-in class every Friday night for $20.

And if that's still too high, plant your feet firmly on the ground at **Sgt. Splatter's Project Paintball** (*54 Wingold Ave., 416-781-0991, sgtsplatters.com*). With its bombed-out buildings and splashy lighting, this indoor arena looks like a movie set. Which it should, since it was created by a set designer.

Photo: Sarah B. Hood

Perhaps you've wondered about those odd-looking installations scattered about the lawns adjacent to the roadway on Ward's Island, something like short metal maypoles with chains dangling to a sort of basket attachment. Those are part of the renowned **Toronto Island Disc Golf** course. Like golf, the game involves a progression from station to station, with competing players attempting to net their flying disks instead of sinking a ball in a cup. There are about 1,400 disc golf courses in the world – of which just under 50 are in Canada. They're used by an avid pro and amateur circuit; the regulating body for all of North America is the **Professional Disc Golf Association** (*5 Dacotah Ave., 416-203-9628, pdga.com*), which is, at the time of writing, located in Toronto, but slated to move to much fancier digs in Georgia. Meanwhile, anyone who's interested can try out the Ward's Island course (being careful not to intrude on an organized competition if one is in progress). It starts next to the fire hall, about a ten-minute walk west of the Ward's Island ferry docks. Those who'd like to get involved officially can call 416-203-7181 to find out about rules and competitions. The two other courses in the Toronto area are in **Etobicoke Centennial Park** off Centennial Park Boulevard, south of Pearson Airport and at **Bronte Creek Provincial Park**. Toronto Island and Etobicoke have been in place since 1980; they were among the first 50 courses in the world.

Greening Your Thumb

Photo: Sarah B. Hood

Even when confined to a window box, we Torontonians love to get our hands into the soil for as much of our short Zone 6b growing season as possible. For some, it's a hobby; for others, one step towards fixing what's wrong with the world.

Civic Garden Centre

This underused facility holds numerous special events and some 7,000 gardening books, all available for loan to the public. You can call them to ask advice from a Master Gardener at 416-397-1345. *777 Lawrence Ave. E., 416-397-1340, infogarden.ca*

Composting Help Line

When your waste ain't wasting away, call the City of Toronto at 416-392-4689.

Cycle Central

Photo: Ontario Tourism, 10200

FoodShare

FoodShare was founded in 1985 to investigate solutions to the growing demand for food banks. Now they spread urban food growing lore and live plants throughout the city. Besides holding their own sale of edible and native plants in early May, they sponsor the **Toronto Community Garden Network**, which links over 100 community garden projects around the city. TCGN hosts a Seedy Saturday on the first Saturday in March to let gardeners buy and trade seeds, especially edible, wild, native, and heritage varieties. *238 Queen St. W., lower level, 416-392-6653, foodshare.net*

North American Native Plant Society

The NANPS exists to conserve and inform people about native species. They organize volunteers to go in ahead of the bulldozers to rescue and relocate plants from areas under development, and they hold an exciting early May plant sale every year. *416-680-6280, nanps.org*

In 1995, *Bicycling Magazine* named Toronto as North America's best city for cycling. About 900 recreational riders are members of the **Toronto Bicycling Network** *(416-760-4191, tbn.on.ca)*, which runs touring rides of 20 to 200 kilometres and some mountain biking excursions. Mountain bikers don't need a club to take advantage of the **Don Trails**, about 20 kilometres of challenging terrain right in the city, the **Rouge Valley** in Pickering, or the **Albion Hills Conservation Area** north of Bolton *(416-667-6299, trca.on.ca)*, with 19 kilometres of trails. Those of a more competitive bent can travel short distances to race in popular offroad events like the **Uxbridge Icebreaker** *(905-852-5544, bikenxs.com)* — an early spring race that all too often literally lives up to its name — and the ever-popular **24 Hours of Adrenalin** *(905-944-9436, 24hoursofadrenalin.com)*, in which teams, or insane solo riders, race to complete the most laps of a wooded course in one nonstop day. It's part of a North American series, of which only four races are held in Canada: two out west, one in Milton's Kelso Conservation Area (June), and one in Barrie's Halton Hills (August). The **Ontario Cycling Association** *(416-426-7242, ontariocycling.org)* is the regulatory body for sport racing and a great source of information about road, track, and offroad events.

Photo: Ontario Tourism, 2590

Joe Rockhead's Climbing Gym Ltd. (*29 Fraser Ave., 416-538-7670, joerockheads.com*) was the first in North America, and is still largest the in Toronto. Their clientele ranges from kids and beginners to the truly hardcore. Some of the establishments that turned up later are **Toronto Climbing Academy** (*100A Broadview Ave., 416-406-5900, climbingacademy.com*), **The Rock Oasis** (*27 Bathurst St., 416-703-3434, rockoasis.com*), and **Equinox Adventures** (*5334 Yonge St., 416-222-2223, equinoxadventures.com*). Once a new climber has a grip on the basics, they might want to join the Toronto Section of the **Alpine Club of Canada** (*905-277-5287, climbers.org*) to find out about climbing the excellent rises in the Toronto region, many of which are along the Niagara Escarpment. **Rattlesnake Point**, only about 45 minutes out of town, is a crowded crag, but often used by beginners. The more extensive **Mount Nemo** is not too much farther, but often much less crowded. In comparison, the challenging **Lion's Head** in Tobermory is much farther away – about 3½ hours north of the city – but many experienced climbers consider it a top location.

Richters

Budding herbalists will relish a visit to Richters greenhouse, about an hour out of the downtown core, to choose from among hundreds of types of herb seeds or plantlets. They handle mail and online orders too. *Goodwood, 905-640-6677, richters.com*

Royal Botanical Gardens

This world renowned facility just outside Hamilton operates a hotline for gardening advice (*905-527-8938, ext. 226, grow@rbg.ca*), while their volunteer Auxiliary runs a sensational plant sale in early May and a spring flowering bulb sale in June. *680 Plains Rd. W., Burlington, 905-825-5040, rbg.ca*

YouGrowGirl.com

Perhaps the liveliest garden information source is this chatty and unconventional Toronto-based website for plant lovers at all levels.

Early Bloomers

Fashion in flowerbeds is as volatile as in any other area, and this city has seen the blossoming and dying off of many horticultural trends. But you can still visit the gardens of the past, at Black Creek Pioneer Village, of course, and at these lesser known locations:

Spadina Historic House and Gardens

This is the biggie, maintained for the past 20 years by local historical garden expert Wendy Woodworth, who holds the formal title of Heritage Horticulturalist for the City of Toronto. The Spadina Gardens (pronounced Spa-DEE-na, unlike the street) include an 1880s flower border and one representing 1915. There are also century-old fruit trees, vegetable plots, a greenhouse, and an array of ever-changing annual beds. *285 Spadina Rd., 416-392-6910*

Photo: Sarah B. Hood

Photo: Ontario Tourism, 11826

The City of Toronto operates an information line just for ice skaters (*416-338-RINK*). There's also a comprehensive city-run program of skating lessons, from beginner to ice dancing to hockey, at arenas all over town. Of course, Nathan Phillips Square is a favourite pleasure-skating location, as is Harbourfront. Slightly less well known is little Devonian Pond – dubbed Lake Devo by Ryerson students – at Gould and Victoria. But nothing beats the lagoons of Ward's Island and even the open bay. Most winters the ice surface freezes thick enough that this is safe in February, but it's not good terrain for experimentation. If you're keen to try, go first to the closed water near the bridge from Ward's to Algonquin Island and get to know some Islanders, because they've studied the conditions for generations. Island skaters warn each other about risky ice: always take their advice. (If you make some friends, you can also ask about Island hockey.)

Toronto, with its safe streets and diverse neighbourhoods, is in many respects a walker's paradise. But once you've donned your sensible shoes, where will they lead you?

• For the past ten years the energetic Shirley Lum and her team of intrepid women guides have been leading Torontonians by foot and bike to the best food treats this city has to offer. Her company, **A Taste of the World** (*416-923-6813, torontowalksbikes.com*), presents inexpensive, year-round walking tours and summer bike tours for non-athletes, including ghost tours and ethnic-food themed events like her popular Chinese New Year outing.

• The **Toronto Field Naturalists** (*416-593-2656*) run an extensive series exploring the natural life of Toronto neighbourhoods, ravines, parks, and cemeteries.

• For less hawks, more shocks, the Toronto Ghosts and Haunting Research Society offers modestly-priced **Haunted Toronto** tours throughout the summer, departing from the steps of the Royal Ontario Museum at 100 Queen's Park Circle (*416-487-9017, ontarioghosts.org/walkingtours*).

• Meanwhile, the Museum has its own series of educational **ROMWalks** (*416-488-5061, rom.on.ca*).

• Heritage Toronto (*416-338-3886, heritagetoronto.org*) runs an annual series titled **Historic Paths**, which focuses on the architecture and history of areas like Cabbagetown, Parkdale, and the Entertainment District.

• The **Ontario Herbalists Association** (*416-536-1509, herbalists.on.ca*) leads outdoor herb identification walks, as well as an excursion to Chinatown herb shops every summer. (At $25 for non-members, these are pricier than some.)

• For the self-starter, the City of Toronto has created a series of **Discovery Walks** (*416-338-0338*) marked by signs that point out the interesting features of neighbourhoods, parks, ravines, and beaches. The full tours can be fairly long, but of course you're free to stop or to diverge from the path whenever the fancy takes you. For downloadable brochures, visit their website (*city.toronto.on.ca/parks/recreation_facilities/discovery_walks/discover_index.htm*).

Campbell House

Built in 1822, Campbell House has a small, pretty, iron-fenced herb garden with dye plants, medicinals, teas, and seasonings of the period. The building itself was originally located in the old city on the site of 300 Adelaide (originally known as 54 Duke Street), but was moved, whole, in 1972; there's a photo of the move in progress inside.
160 Queen St. W., 416-597-0227

Colborne Lodge

A recent restoration project recreated Regency period (1810s) flower and vegetable gardens at the former home of John Howard, who donated the land that is now High Park to the city.
Colborne Lodge Dr. in High Park, 416-392-6916

Montgomery's Inn

Now restored as a museum, this former inn lies within a park; visitors can view a kitchen garden of the 1847 period with heritage varieties of common vegetables like tomatoes and potatoes.
4709 Dundas St. W., 416-394-8113

Scadding Cabin

This snug little log cabin – the oldest surviving residence in Toronto – was built by John Scadding in the Don Valley in 1792. It was moved in the late 19th century to preserve it as a heritage site. The York Pioneer and Historical Society maintains the cabin and its secluded pioneer-style herb garden.
CNE Grounds, south of Dufferin Gates, 416-494-0503

Photo: Sarah B. Hood

Todmorden Mills

The Terry House (which is original to the site) has an 1830s-style flower and kitchen garden. There's also a small "Iroquois Tribute Garden" featuring plants that were important to First Nations life and culture, "... even though there were no Iroquois around here; that's why we call it a 'Tribute Garden'."
Pottery Rd., 416-396-2819

Hawk Eyes

In 1995, Toronto naturalists were delighted to find that a mated pair of peregrine falcons had arrived downtown – the first to successfully nest in southern Ontario in over thirty years. A group of volunteers took it upon themselves to guard the families of Pounce-Kingsley and Victoria (as they became known), and thus was born the Canadian Peregrine Foundation. The CPF watches over urban peregrines, and invites downtown birders to report by email (*diana@peregrine-foundation.ca*) whenever they see peregrine activity over the city. Members were heartbroken in the summer of 2002 when Pounce-Kingsley was killed, probably in a fight with another raptor, and Victoria died soon afterwards. At the time of their deaths they were the oldest nesting pair in southern Ontario, with 29 offspring over eight years. A younger pair, Windwhistler-Spike and Mandy, now frequent some of the same locations. If you want to try spotting falcons, watch the top ledges of Mount Sinai and Princess Margaret Hospitals, the top of the King Edward Hotel, or tall buildings on Bloor from Yonge to Bay. Nests have been spotted behind a pillar on the 19th floor ledge on the east side of 18 King East (often visible from King and Leader Lane), and on the 43rd floor ledge on the south side of the Sheraton Hotel (visible from York and Richmond).
404-250 Merton St., 416-481-1233, peregrine-foundation.ca

Chilled Duck

Have you ever noticed that there seem to be more waterfowl along the shoreline in winter than in summer? Toronto Harbour is home to several species of arctic ducks, which fly south to winter here, then return north every spring. If you pay attention, on any frosty day you should be able to spot at least two or three kinds – apart from the ubiquitous, year-round green-headed mallard – with names like goldeneye, bufflehead, and pintail. Their visits predate European settlement by a long shot; you can recognize them by the sound they make, like the distant chorus of riotous laughter.

Photo: Sarah B. Hood

Green Crusaders

It's no problem finding an organization dedicated to protecting the Toronto environment. The problem is figuring out which one to join.

North Toronto Green Community

Possibly the sweetest of the environmental advocacy groups, operating in the neighbourhood around Eglinton and Yonge. They hold walks that explore the buried streams and rivers of the area, encourage pesticide-free community gardening, and teach about safe handling of toxic household products. But never discount sweetness as a force for change; the NTGC is also the catalyst that drove the introduction of wind-powered turbines in Toronto! *35 Baycrest Ave., 416-781-7663, ntgc.ca*

Seems like artists can't resist the lure of the landscape. Apart from the Music Garden, there's an increasing collection of whimsical **Artists' Gardens at Harbourfront** (*416-973-4000*); 23 at last count. These include Libby Hague's *Whirligig Garden*; Gene Threndyle's slightly disturbing *The Unnatural Garden*, and Soulpepper Theatre's punning *You Can Lead a Horticulture*. Maps are available on site. The little **Toronto Sculpture Garden** (*southwest corner of King and Jarvis, 416-392-1111*) is really more like an outdoor gallery, with exhibits – some pretty far out there – that change seasonally. (A recent installation by Charles Goldman called "Infinitely Intersecting Orbits" consisted of 15 tetherball poles set up so that the imaginary arc of the balls defined infinity symbols. People were supposed to whack the tetherballs.) The privately-maintained garden outside the **Artscape** studio building (*900 Queen W.*) doesn't leap out at you, but it's a gardener's delight, with lots of thriving wild and

Task Force to Bring Back the Don

The Don Task Force is both powerful and effective. It has taken giant strides in cleaning up the river and revitalizing its banks through the planting of some 40,000 trees and uncountable wildflowers. (Links to further defenders of areas like the Taddle Creek, the Humber River, and the Leslie Spit can be found on the Don Task Force website.)
c/o Metro Hall, 55 John St., 23rd floor, 416-392-0401, toronto.ca/don

Toronto and Region Conservation Authority

The TRCA is the guardian of the Toronto ecosystem, especially its watersheds. They run all kinds of hands-on nature experiences and several residential centres.
5 Shoreham Dr., 416-661-6600, trca.on.ca

native plants carefully nurtured in big, generous clumps. Part of the garden is open to passersby, while part is intriguingly hidden from public view by a fence. Not every **Toronto Island** resident is an artist, but the gardens of Toronto's car-free community are inimitable. They may be mainly horticultural (like the sensational site of 4 Second Street, pictured opposite); or structural (like the stripey stick forest on First), or a little of both (like the dead Volkswagen bug used as a planter on Omaha). There are formal garden tours in the summer (416-203-0921 or 416-537-5006); however, there's lots to see if you just stroll among the homes on Ward's and Algonquin Islands. The most spacious and surreal is the grounds of **The Guild Inn** on the edge of the Scarborough Bluffs (201 Guildwood Pkwy.), where the sculptures, ornaments, and entire façades of banks and other buildings have been distributed about a wide grassy parkland. The result is like something out of the Beatles' Pepperland, with a crazy mixture of scales, styles, and proportions.

Winter Gardens

Especially in winter, we crave greenery. Seek it at **Allan Gardens Greenhouse** (19 Horticultural Ave., south of Carlton, west of Sherbourne, 416-392-1111), where palms and bananas unfurl year-round in the evocative 1910 Palm House, while orchids, hibiscus, cactus, and tropical fruit trees abound in the adjoining display greenhouses. **The Music Garden** (475 Queens Quay Blvd. W., 416-338-0338), spearheaded by cellist Yo Yo Ma and designed to mirror the dance sections of Bach's "Suites for Unaccompanied Cello," is an outdoor garden, but it's so creatively designed that you'll find live growth almost all year. It makes a pleasant – though chilly – destination even in cruel February. Same goes for the **Village of Yorkville Park** (south side of Cumberland between Bellair and Avenue Rd.), with its famous, controversial, imported granite rock mountain. Echoing natural conditions (marsh, meadow, pine grove), it has something to offer in all seasons. Just out of town you'll find breathtakingly aromatic jasmine blooming in January in the small but wonderful **Mediterranean Greenhouse** of the Royal Botanical Gardens (680 Plains Rd. W., 905-825-5040, rbg.ca).

Photo: Sarah B. Hood

In case this is not your year for an ecotourism spree in Costa Rica, it's nice to know that the rainforest is also accessible by TTC. You'd need to head to 360 Queen Street East (at Parliament), where a palm-garlanded street sign welcomes you into the **Only in Paradise Cafe**. Run by husband-and-wife team Marcel and Julie, Paradise is pretty much a literal oasis in a neighbourhood that's a little short on amenities of any kind after dark. It was originally located in a much smaller storefront a few steps west, but the Paradise combination of kooky decor and dependable home cooking (in those days they baked their own bread every night) drew enough business to allow them to move to their present digs. They've kept the jungle theme decor, the year-round backyard patio, the odd menagerie (the aquatic turtle has now grown to the size of a dinner plate), and the twisty creative inspiration that makes the place unique. Marcel once installed a bubble machine over the front door, but, he claims, he was asked to take it down when the buildup of stray soapsuds started to make the Queen streetcar skid. He's been known to play a kind of homemade *Wheel of Fortune* with customers at the bar, drawing the blank-letter grid on a giant, fish-filled aquarium with erasable neon markers. He built his own goldfish pond in the open-air jungle patio too, until he discovered that the local raccoons would eat as many as he could stock it with.

Also, you can't eat there, but there's an honest-to-goodness miniature rainforest in the easy-to-miss **Cloud Gardens** on Temperance Street between Yonge and Bay (416-392-1111). The entire park, greenhouse rainforest included, was created as part of a deal between the City of Toronto and the would-be developers of the Bay-Adelaide Centre in the tail end of the downtown office building boom in the late '80s. The project went bust,

Toronto Bay Initiative

A spinoff of the Waterfront Regeneration Trust, TBI protects the shoreline habitat of the City and the Islands, organizing events like wildflower plantings and educational canoe trips.
403-207 Queens Quay W.,
416-943-8080, ext. 227,
torontobay.net

Toronto Environmental Alliance

TEA is one of the most eclectic groups. It helps promote sustainable transportation, smog and pesticide reduction, green power, and green health care.
201-30 Duncan St., 416-596-0660,
torontoenvironment.org

but not before the park was created. Lush and well-planned, the garden sits atop a thin crust of pavement over a parking garage, and features a cooling waterfall fountain as well as a public art installation that somewhat resembles a wall-mounted patchwork quilt. Each "patch" is made of a different type of building material, a tribute to the various construction trades. Meanwhile, the unintentionally PoMo concrete skeleton of the never-finished office tower sulks across the street, vacant window wells staring out at the business district.

Toronto Field Naturalists

Most concerned with living birds, animals, and plants, the Toronto Field Naturalists' homespun newsletter is a treasury of lore about the natural life of the city, and their extensive schedule of walking tours is legendary.
1519-2 Carlton St., 416-593-2656

Waterfront Regeneration Trust

Founded by Tiny Perfect former mayor David Crombie, the Trust is especially concerned with the lakefront, promoting initiatives to improve water quality and spearheading the recreational trail that's ultimately supposed to run along the entire northern Lake Ontario shoreline.
308-372 Richmond St. W., 416-943-8080, wrtrust.com

Island Hopping

Photo: Sarah B. Hood

Some see it as an encouraging sign of a healthy ecosystem, while others view it as just plain yucky. It doesn't much matter which way you look at it, because the annual Toronto Island toad invasion will go on regardless. The American toad (*Bufo americanus*) is a bumpy-skinned little amphibian that's very much at home in these parts. Every spring, after mating, the females each lay thousands of eggs. When they hatch and metamorphose later in the summer, thousands and thousands of thumbnail-sized baby toads set out to migrate from the ponds that have been their homes to the natural areas where they will live as adults mainly on land. Harmless, except to insects, the toads are generally treated with affection by the Islanders. Former City Councillor and Ward's Island resident Liz Amer even has a toad palace in her garden, with spirals of tiny staircases which the gentle creatures will sometimes climb for a little sunshine.

Dining

You can't really point to a single dining experience and say definitively, "That's Toronto!" We don't have an equivalent to Montreal smoked meat, Buffalo wings, or New York cheesecake. Instead, Toronto has inherited the plain home cooking of its early British and Irish settlers, then gradually amplified the repertoire by absorbing the national cuisines of successive waves of immigrants – especially the Italians and the Chinese. Thus dim sum is characteristically Torontonian, as are pizza, pasta, tandoori chicken, tekka maki, and the all-day breakfast.

Also, although we do have a roster of fine chefs, Toronto is not an excellent dining city because of its haute cuisine, but because of its enormous variety. Pick a food: you can probably get it here. So, whereas many other guides list the fanciest and the best, we thought it would be more fun to concentrate on the overlooked and the unusual, along with a few fairly well known places that we just couldn't stand to leave out. As a result, with a few exceptions, the establishments in this section tend to fall into the "under $20" price range. (Many of them aren't *really* unknown, either, since any restaurant that's truly secret doesn't stay in business very long.)

Salad in the Sky

The **Fairmont Royal York Hotel** (*100 Front St. W., 416-368-2511, fairmont.com*) gives new meaning to the phrase "a bed of lettuce." A full 18 stories above the traffic snarl at Front and University, the hotel's apprentice chefs tend an edible garden laid out in custom-designed four-poster beds. Seems executive chef John Cordeaux is also an avid gardener. He insists on an organic-only regime for his herbs, fruits, and vegetables, which end up seasoning Royal York diners' plates. Along with traditional culinary herbs, the garden includes some of the edible flowers that are still all the rage with foodies, plus pears, cherries, and plums.

Back in 2000, Toronto diners started to wonder about the conditions of this city's kitchens — a train of thought that was especially spurred on by Robert Cribb's "Dirty Dining" series in the *Toronto Star*. In response, the City of Toronto's Public Health Department created a program that forces restaurateurs to publicize the results of their most recent inspection.

In fact, the Province of Ontario requires that all food outlets (not just restaurants but, for instance, bakeries and delis) must be inspected annually. If they're designated "High Risk," they get three inspections a year. Before you leap to conclusions, this designation would apply to any restaurant with a wide range of choices on the menu, or to any food facility in a hospital or a day-care centre. "Medium Risk" spots (like fast food outlets) get two inspections annually. "Low Risk" ones (a corner store that serves sandwiches) get just one visit per year.

As of January 8, 2001, all food service facilities must post the results of their most recent inspection: either a green card (for a pass) or a yellow one (a conditional pass, which requires relatively modest changes to meet "green" standards). If they get a red card, the restaurant must close until the problems are fixed. When Public Health authorities suspect an establishment may not be likely to post their card, they'll monitor the place to make sure the sign goes up.

If you can't spot the rating card, or if you want more information, you have the right to request to see the results of the most recent inspection, and every restaurant is required to have a copy on the premises. If you're curious about a particular establishment, you can also check for its inspection results on the City's DineSafe website (*app.city.toronto.on.ca/food2/index.jsp*). If you suspect all is not as it should be in a particular place, you can call the City's Food Service Hotline (*416-338-FOOD*).

There are about 18,000 "food premises" in Toronto, requiring about 33,000 inspections per year. The good news is that less than 1% of Toronto restaurants receive the red rating annually. (Furthermore, the City offers safe food handling courses, and is hoping to make it mandatory for all restaurant owners to become certified, just as Toronto bar servers must undergo training to deal with customers they think should be "cut off" for the night.)

THINGS WE LACK

Unlike many urbanites, Torontonians crave a coffee and a pastry first thing in the morning. Maybe that's why it's really hard to find a place to go after a movie or a play to have a coffee and an excellent éclair or a superb sachertorte. The bakery selection at the coffee chains is often limited to hardy stuff: muffins, brownies, coffee cakes. Those that do carry more elegant fare seldom sell it fast enough to keep it fresh. And once there was a host of cheap and wonderful Hungarian restaurants in town, but now you can barely find two schnitzels to rub together (should you wish to do so, of course). We also lack a Tiki bar that's worthy of the name — certainly nothing that ranks with Montreal's vanished Kon-Tiki.

ROMANCE OVER $30

There's something about its physical location, in a little secluded dip in the road just off Avenue Road, that makes you feel you're in another world while you're dining at **Le Paradis** (*166 Bedford Rd., 416-921-0995*). A faithful local clientele has kept it in business in its out-of-the way corner since 1986. What could be more romantic than a tucked-away authentic French bistro serving such classic selections as *terrine* (chicken and duck liver paté) and *bavette frites*? Order a sip of one of their fine cognacs or armagnacs to finish the meal and warm your heart for post-prandial cuddling.

Gone in a Puff of Smoke

And then there's tobacco. Some of Toronto's early champions of temperance might be puzzled to know that under the current system, children can frequent an establishment where the grown-ups drink liquor, but not one where they smoke cigarettes. Toronto's Smoking Bylaw came into effect in October 1999. (It replaced the disastrous – and quickly repealed – total ban that was so severely flouted as to obliterate previously existing "non-smoking" areas in many places.) The present bylaw is a "multiphase" one, and at the beginning it merely restricted smoking areas to a certain proportion of the space.

As of June 1, 2001, the second phase came into effect, requiring all public places and workplaces to be smoke-free, with certain exemptions. Among these, any establishment that already held a liquor license could choose to designate itself as a bar, as long as it promised not to admit anyone under 19. Other restaurants could serve liquor and admit children, but could not allow smoking. (There's also an option to have a fully enclosed and separately ventilated smoking room, but it can't take up more than a quarter of the dining area.)

But, smokers, beware! In June 2004, the exemption for bars expires and all establishments will have to be smoke-free. The exact date is being contested, but there is a general movement among municipalities to eliminate even these last bastions of nicotine indulgence (on the grounds of health risk for the servers), and Toronto is unlikely to buck the trend.

Haute cuisine may not be this city's strongest suit, but we do have our share of hot shot chefs – like Susur Lee. His Lotus was located in a run-down storefront in a residential neighbourhood; now he operates **Susur** (*601 King St. W., 416-603-2205, susur.com*) in what was once an old-school Italian dining room. He's kept the arched windows and the "restaurant" sign; a small brass plate announces the change of ownership. The interior is – as everyone says – meticulous and minimalist … but with a sense of humour.

Lee has a penchant for Pillsbury Dough Boys, vintage squeaky toys, landscapes on velvet, and he somehow manages to slide them into the rest of the decor in a way that seems to fit with the orchids and the white-on-white design. Maybe that's the secret of his food. A single dinner at Susur could easily cost between $100 and $200, but it's not only exquisite, *it's also funny*. In the same way that a punch line makes you laugh because you don't expect it, Lee's food delights with surprise; his gentle, off-the-wall creative imagination makes him truly amazing.

Like Castor and Pollux, the two other most obvious stars of Toronto chefdom have led linked careers. Together, Jamie Kennedy and Michael Stadtlander made Scaramouche one of the best places in town, and cofounded the organic growers' market Knives and Forks. The list of their individual endeavours – Stadtlanders, Nekah, Palmerston's – has been likewise stellar. Most recently, Kennedy took over the restaurant atop the Royal Ontario Museum, known simply as **JK ROM**. (It closed as of fall 2002 for the ROM's extensive renovations.)

Stadtlander has pursued the ideal of local ingredients to its only logical conclusion: his own 100-acre **Eigensinn Farm** near Collingwood, Ontario (*RR#2, Singhampton, 519-922-3128*). There, he and his wife Nobuyo book intimate meals for barely a dozen people at a time, feeding them largely upon produce they raise themselves. In 1998, they experienced a brief bout of unpleasantness when undercover police officers posing as a honeymoon couple charged them with selling wine without a license. (The Stadtlanders had erroneously made a profit of $1.50 on the bottle, which they thought they were selling at cost. Charges were subsequently

ROMANCE UNDER $30

You may end up deciding you can't stand each other after confronting the tapas menu at **Oasis** (*294 College St., 416-975-0845*) together, but isn't it better to find out sooner rather than later? They offer eight- and ten-item specials, which you choose from a list of 68 possible little dishes, like quinoa salad, Thai coconut rice balls, seafood cakes with wasabi sour cream, and mashed yams with maple syrup. Many choices are vegetarian, but there are three kinds of aphrodisiac mussels. And if you negotiate the challenges of agreeing dropped.) In 2002, the London-based *Restaurant* magazine named Eigensinn as the ninth best restaurant in the entire world; lately, Stadtlander also hosts a TV show on Food Network Canada.

Who's Really Who?

Unless it's obviously a McDonald's, a Red Lobster, or a Swiss Chalet, we diners tend to perceive each restaurant as a separate entity. But of course many places that look like one-offs have been carefully engineered to *seem* unique. Some of these may be exquisitely individual in their own right, while others may be the jumping-off point to an entire franchise operation.

An example of the first category would be Oliver Bonacini. That's not one person but two: Peter Oliver and Michael Bonacini, who run some of the ritziest spots in town. Their upscale empire began with the no-longer extant North Toronto favourite Oliver's Bistro. Now they own the minimalist mecca **Canoe**, the radiantly rustic **Auberge du Pommier**, the vibrant **Jump**, the cheerfully classy **Biff's**, **Steakfrites** (with its live ficus tree growing up through several stories of the building), and the recently opened **Oliver & Bonacini Café Grill** at Bayview Village.

There are probably lots of habitués of the toney business bistro **Reds** in First Canadian Place who don't realize that it's a cousin of the much more laid-back **Jack Astor's Bar and Grill**. Both are creations of SIR CORP, which also runs **Soul of the Vine**, **Far Niente**, **Alice Fazooli's**, **Canyon Creek Steak and Chop House**, **Armadillo Texas Grill**, **Leoni's**, and **Al Frisco's**. (It's moved now, but back in the late '80s, when it was on the north side of Adelaide east of Duncan, their **Loose Moose** was the very first pioneer of what is now the almost-too-exuberant nightclub scene. In those days, while the rest of the buildings in the area were still darkened industrial warehouses, would-be-clubbers would pack the sidewalk for a block hoping to get into the ground-level night spot.)

Also carefully designed for their audience tastes are the Prime Restaurants: the **East Side Mario's** chain, **RD's** (originally "Red Devil") **BBQ & Blues**, **Pat & Mario's**, **Fionn MacCool's Irish Pub**, **Esplanade Bier Markt**, and **Casey's Bar and Grill**. Five "Duke" pubs are owned by Imago Restaurants. These are the **Duke of**

on an order, you'll have the fun of sharing a feast of intimate finger foods in a cozily dim setting. If you go to **Fez Batik** (*129 Peter St., 416-204-9660, bandofgypsies.com*) early in the evening, you'll find its four floors virtually empty, but as 10 p.m. rolls around, it heats up into the popular club that it is. Before the throng arrives, you can snuggle up with pillows and carpets in the Moroccan lounge or next to the fireplace and share combinations like the Gypsy Platter, with its bruschetta, olives, pepper jelly, and optional chorizo.

Kent (*2315 Yonge St.*), the venerable **Duke of York** (*39 Prince Arthur Ave.*), the **Duke of Argyle** (*86 John St.*), the **Duke of Westminster** (*First Canadian Place*), and the **Duke of Richmond** (*20 Queen St. W.*). (But they're not related in any way to any of the other Duke-named pubs.) And if a pub has the word "firkin" in the name, it's a member of the Firkin Group of Pubs. But you already knew that.

Quick Fixes

We rail against them, but there's still something wonderful about fast foods: those comforting instant meals that you can eat with your hands. But hamburgers and hot dogs don't always cut it. Here are our suggestions:

Photo: Sarah B. Hood

• As fast as you can say *ena spanokopita, parakalo*, the ladies behind the counter at the quarter-century-old **Athens Pastries** (*509 Danforth Ave., 416-463-5144*) will slice you off a warm, soft slab of filo pastry filled with salty spinach (*spanokopita*) or feta cheese (*tiropita*), fragrant with olive oil. Meanwhile, neighbourhood residents will be ordering up bigger quantities to take home for the family. Don't forget to say *efharisto*.

Photo: Sarah B. Hood

WHERE TO CLOSE A DEAL

For old-school, dimly-lit opulence, you can't beat **Barberian's Steak House** (*7 Elm St., 416-597-0335*). Located moments from the seats of Toronto power, it serves up steaks, wines, and scotches in a reverently hushed room hung about with venerable oil paintings. In a more contemporary vein there's **Fusion** (*First Canadian Place, lower level, 416-368-3692*), with its fresh, urban look and its well stocked bar. Under chef Joe Lui, the menu follows the fusion theme, with osso bucco, pad thai, and popular fish specials.

PERFECT PATIOS

A hangout for the artists and media types who frequent the Liberty Street neighbourhood, the **Liberty Café** (*25 Liberty St., 416-533-8828*) is never more inviting than at dusk on a weekend with the first strains of a small jazz or Latin act starting to play. Arranged around a corner, the patio is overhung with greenery, and regulars linger for hours. More like a back porch, really, the patio of the **Old York Bar and Grill** (*167 Niagara St., 416-703-9675*) may be right across the street from the slaughterhouse, but somehow seems much more idyllic. Great on a summer evening with burgers, beer, and just the hint of a sunburn from a day in the park. In the east end, **Tango Palace** (*1156 Queen St. E., 416-465-8085*) has a secluded backyard deck with lots of tree cover where, over morning coffee, patrons can watch Tai Chi practitioners or kids in the playground in the neighbouring park. One house rule: no flicking of spent cigarettes, so they don't make *another* car explode.

• Some people call them "Shanghai Subs." Others, more accurately, call them "Saigon Subs." You can call them whatever you want, but the substantial pre-made Vietnamese cold cut sandwiches on a fresh crusty bun – usually priced at $1 – are a bargain by any name. They're generally garnished with lightly pickled veggies, and the servers will add fish oil and hot chili sauce unless you ask them not to. Roast pork is recommended, but, like other deluxe fillings, it usually costs an extra 50 cents. Other choices include tofu, meatball, shredded chicken, marinated tuna, and bologna-type meat. They're available at many outlets, including **Banh Mi & Che Cali** (*318 Spadina Ave., 416-599-8948*) and – right next door – **Banh Mi Nguyen Huong Food Co. Ltd.** (*322 Spadina Ave., 416-599-4625*).

• Kensington Market offers almost too many munching opportunities to list, but among our favourites are the "spinagels" and "spudagels" on the cash counter at **My Market Bakery** (*172 Baldwin St., 416-593-6772*). These squashy spinach- or potato-filled treats aren't true bagels at all; they're really a rich, flaky savoury pastry. For a meatier hit, there's **Jumbo Empañadas** (*245 Augusta Ave., 416-977-0056*), where you can get the genuine Chilean variety, baked and stuffed with chicken and boiled egg, beef and boiled egg, or veggies. There's also a fried empañada with cheese.

Buffets, the Appetite Slayers

All-You-Can-Eat is likely an American invention, and it's a staple of bland commercial chains. But with Toronto's multicultural vitality, the big buffet idea is available in multiple variations. And many's the grad student who's been grateful to pad out a diet of KD and sidewalk sausages with an occasional binge at one of these:

• Fragrant lemongrass soup and unlimited shrimp chips are among the treats at **Young Thailand** (*165 John St., 416-593-9291; 81 Church St., 416-368-1368, young-thailand.ca*). Admittedly the pad thai gets a little limp on the hot table, but, hey, you can have as much as you like!

Photo: John Hood

• It isn't shabby chic; it's just plain shabby. Nonetheless there's something compelling about the Chinese food buffet at **Flamingo House Chinese Restaurant** (*446-448 Parliament St., 416-929-5576*). Maybe it's because so many people from the less monied parts of this neighbourhood are so pleased to have such bounty at these prices. (The lunchtime take-out is a steal.) There's always a good hot-and-sour soup and an honest fried tofu with green veggies. Lots of the other dishes are battered, deep-fried, and served in bright red sweet-and-sour sauce, but there's ice cream for dessert and, of course, fortune cookies. If you're making a special trip, call first, because they host a surprising number of private events.

Photo: Ontario Tourism, 13200

ROOMS WITH A VIEW

Diners who consider the wait for the CN Tower elevator to be too long have many other choices. For example, Chef Anthony Walsh presides at **Canoe** (*66 Wellington St. W., 416-364-1212, oliverbonacini.com*), where local and organic ingredients star atop the TD Tower. It's on the 54th floor, to be exact, and it looks south over Lake Ontario and east to the Niagara escarpment. Perched above the shoulder of the SkyDome, patrons oversee the Islands and watch planes approaching two airports, perhaps while enjoying a sunset drink. **Oasis on the Lake** (*2161 Lakeshore Blvd. W., 416-259-3756*) still has the brick archways, stucco walls, and exposed wooden beams of its earlier incarnation as Argentinian steakhouse Casa Mendoza. Almost invisible from the road, and set back amongst '50s

Photo: Sarah B. Hood

bungalows on the notorious old motel strip, it's nestled on the curve of the bay, and allows for a unique view of the islands, the harbour, and the downtown core. (The menu is heavy-duty steak and seafood.) Perched on the cusp of the St. Clair escarpment, the renowned **Scaramouche Pasta Bar/ Restaurant** (*1 Benvenuto Pl., 416-961-8011*) reveals a cascading southward prospect over the centre of the city. But be warned: it's unquestionably upscale. Those whose pocketbooks don't stretch to the above suggestions can head for the elevators to the top floor of the **Clarke Institute of Psychiatry** (*250 College St.*). For the price of a modest cafeteria lunch, they'll enjoy a 360-degree panoramic vista from the university district, including the lake.

• Indian food lends itself especially well to the buffet concept, and there are lots to choose from, although the menus are pretty standard. Expect to find steamed basmati rice, tender naan bread, and half a dozen meat or vegetable dishes. Dessert is most likely rice pudding or *gulab jamun* (small dough balls in a sweet, rose or cardamom-seasoned syrup). Some of the standouts are **Sangam** (*788 Bay St., 416-591-7090*), **Haandi** (*1401 Gerrard St. E., 416-469-9696*), **Skylark**, a haunt of Hawksley Workman (*1433 Gerrard St. E., 416-469-1500*), and **Nataraj** (*394 Bloor St. W., 416-928-2925*).

• It's a great restaurant anyway, but **Sushiman's** (*26 Richmond St. E., 416-362-8793*) once-a-month, all-you-can-eat sushi nights ($26 per person at last report) are amazing. They normally fall on the last Saturday of each month (but may be rescheduled to coincide with New Year's Eve, for example). There are two sittings: 6 and 8 p.m.; of course, you must call for reservations.

Fun on a Bun

Since the legendary Earl first called for his meal to be served between slices of bread, humankind has developed endless permutations on the classic sandwich. Here are some unbeatable Toronto riffs on the theme.

• Hearty and juicy are understatements for the sweet veal and meatball sandwiches that they turn out at **California Sandwiches** (*244 Claremont Ave., 416-603-3317*). The drill is this: you line up at the little window inside the side entrance and place your order. It soon turns up, hot and foil-wrapped. Some people choose to dine in, but most prefer to eat on the run. A haunt of Maple Leafs players, it's also beloved by the local constabulary, so if you see a cop car parked out front you know it's not a B&E: just a craving for a cheesy, saucy, messy, meaty, yummy Mediterranean sandwich!

• There really was a **Dangerous Dan**, and his Queen/Broadview diner (*714 Queen St. E., 416-463-7310*) is a favourite of east-end carnivores (though he does offer five varieties of "Tree Hugger Burgers"). Besides a clot-forming array of ribs and steaks, it's perhaps best known for the daunting Coronary Burger, featuring two half-pound beef patties, bacon, and cheese … topped off with a fried egg. Comes with fries, gravy, mayo, and pop. Anyone for a bypass?

• It's no secret that College Street's Bar Italia serves delectable Italian sandwiches, but only a few denizens of the Queen and Parliament area know about **Peter's Cajun Creole Pizza** (*181 Parliament St., 416-368-8099*). When we first saw the sign, with its happy little alligator chefs, we thought: "Oh well … doomed." But Peter's excellent spicy pizzas have established him as a neighbourhood fixture. However, the real secret treat is his sandwiches, with fresh combinations of arugula, roasted peppers, eggplant, zucchini, capicollo, provolone, and other Italian favourites. Eat in (if any of the half-dozen or so seats are free) and it comes with a masterful mixed green salad with balsamic vinaigrette. All for as little as $3.75!

Photo: Ontario Tourism, 13103

SUSHI AND BEYOND

In Toronto, there seems to be a sushi bar on every corner. If forced to choose a favourite, we would have to name **Sushi On Bloor** (*515 Bloor St. W., 416-516-3456*) for freshness and generosity – their "Sushi Silver" is a good deal. **Sushi Bistro** (*204 Queen St. W., 416-971-5315*) has an imaginative selection of giant sushi rolls. (Then again, there's some fun to be had by ordering the plastic-wrapped packets at **Sushi-Q** in the basement food court of the Eaton Centre. It's not the best – and they charge extra for ginger! – but eating in the milling throng with those giant video screens blaring adverts on two sides is as close as you can get to the *Blade Runner* experience … without the perpetual rain.) In a different price scale entirely is clubland's soigné **Di.ferent By Edo** (*257 Adelaide St. W., lower level, 416-977-8744*), with its fusion-flavoured sushi, tempura, and seafood. **Okonomi House** (*23 Charles St. W., 416-925-6176*) serves no sushi whatsoever; instead they have a selection of eggy Japanese pancakes called *okonomiyaki.*

No Animals Were Harmed in the Cooking of These Dinners

• The long-established **Annapurna** (*1085 Bathurst St., 416-537-8513*) is as tranquil as it gets, from the service to the decor to the very accommodating vegan-friendly menu, a combination of South Indian food (like the crispy fermented lentil flour pancakes known as *dosai*) and generic North American vegetarian choices. The menu is even okay for strict, non-garlic-eating Buddhists. The staff are volunteers associated with the Shri Chinmoy Meditation Centre in the same building. If you want to go a step further into South Indian vegetarian cooking, try **Madras Durbar** (*1435 Gerrard St. E., 416-465-4116*), which makes the ultimate crispy, lacy dosai.

Photo: Sarah B. Hood

• From noon to 2:30 p.m. and 6 to 8:30 p.m. Monday through Saturday, **Govinda's Dining Room** at the International Society for Krishna Consciousness (*243 Avenue Rd., 416-922-5415*) lays out a vegetarian feast for all comers. When it's gone, it's gone, so arrive promptly. However, you decide how much to pay – cash only.

• Cheese blintzes and boiled whitefish are among the most popular items at **United Bakers Dairy Restaurant** (Lawrence Plaza, *506 Lawrence Ave. W., 416-789-0519*), which is meatless in the kosher sense of the definition. It was founded in 1912 by Aaron and Sarah Ludovsky and remains in the hands of their grandchildren Philip and Ruth. For many years located at 338 Spadina, the restaurant moved north with much of the Jewish community; its name remembers an early attempt to organize bakeries in Toronto.

• You might want to do a couple weeks of cleansing before you actually order anything at **Fresh by JuiceForLife** (*521 Bloor St. W., 416-531-2635; 336 Queen St. W., 416-599-4442; 894 Queen St. W., 416-913-2720, juiceforlife.com*). Don't get us wrong; it's great and all, but their healing cocktails and various vegan solid food selections are so extremely potent that they may shock your system if it's not prepared.

• **Cafe 668** (*668 Dundas St. W., 416-703-0668*) is an outstanding – though tiny – Vietnamese Buddhist vegetarian spot. The owners don't eat garlic or onions, but you can have them if you ask. Don't confuse it with the *other* Buddhist vegetarian spot right next door.

• Against all odds, we're pleased to report **Hey Good Cooking** (*238 Dupont St., 416-929-9140*) has survived for many years in a location that had quickly wiped out a previous half-dozen or so occupants. Must be the extremely cheap and good vegetarian fare, their yummy green salad dressing, or their bustling side business in the take-out line.

More Than Breakfast, Not Quite Lunch

Photo: Sarah B. Hood

A step up from over-easy, bacon, brown toast, and coffee is that blissful meal invented especially for lazy, sociable weekends: brunch. Of course, on perfect brunch days, everybody wants to eat out, so you must be quick off the mark to get seated and served before everything gets too chaotic. One spot that seems to handle the crunch well is the evocative **Lakeview Lunch** (*1132 Dundas St. W., 416-530-0871*), with its cozy, dim, old-fashioned booths and its antique movie memorabilia.

Unexpectedly for its nondescript location, **The Star on Queen** (*912 Queen St. E., 416-469-0414*) offers up beautifully presented and perfectly cooked brunches –

booth rooms. In contrast, **E Zone** (*170 Spadina Ave., 416-598-2042*) has a playroom ambiance, with hot-coloured plastic furniture and fixtures, as well as a tasty menu. They also rent out popular games at $1 each. (Tip: One frequent bubbler cautions that: "Usually attitude of wait staff is inversely proportionate to quality of drinks served.") Confirmed bubble tea aficionados might like to branch out into a similar beverage, the syrupy Indian *falooda*, which has jellylike *tukmaria* seeds floating in it. (Yum!) It's available at **Punjab Food and Sweets** (*1448 Gerrard St. E., 416-466-4647*), **Lahore Paan Centre** (*1431 Gerrard St. E., 416-462-3293*), and other locations.

eggs Florentine, seafood, and so on – in an unassuming space that only seats about 25 people at a time. That's because its Escoffier chef/owner decided he just didn't want to fuss any more, so when the place is full, it's full. The best Jewish knosh is at the **Free Times Café** (*320 College St., 416-967-1078*). Owner Judy Perly (related to Toronto's famous mapmaking family) serves up a feast of blintzes, stewed fruit, bagels, and other traditional treats, accompanied by live klezmer in the back room. At the gently upscale, sunny **Swan Diner** (*892 Queen St. W., 416-532-0452*), the

Photo: Sarah B. Hood

cheerful and usually efficient staff shuck oysters before your eyes and serve 'em with a choice of three condiments: red wine, hot pepper, and horseradish. Lots of other good choices too, so don't be daunted by the knot of people standing at the door – the line moves fast. If you run out of patience, just step a little way down the street to the more modest but equally charming **Cafe Bernate** (*1024 Queen St. W., 416-535-2835*). Finally, your two authors have a disagreement over the topic of banana pancakes. One of us holds that the best are to be had at **Aunties + Uncles** (*74 lippincott St., 416-324-1375*), while the other of us roots for the nearby **Bellevue Diner** (*61 Bellevue Ave., 416-597-6912*). You'll just have to try both and let us know.

The Diners Time Forgot

So many diners – from the wonderful The Brothers on Yonge to Yorkville's retro pastiche known as 4-Ds – have gone the way of cherry cola from the fountain! And of course, no new place is ever as good as the genuine oldies. The very best and most authentic – the one that makes KOS, Mars, and Stem look like chi-chi poseurs – is the inconspicuous **Avenue Open Kitchen & Deli** (*7 Camden St., 416-504-7431*), where you can sample hearty, rib-sticking eggs, peameal bacon, and potatoes alongside city roadworks crews. The out-of-the-way **Canary Grill** (*409 Front St. E., 416-364-9943*) is such a classic that it's constantly being used as a film location. **Gale's Snack Bar** (*539 Eastern Ave., no telephone*) is reputed to be the very cheapest in town ("the most expensive thing on the menu is a pack o' smokes," one fan reports). And everybody has a local favourite. Some extol the virtues of the peameal "steaks" at **New York Café Restaurant, Bar & Eatery** (*757 Broadview Ave., 416-778-4444*). Others love the **Sunset Grill** in the Beaches (*2006 Queen St. E., 416-690-9985*) for its very late hours. The **Homeway Soda Bar** (*955 Mount Pleasant Rd., 416-488-3242*) is another of those beloved throwbacks to an earlier era. And – whereas they no longer attract line-ups of yuppies outside the door on weekend mornings, as they did in the '80s – **People's Bar & Eatery** (*270 Dupont St., 416-925-3258*) is still serving up the real deal.

PAN-ASIAN PANOPLY

Many Toronto sushi bars are actually Korean-owned, but if you want straight-up Korean fare, head to Bloor Street West between Bathurst and Christie. We recommend the tranquil, child-friendly **Korean Village** (*628 Bloor St. W., 416-536-0290*) with its huge menu and plentiful, free side dishes. The cheap 'n' cheerful **Buk Chang Dong Soon To Fu** (*691 Bloor St. W., 416-527-0972*) serves a more limited choice of seafood, beef, pork, and dumplings in various combinations. The back of the laminated menu is in Korean only; it lists rice dishes, sides, and soups that don't appear on the English side. To satisfy your next big yak attack, you

Photo: Sarah B. Hood

Girls with Grills

Photo: Sarah B. Hood

might choose either **Little Tibet** (*712 Queen St. W., 416-306-1896*) or **Everest** (*232 Queen St. W., 416-977-6969*). **Pho Hung** (*350 Spadina Ave., 416-593-4274; 200 Bloor St. W., 416-963-5080*) is a good pick for Vietnamese food, but we've been puzzled for some time about their trademark, which is a laughing cow — oddly similar to the one on the label of *La Vache Qui Rit* cheese. The management claims there's no link between the cheese and the restaurant. They point out that the cheese cow has one earring, whereas theirs has two. Instead, they tell us, the cow signifies the beef soup for which Pho Hung is named.

Sometimes it seems like all you have to do in this town to make a splash with your eatery is give it a retro girlie name and serve breakfast. We can't explain it, but here are a few examples: **Betty's** (*240 King St. E., 416-368-1300*) – formerly The Betty Ford, until they got "that really nasty letter" – is a haunt of students, journalists, bike couriers, and so on. It's really a pub with a wide beer selection, plus good all-day breakfasts. **Mimi's** (*218 Bathurst St., 416-703-6464*) is that dusty-looking window with the line-up of chicken-and-egg-shaped ceramics. To say it's small is an understatement. Eating breakfast there (do they serve other meals?) is about like when you go over to your friend's really cluttered apartment and you're both a bit hung over so she makes you eggs. We're surprised they even have a phone. But it's great. Honestly. **Mitzi's** (*100 Sorauren Ave., 416-588-1234*) is the Parkdale place with the patio and the big brunch line-ups. Like Barbie, she's *so* popular that she has a little sister – predictably named **Mitzi's Sister** – already in a second home that was once the classic Tennessee (*1554 Queen St. W., 416-532-2570*). What is it called? **Maggie's**. What do they serve? All-day breakfast. All right, they do other meals too. But we rest our case (*400 College St., 416-323-3248*).

Photo: Sarah B. Hood

Photo: Ontario Tourism, 12256

Chinese food is a whole world of regional styles and variations, and apparently, we've got 'em all. For rich, sweet Peking Duck, try **Champion House** (*486 Dundas St. W., 416-977-8282; 25 Watline Ave., 2nd floor, Mississauga, 905-890-8988*). For cheap and delicious noodle bowls, there's **King's Noodle** (*296 Spadina Ave., 416-598-1817*).

Seafood is the specialty at the perennially popular **Eating Garden** (*41 Baldwin St., 416-595-5525, eatinggarden.com*); their shrimp and banana spring rolls get high marks. Open late, **Swatow** (*309 Spadina Ave., 416-977-0601*) has great *congee* (rice porridge) with seafood chunks. The cutthroat food-court competition that used to prevail at Dragon City has moved south to the basement of **Chinatown Centre** (*222 Spadina Ave.*). All the vendors offer a four-items-for-$2.99 special (rice or noodle counts as an item). Each counter presents quite different fare, and the offerings range from the pedestrian (fried chicken) to the more adventurous (sausage-stuffed bitter melon), with lots

BOILING POINT

Most non-Chinese folks still haven't really figured out "hot pot" (known in Singapore as "steam boat"). It's essentially an Asian variant on the fondue theme, served for about $10 a person. When you order, a hot plate with a broth bowl is brought to the table. (You can have it spicier or blander, or both, in a divided bowl.) Then they pile the table with raw seafood, noodles, sliced beef, tripe, chicken, tofu, eggs, vegetables, and so on, and arm you with ladles, chopsticks, and mesh baskets. It's up to you to cook your own dinner communally, and you can have more of anything you like — or specify in advance the things you don't want. Added participatory fun comes from the opportunity to blend your own

Photo: John Hood

sauces from canisters of red and black bean sauce, vinegars, oils, soy sauces, and garlic — which may be out of sight until you ask about them. Our recommended hot pot outlet is **Lucky Dragon** (*418 Spadina Ave., 416-598-7823*), open until almost dawn. There's a "northern Chinese" variant at the **Great Khan Mongolian Grill** (*7131 Kennedy Rd., Markham, 905-947-8288*), where you can also sample meaty all-you-can-eat Mongolian barbecue.

Tip #1: Normal cooking rules apply, so don't lick the utensils you use to handle the raw meats unless you like to live dangerously.

Tip #2: Pork or fish balls are done when they float to the top.

of choices for the vegetarian who likes tofu. Then there are the yummy barbecue places — if you have no trouble walking past cooked whole beasts hoisted on meathooks in the window — like **Sing Sing B.B.Q. House** (*351 Broadview Ave., 416-778-8029*). Among the myriad outlets for dim sum, the never-ending buffet "à la cart," we especially like **Golden Mile** (*421 Dundas St. W., upstairs, 416-260-1818*) and **Pearl Court** (*633 Gerrard St. E., 416-463-8778*). For the stuffy, sweet, meat-filled curry buns, the classic outlet is **Yung Sing Pastry** (*22 Baldwin St., 416-979-2832*), but there are many others, like **Miao Ke Hong Bakery** (*345 Broadview Ave., 416-463-6388*).

Photo: John Hood

Like Chinese cuisine, the delights of South Asian food are a universe unto themselves, especially here where every region is amply represented. Relaxed and dependable are **Curry Twist** (*3034 Dundas St. W., 416-769-5460, currytwist.com*), **Sher-E-Punjab** (*351 Danforth Ave., 416-465-2125*), and **Woodlands** (*177 College St., 416-593-7700*). More elegant are the lovely **Indian Rice Factory** (*414 Dupont St., 416-961-3472*), **Kama Classical Indian Cuisine** (*214 King St. W., 416-599-5262*), and **Cuisine of India** (*5222 Yonge St., 416-229-0377*). **Bar-be-que Hut** (*1455 Gerrard St. E., 416-466-0411*) is the temple of the tandoor, featuring oven-baked meats like the dear but delectable shrimp tikka. You can enjoy similar cuisine of Pakistan under the colourful tent at **Lahore Tikka House** (*1365 Gerrard St. E., 416-406-1668*). Seriously spicy Tamil fare reigns at **Rashnaa** (*307 Wellesley St. E.,*

Photo: Sarah B. Hood

QUEEN VANIPHA

It's a dramatic instance of the ill wind that blows good. In 1980, would-be medical professional Vanipha Southalack arrived from Laos as a refugee and promptly, with members of her family, took charge of the kitchens of the newly-opened Rivoli and Queen Mother, just as Queen West was beginning to buzz. In those days, Thai food was so little known that the BamBoo Club menu featured "Thai Spicy Noodles" rather than "Pad Thai." But with the influx of fugitives from the horrible political situations of Cambodia and neighbouring areas, Toronto quickly

learned the taste for spring rolls, satay, and other Thai and Laotian treats. Southalack pioneered Vanipha in Kensington Market — now **Ban Vanipha** (*638 Dundas St. W., 416-340-0491*). Among the many other places that rode the lemongrass wave, we've always had a soft spot for **Satay on the Road** (*2306 Queen St. E., 416-698-8618; 1570-1572 Bayview Ave., 416-440-0679; 2003 Avenue Rd., 416-488-5153, satayontheroad.com*). Also, the coconut soup is good at **Somporn Thai Cuisine** (*2961 Dundas St. W., 416-604-0062*) but we'll confess we just enjoy getting to say the name.

416-929-2099), while unassuming little **Kabul Kebab House** (*1324 Gerrard St. E., 416-466-6000*) prepares the cuisine of Afghanistan: meat kebabs, cinnamon-spiced rice, and the filling steamed dumplings known as *mantoo*. For delicate and unusual spicing, we think the prize might have to go to **Elixir** (*522 Bloor St. W., 416-597-2915*), with its Persian/Indian fusion.

And then there's the streetside snack trade. We haven't found better samosas than those at **Narula's Chat, Dosa & Thali House** (*1438-A Gerrard St. E., 416-466-0434*). The crispy, chewy, delicately-seasoned vegetarian pockets are baked fresh about once a week, but not on a particular day; just, we're told, "whenever we run out." In the same neighbourhood there's a lively competition among several *paan* houses, all open late, usually blaring *bhangra* and surrounded by knots of young fellows on the sidewalk. The attractions? Barbecued corn with hot spices and lime juice, the Indian ice cream known as *kulfi*, and *paan*, a blend of ingredients like cumin, candied anise, slivered betel nut, and tobacco, all wrapped up in a betel leaf. *Paan* is meant to be chewed at leisure like a tobacco plug, and it produces a similarly juicy effect; it's also a mild stimulant. **Lahore Paan Centre** (*1431 Gerrard St. E., 416-462-3293*) is one of the most thriving paan locations.

Caribbean food is adapted from African cuisine, but it's also heavily influenced by East Indian recipes — especially in Guyana and Trinidad. **Bacchus Roti** (*1376 Queen St. W., 416-532-8191*) is Guyanese-run, and their excellent roti shells are made fresh. Try the shrimp! East-Indian Trinidad was the place of origin for the fried, chickpea-stuffed treats known as doubles, and Ali of **Ali's West Indian Roti** (*1446 Queen St. W., 416-532-7701*) claims to have been the first to bring them to Toronto. He's one of the few to offer delectable, chewy, conch-filled roti. Other notable roti shops include **Vena** (*646 Queen St. W., 416-504-8485; 1263 Bloor St. W., 416-532-3665*), and **Caribbean Roti Palace** (*744 Bathurst St., 416-533-7466*).

Photo: Sarah B. Hood

Jamaica is the home of flamingly spicy jerk chicken or pork, and **The Real Jerk**'s colourful dining room (*709 Queen St. E.. 416-463-6055*) has long been a mecca for jerk fans. For casual take-away, it's **Mr. Jerk** (*209 Wellesley St. E., 416-961-8913; 1552 Eglinton Ave. W., 416-783-1367; 1166 Morningside Ave., 416-724-9239; 1347A Lawrence Ave. W., 416-248-8609*). Then there are the two, unrelated Iries. **Irie Caribbean Restaurant & Caterers** (*808 College St., 416-531-4743*) is more traditional and liable to be

BACK TO OUR ROOTS ... AND LEGUMES AND RICE

Toronto's African communities have been growing over the past decade — especially the Somali community, well represented at establishments like **Café Sinai** (*1801 Lawrence Ave. E., 416-285-8005*), which dishes up Somali goat meat and rice with homemade hot sauce and fruit juices. Neighbouring Ethiopia, with its stewed meats and vegetables served atop an edible dish of *injera* bread, gives us and the long-established **Queen of Sheba** (*1051 Bloor St. W., 416-536-4162*), among others. **Boujadi** (*999 Eglinton Ave. W., 416-440-0258, boujadi.com*) is Moroccan, and the word everyone seems to use to describe it is "intoxicating." (All their meat is kosher.) The also-burgeoning Nigerian community boasts **B's Place** (*2133 Jane St., Unit 1, 416-242-8858*), while you can sample Congolese fare at **Faubourg Restaurant, Buffet & Bar** (*2362 Danforth Ave., 416-421-8933*).

DAIRY GHOST

For the past two decades diners in the university neighbourhood have enjoyed the moderately priced **John's Italian Caffe** (*27 Baldwin St., 416-598-8848*), but they've been puzzled by the Hebrew lettering on the window. It seems it's a case of new management having the good sense to maintain a little piece of area history on their premises. You see, at one time John's expanded into the spot that had previously been Mandel's Dairy. We're no Yiddish scholars, but we did our best to puzzle it out and can report with some confidence that the text translates as "Butter, cheese, cream, eggs. Fresh every day."

playing Bob Marley, whereas **Irie Food Joint** (*745 Queen St. W., 416-366-4743*) is more urbane and liable to be playing technojazz. We also like the venerable **Albert's Real Jamaican** (*542 St. Clair Ave. W., 416-658-9445*) and the homey **Island Foods** (*1182 King St. W., 416-532-6298*), while the destination for Jamaican patties is **Patty King** (*187 Baldwin St., 416-977-3191*), where they're baked fresh daily. Among other islands represented by Toronto eateries is St. Lucia, which gives us the subtle spicings of **Soul Food** (*582 Lansdowne, no telephone*).

That's Amore

With our huge Italian population, Toronto may have more fine and more varied Italian restaurants than those of any other national cuisine – with the possible exception of Chinese. To rattle off a list of some of the best in the downtown area: **Romagna Mia Osteria Pizzeria** (*106 Front St. E., 416-363-8370*) is a higher-end North Italian spot known for its risotto, veal, and seafood. Milanese **Toula**, in the Westin Harbour Castle Hotel (*1 Harbour Sq., 38th Floor, South Tower, 416-777-2002*), has a top-floor harbour view. Celebrity-spotting is one of the attractions of the romantic **Sotto Sotto Trattoria** (*116-A Avenue Rd, 416-962-0011*), with its pastas and grilled meats. Located in a charming house with an appropriate white-and-blue interior, **Adriatico** (*14 Dupont St., 416-323-7442*), as its name suggests, specializes in seafood. And we've long enjoyed the oasis on Yonge Street that is **Caffe Volo Pasta Ristorante** (*587 Yonge St., 416-928-0008*), an unexpected haven in a hectic strip, though less swanky than those listed above. Narrow **Terroni** (*720 Queen St. W., 416-504-0320*) serves thin-crust pizzas that are a favourite with west enders.

Along St. Clair, **Ferro** (*769 St Clair Ave. W., 416-654-9119*) is a destination for the chic pool-table crowd, with a varied menu, filling portions, and – according to our sources – the best pizzas in the city. **Marcello's Pizzeria** (*1163 St. Clair Ave. W., 416-656-6159*) serves excellent, moderately priced pastas and meat mains, but their pizza is a standout. Nearby **La Bruschetta** (*1317 St. Clair Ave. W., 416-656-8622*) is not only the genuine article, but a favourite of Tom Cruise's.

Further north, **Grano** (*2035 Yonge St., 416-440-1986*), with its warm, creative decor and great menu, gives the impression of an elegant and convivial family affair to which you've been invited. The Columbus Centre (*901 Lawrence Ave. W., 416- 789-5555*) features several eating spots, of which the most gracious is **Ristorante Boccaccio**, equally wonderful for a long and leisurely lunch or a splendid dinner.

OPA!

There are Greek restaurants in other parts of town, but we still think it's worth going out to the Danforth. On Saturday nights the neighbourhood's really crowded with "tourists"; Sunday is when Greek families go out to eat; the rest of the week is much quieter. In our opinion, if what you want is a big souvlaki dinner, just head for **Astoria Shish Kebob House** (*390 Danforth Ave., 416-463-2838*), the one with the mermaid fountain. For the less-common chicken souvlaki on a pita at lunchtime, try the unpretentious **Asteria Souvlaki Place** (*292 Danforth Ave., 416-466-5273; 679 Danforth Ave., 416-463 9765*).

Athenian Garden Restaurant *(526 Danforth Ave., 416-465-4001)*, with its tasty take-out tzatziki, used to be a favourite with former *NOW* restaurant critic and caterer Byron Ayanoglu — who was himself raised on Greek fare. A little more upscale and out-of-the-way is **Ellas** *(702 Pape Ave., 416-463-0334)*. Perhaps our favourite, for its fish soup and delightful baked-on-premise *mezes*, is **Pappas Grill** *(440 Danforth Ave., 416-469-9595)*, although it's not as fancy or popular as places like **Myth** *(417 Danforth Ave., 416-461-8383)*.

In the east end, a rather barren stretch of Queen is enlivened by **Pulcinella Trattoria Napoletana** *(1590 Queen St. E., 416-463-5373)*, decorated with icons of its Commedia dell'Arte namesake, which dishes up Neapolitan charm and homemade pastas. And, although we haven't yet visited **Michelangelo's Fine Italian Cuisine** *(1910 Gerrard St. E., 416-698-4891)*, we've witnessed near-swooning at the mention of their gnocchi with gorgonzola.

On a different scale entirely, the former Ford assembly plant is home to **Café Faema** *(672 Dupont Street, 416 535 1555, faema.net)*, named for and owned by the manufacturers of excellent espresso machines. Sunny and pretty, it's a cheerful spot for an afternoon business meeting over coffee and light fare. People still flock to **Camarra's Pizzeria & Restaurant** *(2899 Dufferin St., 416-789-3221)* for the legendary old-fashioned pizza, while **Bitondo Pizzeria & Sandwiches Ltd.** *(11 Clinton St., 416-533-4101)* has been luring downtown folks with their unforgettable panzerotti for almost 40 years. There's also a certain robust charm about **Pizza Gigi**'s *(189 Harbord St., 416-535-4444)* thick-crust products, and you can watch the Central Tech students compete on the video machine while someone heats up your slice.

Latin Licks

A growing South American population has recently been swelling the ranks of places serving food from Spanish-speaking lands; this is one of the most eclectic categories. Be warned that a mariachi band may actually stop at your table and play romantic songs to your and your sweetie at **Jalapeño** (*725 King St. W., 416-216-6743, jalapeno.ca*). However, it may be worth the risk to taste their oh-so-genuine high-end Mexican, with sophisticated hot sauces and real *mole* –

the Mexican savoury chocolate sauce. **El Sol** (*1448 Danforth Ave., 416-405-8074*) is a northwestern Mexican cantina that's so authentic it has cactus on the menu. Owner Yolanda also has an interest in promoting Mexican crafts and artwork, and occasionally offers cooking lessons. **El Penco** (*573 King St. W., 416-979-7287*) is a tiny little Ecuadorian lunch counter where you can eat a good hot meal for as little as $5. Also minuscule is the trusty, Salvadorean **Tacos El Asador** (*690 Bloor St. W., 416-538-9747*). Nudged in among a row of houses on a residential street, **Julie's Cuban Restaurant** (*202 Dovercourt Rd., 416-532-7397*) is actually a bit more upscale than it sounds, with good, Cuban-inspired tapas, delectable shredded meat, and a nice patio. Peruvian **El Bodegon** (*537 College St. W., 416-944-8297*), in its unobtrusive corner location, features mouthwatering ceviche: marinated squid, octopus, shrimp, fish, and clams, or (in the Ecuadorian variation) shrimp alone. **97 Bistro and Tapas Bar** (*97 Danforth Ave., 416-778-0007*) is a Spanish-from-Spain spot with live flamenco on the weekends. We might as well have included **New York Subway** (*520 Queen St. W., 416-703-4496*) under Indian food, because it's fusion at its weirdest. We decided it belonged here though because it has the feeling of a San Francisco taqueria, with vinyl decor, quick service, and minimal seating. What do they serve? Burrito-shaped food with Indian spices: real cheap, real good, and lots of choices for vegetarians.

PORTUGUESE PLENTY

One of our friends, a bike courier, has pretty much detached himself from his traditional Portuguese family, except, he says: "I go home for the rabbit." Portuguese cuisine is also famous for what it does with salt cod – while world stocks hold out. The take-out barbequed chicken and other meats from **Churrasqueira Oliveira** (*898 College St., 416-537-7133*) come highly recommended, as do those from **Churrasco of St. Clair** (*679 St. Clair Ave. W., 416-658-0652*). If you can find a seat on the patio, there's nothing so pleasant as chatting away a sunny afternoon over plates of seafood at **Amadeu's** (*184 Augusta Ave., 416-591-1245*), where you may spot *NOW Magazine* food critic Steven Davey. Way upscale is seafood site **Chiado** (*864 College St., 416-538-1910*), which many consider to rank among the top restaurants in the city.

Floor Show

On a summer Saturday afternoon, it's fun to sit on the sidewalk and watch the crowd go by. At **Louie's Coffee Stop** in the heart of Kensington (*235 Augusta Ave., 416-593-9717*) you can literally sit *on the sidewalk* (with a stool, of course) as you sip cappuccino or latte and munch biscotti, edging over occasionally to let a bicycle or bundle buggy pass by.

Photo: Ontario Tourism, 11934

EATING IN

But maybe you don't have the energy to venture out for your next meal after all. Used to be that delivery choices were mainly limited to pizza, chicken, and Chinese. Now you can order out for oysters, sushi, Cajun, Caribbean, or whatever else your tummy desires. Two different outlets have assembled a stable of excellent restaurants and will pick up an order for a modest fee: **SuperWaiter** (*416-782-7877, superwaiter.ca*) handles such spots as Aida's Falafel, St. Louis Bar and Grill, Bacchus Roti, Rancho Relaxo, and Shopsy's. The slightly more upscale **Restaurants on the Go** (*416-932-3999, restaurantsonthego.com*) delivers Whistling Oyster, Mövenpick, Masquerade, Il Fornello, and dozens of others. In both cases you can place an order either by phone or online.

Photo: Sarah B. Hood

Shore Dinner

There's only one good place to eat on the Toronto Islands, and that's **The Rectory Café** (*416-203-2152, torontoisland.org/rectory*). A year-round sanctuary of calm – if it's not between owners – it generally offers excellent coffees, fresh baking, ample breakfasts, and delicious hot meals, all a few minutes' walk west of the Ward's Island ferry docks. Lovely in the summer, it's also haunting on a softly sunny January afternoon when the lake is frozen, the trees are skeletal, and the fireplace is roaring. (For ferry service information, call 416-392-8193.)

Just Watch Out for Falling O's

Photo: Sarah B. Hood

Who would have thought when they built the new graduate student residence at the University of Toronto that it would include a restaurant with interesting architectural detailing (like the wooden-bowl sinks) and a fresh, light menu? **SpaHa** (*66 Harbord St., 416-260-6133*) is named for the intersection it sits on, Spadina at Harbord.

Cast of Theatre Smith-Gilmor's *The Serpent Woman* (1991)

Painting and poetry and performance on the streets and in the storefronts, on balconies and buses, in the parks and the pubs, and drilled into the very pavement. You can't get away from it: this city's all about the arts.

Hippie Lit

Senator David A. Croll Apartments, the staid seniors' residence at the corner of Bloor and Huron Streets, has a slightly more notorious past. From 1968 to 1975, this was the home of Rochdale College, an experiment in alternative education and communal living. A failed experiment, actually, since Rochdale quickly fell victim to ad hoc anarchy and a regime of drug deals and overdoses, three of them fatal. But out of this tumult came one of our most venerable publishing houses.

Coach House Press, the baby of Stan Bevington, started at 317 Bathurst Street. When the area was slated for slum clearance in 1968, the press moved right in behind Rochdale, at the rear of 401 Huron Street. Bevington even lived in the college, and the new neighbours mixed quite nicely, with a free flow of writers and artists moving from one establishment to the other. Over the years, the press has published early works by CanLit superstars Michael Ondaatje and Margaret Atwood. After a brief demise, it was renamed Coach House Books in 1996.

Storied Street

Everyone lives on Brunswick Avenue sooner or later. This was the first line in Katherine Govier's short story collection *Fables of Brunswick Avenue.* And she should know, having lived at house number 411 while writing some of those stories. Brunswick has been home to a surprising number of writers. Dennis Lee wrote *Civil Elegies and Other Poems* at 474, and Marian Engel penned *Bear* at 338. Morley Callaghan lived at 456 when he knocked off two novels: *They Shall Inherit the Earth* and *More Joy in Heaven.*

Any talk about local literature begins and ends with the same tomes: *In the Skin of a Lion* by Michael Ondaatje. Margaret Atwood's *Cat's Eye. Fugitive Pieces* by Anne Michaels. Time for something new? Here are ten titles for all tastes.

• From Allan Gardens to the (Metropolitan) Zoo, Lynn Crosbie's *Alphabet City* is a suite of poems that offers an intensely personal geography. Look for it in her collection *Queen Rat.*

• Hugh Garner's 1950 *Cabbagetown* is a gritty narrative about being down and out at Dundas and Sherbourne.

• *Moody Food*, a novel by Ray Robertson, is both an anthem and elegy to rock 'n' roll. Local boy Bill Hansen meets charismatic southerner Thomas Graham and together they take a wild, drug-fueled ride through 1960s Yorkville.

• Nalo Hopkinson's *Brown Girl in the Ring*, infused with Caribbean folklore, visits a future Toronto where only the poor, the powerless, and the predators remain after the wealthy have fled to a safe suburban outer circle. It won the Warner Aspect First Novel Contest, and it climaxes with a supernatural duel atop the CN Tower.

• *King Leary* by Paul Quarrington is a novel about the life and times of Percival Leary, an old-time star player for the Toronto Maple Leafs (note that spelling: this must be fiction). This odd, heartbreaking hockey tale won the Stephen Leacock Award for Humour in 1987.

• In Guy Gavriel Kay's Tolkienesque *The Summer Tree*, a party of unwitting adventurers vanishes from the middle of Philosopher's Walk right into a world of wizards and enchantment. It's the first book in Kay's Fionavar Tapestry trilogy, which also includes *The Wandering Fire* and *The Darkest Road.*

• Tough breaks and heartaches are the daily fare of the *Nine Men Who Laughed*, Austin Clarke's bitter story collection about West Indian immigrants trying to beat the odds.

• Acting Detective William Murdoch investigates a grisly murder in which his estranged father is the prime suspect in author Maureen Jennings' *Let Loose the Dogs*. Set in

Photo: Susie King

CIVIC TONGUE

In 2001, Dennis Lee became our city's first-ever Poet Laureate. Best known for his children's verses *Alligator Pie* and *Jelly Belly*, Lee has also written a handful of adult works. *Civil Elegies and Other Poems*, which won the Governor General's Award in 1972, is deeply rooted in Toronto. Poems in the book include "Brunswick Avenue" and "High Park, by Grenadier Pond." After his official appointment, Lee told reporters he's not going to start figuring out rhymes for "budget crisis."

Victorian Toronto, these moody mysteries are as authentic as they are engaging. This is the fourth book in the series that includes *Under the Dragon's Tail*, *Except the Dying*, and *Poor Tom is Cold*.

• Daniel Jones's posthumously published *The People One Knows* is an almost-autobiographical assembly of vignettes set in the early '80s Queen West arts scene.

• Take a ride around the old Canadian National Exhibition with *Wild Mouse*. Three stories by Derek McCormack and five poems by Chris Chambers feature a freak, a carny, and a Ferris wheel. Silly and sad in the way good nostalgia should be, the book also has great black-and-white photos.

Photo: Courtesy Estate of Milton Acorn

A REAL NUT

Milton Acorn truly lived the life of the poet. Born in Charlottetown, P.E.I., the cigar-chomping, working-class writer lived all over the country. His time in Toronto was not without incident. Like the summer of 1962, when he tried to read his poems aloud in Allan Gardens and was ticketed by a plainclothes cop. We're not too clear on what the actual charge was, but Acorn returned with friends the next week and read again. Again, he was ticketed. This scene repeated itself every weekend that summer, with the press capturing the whole free speech fiasco.

Through most of the 1970s, Acorn lived and worked in a room at the down-at-the-heels Waverley Hotel at College and Spadina. Actually, he lived in many rooms. Seems Acorn was convinced the RCMP, suspicious of his left-wing political views, was bugging his room, so he constantly moved around in the hotel to keep the spies at bay.

Good Things in Small Packages

In this city, the small press is big stuff. Independent publishers of mags, zines, and books are a healthy, hyper-literate bunch. Take *Taddle Creek* (*taddlecreekmag.com*), a twice-a-year magazine showcasing some of the city's best young writers and often featuring fantastic historical essays by Alfred Holden.

Kiss Machine (*kissmachine.org*) is Emily Pohl-Weary's irreverent zine of arts and culture, which features theme issues like sex and condiments (#3) or hospitals and aliens (#4). *She's Got Labe* (*shegotlabe@hotmail.com*) is all about sex, sex, sex. Articles cover Kegel exercises and the mysteries of female ejaculation. One issue even came with a blue tickle feather.

Illustrator Ian Phillips designs beautiful books at Pas de Chance (*interlog.com/~ian/*). Examples of these meticulously crafted *objets* include Elissa Joy's *Quiceñera*, a collection of 15 poems with a hand-printed cover on Japanese wood paper and 3D peek-a-boo eyeballs that stare out every time you turn the page. Local authors lend their talents, but not their names to Emily Schultz's *Pocket Canon* (*24hourarcade.com/pocketcanon*). The first in this series of anonymously-written chapbooks was *Anaïs*, a delicious spoof of Ms. Nin's sexcapades.

Photo: Tony Makepeace

The Annex has been a literary neighbourhood for a long time. So long, it's easy to forget all the writers who worked here. Recently, the city has been providing some helpful hints.

• Gwendolyn MacEwan Park, on Walmer Road, north of Bloor, is named for the Governor General's Award-winning poet. MacEwan (1941-1987) wrote otherworldly verse, often steeped in myth and magic. She also lived most of her life in the Annex and was known for feeding the numerous stray cats around the streets.

• Matt Cohen Park sits at the southeast corner of Bloor and Spadina. Fitting, since Cohen (1942-1999) called Spadina "the spine of the cosmos." Best known for his GG-winning novel *Elizabeth and After*, Cohen also wrote children's books under the name Teddy Jam.

Photo: Christina Harling

• Hidden away behind a string of houses, bpNichol Lane runs north of Sussex Avenue and east of Huron Street. Named for experimental poet and small press editor bpNichol (1944-1988), the laneway features one of his concrete poems (literally!), drilled right into the ground.

Photo: Howard Akler

A, E, I, O, U, AND SOMETIMES $

Eunoia is the shortest English word to use all five vowels. It's also the title of one of the best-selling poetry books in Canadian history. Written over seven years by Christain Bök, each chapter of *Eunoia* is devoted to a single vowel. Chapter A, for instance, offers this line: "Hassan can watch cancan gals cha-cha-cha, as brass bands blat jazz razzmatazz (what a class act)." The surprise hit of 2001, *Eunoia* has sold 15,000 copies where a "successful" Canadian poetry book tops out at 500. The book also won the $40,000 Griffin Poetry Prize for 2002.

Where do you go to find letters and doodles by *Peter Rabbit* creator Beatrix Potter? The book General Wolfe was reading the night before he died on the Plains of Abraham? Prints by William Blake? In this city, you just have to visit your local library. Our public library system is the busiest in North America, and 1.3 million Torontonians hold library cards. The most valuable book in the system, housed at Toronto Reference Library, is *The Birds of America* by James Audubon, valued at $2.2 million. Here's where to look for other gems.

Archives of Ontario

Founded in 1803, the Archives of Ontario hold provincial records including Census documents, vital statistics, land records, maps, photos, and memorabilia relating to Ontario people and businesses. They boast that their printed material alone would fill 45 miles of one-foot boxes. Highlights of the collection include original letters from the likes of Mahatma Gandhi, Florence Nightingale, George Washington, and Friedrich Nietszche.
77 Grenville St., 416-327-1600, archives.gov.on.ca

Arthur Conan Doyle Collection, Toronto Reference Library

Toronto boasts the only special library collection devoted to author Sir Arthur Conan Doyle and the world's second largest collection of memorabilia relating to his most famous creation: Sherlock Holmes. (In fact, the material is displayed in a room that strangely resembles The Master's Baker Street digs.) And nobody could be more pleased about the collection than The Bootmakers of Toronto (c/o 5 Brownlea Avenue, M9P 2R5), Toronto's avid Sherlockian society. Named for the maker of Sir Henry Baskerville's boots in the famous tale of *The Hound of the Baskervilles*, the society meets every second month – usually at the library – to discuss matters of interest to students of the great detective. A year's membership costs $25.
789 Yonge St., 416-395-5577, tpl.toronto.on.ca

DOGGIE TALE

Like *Black Beauty* and *Lassie Come Home*, the 1893 novel *Beautiful Joe*, about an abused dog who finds loving treatment, has wrung rivers of tears from young readers. Written as a call for kindness to animals, it was the first Canadian book to sell more than a million copies. Author Margaret Marshall Saunders (who wrote under her middle name in an age that still didn't quite countenance women authors) lived and wrote at 62 Glenowan Road in north Toronto. (By the way, her book has nothing whatsoever to do with the 2000 Sharon Stone film of the same name.)

Canadiana Branch, North York Central Library

This is the jackpot for people who are interested in researching their family history in Ontario. Besides general Canadian historical holdings, the library houses the collections of the Ontario Genealogical Society, the Toronto Division of the Jewish Genealogical Society of Canada, the Canadian Society of Mayflower Descendants, and la Société franco-ontarienne d'histoire et de généalogie de Toronto.
5120 Yonge St., 6th floor, 416-395-5623

City of Toronto Archives

Photo: Howard Akler

If you've ever seen the end of *Raiders of the Lost Ark*, you know what the viewing platform at the Toronto Archives looks like. In case you haven't, it's a window in the wall that gives you a sobering view of a cavernous two-storey room crammed with identical brown cardboard boxes, the repository of all things related to running the city. Yes, there's plenty of dull stuff here – like council minutes going back to the year dot – but there's also a sensational photo collection, including 40,000 shots taken by *Globe and Mail* photographers. The research room is always humming with folks checking out TTC records, diaries, and other documents in the collection, whose earliest item is likely the 1792 plan of Toronto Harbour.
255 Spadina Rd., 416- 397-5000,
city.toronto.on.ca/archives/

AS I SAY, LYING

Young Billy Falkner came to Toronto from Mississippi in July 1918. He had wanted to be a pilot and fight in the First World War. He first tried to enlist in the U.S. Air Force, but did not meet the height requirement, so he headed north. Hoping to increase his chances, he faked a British accent and changed his name to the more formal-sounding William Faulkner. He was accepted by the Canadian Air Force and was sent to Long Branch for basic training. In September, he was shipped to Wycliffe College on the University of Toronto campus to study engine repair and navigation. Two months later, the war ended.

Faulkner returned home a changed man. Or rather, he returned home pretending to have changed. He had photos of himself in an officer's uniform, even though he was only a cadet. He boasted of solo flights despite never having earned his wings. He even affected a limp and alluded to a mysterious crash landing. War hero or no, young Billy really had honed his talents in Toronto, talents that would serve him well in his later career as a writer of brilliant fiction.

Merril Collection of Science Fiction, Speculation, & Fantasy

Judith Merril was an American science fiction writer and editor who came north with the influx of Vietnam War draft dodgers. Our gain! She moved into the notoriously bohemian Rochdale College, along with her formidable sci-fi collection, then groovily named the Spaced Out Library. It has ballooned into a 57,000-item research collection that's especially important for its original art and perishable pulp magazines dating back to the '20s. (The library holds the Fantastic Pulps Show and Sale on the last Saturday of April where die-hard fans can drool over such literary classics as the early editions of *Weird Tales, Doc Savage,* and *Spicy Adventure Stories.*)
239 College St. 3rd Floor, 416-393-7748, tpl.toronto.on.ca

BURIED AFFECTION

Folklore and children's stories may have been her life, but Joan Bodger's personal history was no fairytale. The beloved pioneering story collector and teller suffered great losses through illness and death in her immediate family, but she was never daunted, and shone as a beacon of wisdom and humour to her many friends right to the end of her life. Apparently typical of her courage, inventiveness, and loyalty is the story of how she buried her husband Alan Mercer. As he was nearing the end of his life, the couple decided that his ashes should rest in some Toronto cultural institution. Thus, when the Lillian H. Smith Library (destined as the home of the Osborne Collection of children's books) was under construction, Bodger — perhaps on the theory that it's easier to get forgiveness than permission — made her own, quite unofficial arrangements to bypass the construction barricades and personally deposit her late husband's ashes in the foundations, where they rest to this day.

Osborne Collection of Early Children's Books

Photo: Sarah B. Hood

Once upon a time there was a marvelous library with over 70,000 children's books and related items. Many date from the days before there really were books for kids: like "horn books" – little inscribed plaques for teaching first letters and prayers, tiny, readable "thumb bibles," and the earliest flash cards, from the late 1700s. There are also woodblocks and original illustrations; book-related games, lots of contemporary children's fiction, and a 14th-century vellum illustrated and hand-lettered edition of *Aesop's Fables,* the oldest book in any Toronto public library. (We know it's there, and we know it's lovely, because the library happily showed it to us when we went for a visit.)
239 College St. 4th Floor, 416-393-7753, tpl.toronto.on.ca

Parkdale Library

A particularly good collection relating to Black history and Caribbean Canadian culture, due in large measure to the pioneering efforts of the revered Dr. Rita Cox.
1303 Queen St. W., 416-393-7686, tpl.toronto.on.ca

Thomas Fisher Rare Book Library

Half a million books and other documents, including a 3,800-year-old cuneiform tablet, 14th-century cabbalistic works, Galileo's handwritten notebooks, and the extremely rare (11 known copies) "Wicked Bible," with the typo "thou *shalt* commit adultery," as well as maps, theatre programmes, chapbooks, and prints. And if you have a legitimate research project, they'll encourage you to handle almost anything in the collection — with your bare hands!
120 St. George St., 416-978-5285,
library.utoronto.ca/fisher

The United Church of Canada/Victoria University Archives

Housed in this quiet, medieval-style building are the records of that most Canadian of denominations, the United Church of Canada, as well as the churches that were merged to form it, and documents relating to the history of Victoria University.
73 Queen's Park Cres. E., 416-585-4563,
vicu.utoronto.ca/archives/archives.htm

Urban Affairs Library

A companion and complement to the City of Toronto Archives, this sunny, airy reading room houses books, directories, planning documents, and other materials related to the building of the city.
Metro Hall, 55 John St., 416-395-5577,
tpl.toronto.on.ca

ANNE OF HIGH PARK

The name of Lucy Maud Montgomery is virtually synonymous with Prince Edward Island. But the *Anne of Green Gables* author actually lived out her last years in Toronto. In March 1935, the Montgomery family moved into a house she ominously called Journey's End, at 210 Riverside Drive, not far from High Park. Splitting time between writing and caring for her husband, who was in fragile mental health, Montgomery soon fell ill herself. She had a nervous breakdown in 1940 and never wrote another word. She died in 1942.

Words for Sale

If you're looking for something good to read, you don't always have to hit the nearest bookstore. Try **Canzine** (*brokenpencil.com*), the annual festival of all things independent and photocopied. A lesser known, but equally inspired, gathering is the **Cut 'n' Paste Fair** (*comeaumichael@hotmail.com*), the apotheosis of the do-it-yourself aesthetic. For old newspapers, magazines, postcards, and other ephemera, you can't beat the **Old Paper Show and Sale** (*416-410-1310*), held spring and fall at the Harbourfront Antique Market. Indie publishers hock their wares twice a year at the **Small Press Book Fair** (*torontosmallpressbookfair.org*) and, in 2003, the first-ever **Toronto Comic Arts Fair** (*torontocomics.com*) was penciled into artists' schedules. And lastly, there is **Word on the Street** (*thewordonthestreet.ca*), the city's biggest literary event. Held on the last Sunday of every September, WOTS commandeers seven blocks of Queen West, between Spadina and University, where readings are staged, author signings are scheduled, and publishers and bookstores show off and sell all manner of books.

WILDE TIMES

Robert Ross was the grandson of Robert Baldwin, an early advocate of responsible government in these parts. Born in 1869, he spent the first three years of his life in the area near Dufferin and St. Clair before the family moved to England. As a 17-year-old at Oxford, he met and seduced a man nearly twice his age: Oscar Wilde. The affair was over within months, but their friendship lasted a lifetime. Ross stuck by his infamous friend through obscenity trials and exile, and was named literary executor after Wilde's death in 1900. Ross died in 1918 and asked that his ashes be interred with Wilde's, but his high society family refused and it took over 30 years before Ross's last wish could be fulfilled.

Looking through the local media, it sometimes seems our art has never got past the Group of Seven. Nothing could be further from the truth. Here are a few who've made their mark.

• His work is lovely and utterly useless: cardboard replicas of everyday appliances, made from the box they came in; marble carvings of Styrofoam containers. James Carl walks the line between art and consumption. He also curates *The Balcony*, an ongoing series of easily-reproduced images that hang from his apartment balcony at 183A Augusta Avenue in Kensington Market. Participants have included General Idea's AA Bronson and 2001 Governor General's Award winner Tom Dean.

• Glen Crumback's drawings are often compared to those of Winnipeg star Marcel Dzama. One of the major differences is that Crumback's work contains original drawings and found images. The result is immediately surreal and oddly touching.

• Diverse as they come, Germaine Koh makes ordinary objects extraordinary. Her diary excerpts have been published as classified ads and she once devised a machine that translated computer keystrokes into smoke puffs of Morse code. She also hosts *weewerk*, a series of twice-a-month art salons in her small apartment.

• Tayna Read is the creator of Mr. Nobody, a cat-like cartoon whose simple, beatific existence is inevitably at odds with modern technology. Mr. Nobody has been mass-produced on T-shirts and meticulously hand-drawn on single sheets of paper. He has been featured in old-style animated cartoons and recreated as a giant robot – called Nobot, naturally.

LIKE A BAT OUT OF HELL

Do the undead like to toboggan? Probably not, if we base anything on Bram Stoker's experience. In February 1884, the *Dracula* author was in town as stage manager for Henry Irving's travelling theatre troupe. Invited to Riverdale ravine with the Toronto Toboggan Club, Stoker would fly downhill and repeatedly fall off the sled. He kept trying, but the toboggan was just too bloody fast.

CAFFEINE DREAMS

• A senior artist by any standards, Jamaican-born Winsom is best known for her fabric art – she studied traditional textile symbology across Africa – and for her paintings and installations on spiritual themes. Inspired by the ancient religions of the Ashanti, Carib, and Arawak peoples, her installations often incorporate altars or gateways between this plane and the spirit realm. (One such outdoor work was promptly struck by lightning.) Her work has been shown at the AGO, across Canada, and internationally, and she has a great gallery at *winsomwinsom.com*.

• Kika Thorne's videos have been described as "low-tech documents of the underclass." Basically, this means her work veers between the personal and the political. Her guerrilla style was perhaps best showcased in *Mattress City*. The eight-minute video, shot with frequent collaborator Adrian Blackwell, covers a 1998 megacity protest in which a group of activists staged a public bed-in at Nathan Phillips Square.

• If there's a more intelligent humorist in Canada than Mike Constable, we have yet to meet them. The bearded and beret-topped activist spent about a quarter-century curating  political art at Partisan Gallery. A cartoonist for magazines from the *Canadian Tribune* to *Saturday Night* to *The National Post*, he's also created just about every satirical giant puppet you've ever seen at a political demonstration in this town. Constable's sly, piercing wit belies dogged dogmatism; some of his wicked animations are posted at *web.net/~animated*.

Photo: Bryce Duffy

• No one else in the city – perhaps no one in the world – has elevated knitting to such a high level of artistic ingenuity and off-the-wall creativity as Janet Morton. Javacheff Christo made a reputation wrapping buildings and islands in plastic, but Morton thinks nothing of knitting a house cozy – sort of like a tea cozy, but much, *much* bigger. Some of her quirkier projects have included neck warmers for giraffes and sweaters for plastic snakes. She also spent a week in a store window, where passersby could watch her knitting the news of the day into a gigantic scarf-like document.

• Anyone who's spent any time at all downtown knows Barbara Klunder, who's made her joyfully spiky and swirly style of illustration the virtual trademark of Toronto. She created the signature look of the BamBoo Club, right down to the matches, and *NOW Magazine*'s Deirdre Hanna has called her "Toronto's patron saint of the good-cause T-shirt." Her multimedia gallery work is invariably filled with verbal as well as visual puns; she's even created a typeface, and the Rolling Stones came to her to design the merchandise for their *Voodoo Lounge* tour.

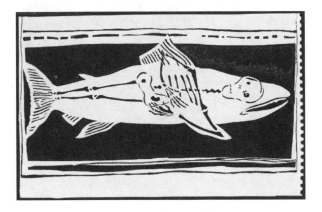

Art Bar Poetry Series
*Victory Café, 581 Markham St.,
416-516-5787, artbar.org*

Cryptic Chatter
*Renaissance Café, 1938 Danforth
Ave., 416-698-6188*

I.V. Lounge Reading Series
*I.V. Lounge, 326 Dundas St. W.,
416-593-5105*

Lexiconjury
*The Pilot Tavern, 22 Cumberland St.,
416-923-5716*

The Scream in High Park is
an annual July reading in the
great outdoors. *the scream.ca*

Syntactic Sunday
*Free Times Café, 320 College St.,
416-967-1078*

**U of T Bookstore
Reading Series**
*214 College St.,
416-978-7900 ext.9*

Bookstores

Acadia Books

Great shop for out-of-print art books.

232 Queen St. E., 416-364-7638

Annex Books

Looking for CanLit? Look no further.

1083 Bathurst St., 416-537-1852

Another Man's Poison

All about design, collectibles,
and architecture.

29 McCaul St., 416-593-6451

Another Story

General, kids, and educational books.

164 Danforth Ave., 416-462-1104

**Bakka Science Fiction
Book Shoppe**

Ray guns and cyberpunk.

598 Yonge St., 416-963-9993

Balfour Books

Used book shop strong on art and lit.

601 College St., 416-531-9911

**Ballenford Books
on Architecture**

Building a collection?

600 Markham St., 416-588-0800

Seth, the ubiquitous, one-named magazine illustrator, also happens to be one of our best-known comic book artists. Hs graphic novel, *It's A Good Life If You Don't Weaken*, is filled with pages of moody and evocative city scenes. But in 2002, Seth moved to the nearby town of Guelph, so there's open competition for top spot. Here are four candidates.

• Matt Blackett (*mattbcomic.com*) has been self-publishing his mini-comic, *M@B*, since 1998. Snatches of dialogue and mundane moments add up to a complete, three-panel diary of Blackett's life. In 2003, eight issues of his comic were collected in a volume called *Wide Collar Crimes*.

• Her 2000 graphic novel, *Can of Worms*, is Catherine Doherty's autobiographical tale of the adopted artist's search for her birth mother. Wordless save for reprinted correspondence, the story has the perfect pacing of a silent movie.

• If you dropped the old *Pogo* comic strip into modern consumer society, you'd get *Enter Avariz*, Marc Ngui's 2003 book. But Ngui (*bumblenut.com*) also knows his local history. His comic strip tour of Cabbagetown appeared in the *Toronto Star* in 1999. Future tours will cover the Humber River and the old town of York.

• Another comics artist interested in history is Diana Tamblyn. Her biography of insulin founder Frederick Banting first appeared in the acclaimed anthology *SPX 2002*. One year later, Tamblyn (*speedlines.com*) published an expanded edition under her own imprint.

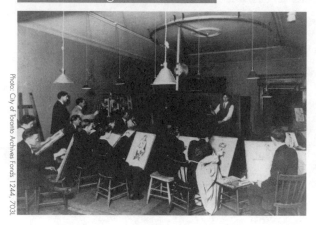

Photo: City of Toronto Archives Fonds 1244, 703I.

The art community has been centred on Queen West for so long now it's easy to assume that has always been the case. Not so. In the late 19th century, artists gathered in the Yonge and Adelaide area. The centre of bohemia was the old Toronto Arcade, a three-storey structure at 131-139 Yonge Street. With shops on the ground floor and a peaked glass roof to let in natural light, the Arcade was an early version of the Eaton Centre. Top floor studios were rented out for five dollars a month. There was no gallery system at this time, so recognition came only through self-promotion in art clubs such as the Toronto Art Students League, which held drawing classes and meetings at 56 King East. A sketch group called Little Billie met in the back room of a joint called McConkey's, at 27 King West. Art supply shops like Art Metropole and Matthews & Brothers, both on Yonge, would occasionally hold exhibitions.

The Beguiling
One of North America's best comic shops, specializing in independent comics, manga, and original art.
601 Markham St., 416-533-9168

Photo: Sarah B. Hood

Book City
Friendly independent chain has thrived in the face of the superstores.
501 Bloor St. W., 416-961-4496;
348 Danforth Ave, 416-469-9997;
1950 Queen St. E., 416-698-1444;
2350 Bloor St. W., 416-961-9412;
1430 Yonge St., 416-961-1228

Chapters
Flagship store for the Canadian chain.
110 Bloor St. W., 416-920-9299;
other locations

Contact Editions
The biggest used book shop in town.
759 Mount Pleasant Rd.,
416-322-0777

The Cookbook Store
Whatever your taste.
850 Yonge St., 416-920-2665

David Mirvish Books on Art
Browser's delight.
596 Markham St., 416-531-9975

A Different Booklist

African and Caribbean selection.
746 Bathurst St., 416-538-0889

Glad Day Bookshop

Long-time stop for gay
and lesbian books.
598-A Yonge St., 416-961-4161

Indigo

Books, candles, coffee, more books.
55 Bloor St. W., 416-925-3536;
other locations

Jamie Fraser Books

Pulp magazines, out-of-print mystery
and sci-fi, and scattered movie books.
427-A Queen St. W., 416-598-7718

Letters Bookstore

Over 30 years of small press.
77 Florence St., 416-537-5403

McBurnie and Cutler

Classic used book shop, with good
local history section.
698 Queen St. W., 416-504-8873

Nicholas Hoare

Fireplace, comfy chairs, and books.
45 Front St. E., 416-777-2665

Pages Books and Magazines

Hip lit and culture.
256 Queen St. W., 416-598-1447

Pandemonium Books and Discs

The best book shop in the Junction.
And the only one.
2862 Dundas St. W., 416-769-5257

Arts Enclave

Photo: Sarah B. Hood

The elegant arched doorway at 14 Elm Street is the entrance to a select society: the Toronto Arts & Letters Club. Formed in 1908, it has been both a home for senior artists and a social club for other professionals who may not practice the arts, but appreciate them. Inside, there's a grand dining hall, much like a smaller version of the quasi-Medieval Great Hall at Hart House (no surprise; they used some of the same building materials), plus meeting rooms, a bar, and a library. Throughout, the walls are covered with photos and artwork reflecting the careers of illustrious past members like former Governor General Vincent Massey, composers Healey Willan, Louis Applebaum, and Sir Ernest MacMillan, the Group of Seven, author Robertson Davies, music festival founder Nicholas Goldschmidt, playwright, performer and producer Mavor Moore, and eminent theatre critic Herbert Whittaker, to name a very few.

Sacred Images

A hidden trove of Group of Seven artwork is to be found at St. Anne's Anglican Church (*270 Gladstone Ave., 416-536-3160*), designed by Ford Howland in a – for the time and place – very offbeat domed Byzantine style. In 1923, painter J.E.H. MacDonald was commissioned to decorate the interior, and he brought along his GO7 buds Frederick Varley and Franklin Carmichael to help him produce 17 murals on the life of Jesus Christ, as well as local sculptors Frances Loring and Florence Wyle to embellish the interior ceiling.

More Than Meets the Eye

Photo: Sarah B. Hood

Want to see one of the city's secret attractions? Easy. Just walk down the first alley off Portland Avenue, south of Queen Street; the walls are covered in graffiti, pieces, and throw-ups as far as the eye can see. Graf artists from all over come to Queen between Bathurst and Spadina, looking to leave their mark, like TRIK, who made his name by tagging high up on the Bathurst Street Bridge.

But not everyone is impressed. Take Staff Sergeant Heinz Kuck, who heads the police Graffiti Eradication Program. Using a team of volunteers and students doing mandatory community service, Kuck has reclaimed over 16,000 square feet of downtown city space. As far as he's concerned, graf artists are vandals who often get off easy with a mischief charge and fine.

Then there's someone like Duro III. An artist with over 400 murals (legal and illegal) to his credit, he has moved from the simple world of tagging to owning his own multimedia company, Vengence9. His clients include HMV Canada and Absolut Vodka.

Cartoon Characters

About 130 cartooning connoisseurs are members of the Toronto Animated Image Society (*37 Hanna Ave., 416-533-7889, awn.com/tais*), an organization that promotes the skills and appreciation of animation. They hold screenings and classes, and offer members a discount on related arts supplies. They also hold an annual picnic on Toronto Island, where, we expect, they hold animated conversations. (Sorry.)

She Said Boom
Used books and CDs.
372 College St., 416-944-3224;
393 Roncesvalles Ave.,
416-531-6843

Silver Snail Comic Shop
Oldest comic store is still your one-stop X-Men shop.
367 Queen St. W., 416-593-0889

**This Ain't the
Rosedale Library**
It sure ain't. Lots of lit and gender studies.
483 Church St., 416-929-9912

Toronto Women's Bookstore
A quarter century strong.
73 Harbord St., 416-922-8744

**University of
Toronto Bookstore,
St. George Campus**
More than just textbooks.
214 College St., 416-978-7900

Uprising
Anarchist, activist, and upstairs.
685 Queen St. W., 2nd floor,
416-516-2966

World's Biggest Bookstore
Toronto's original mega-store, just off Yonge.
20 Edward St., 416-977-7009

Photo: Min Sook Lee

ART AND TRASH

In August 2000, the city teamed up with the Toronto Environmental Alliance and the Canadian Union of Public Employees to present the *Garbage Collection*, a trio of painted garbage trucks. Using themes of air, earth, and water, each truck would illustrate the importance of co-operation between unions and environmentalists. But when one mural portrayed two politicians swapping money and a trash train heading out of town, the truck was quickly whitewashed. Too controversial, considering the city was being roundly criticized for sending trash to an abandoned mine in northern Kirkland Lake.

Photo: Sarah B. Hood

For most of the year, strollers, bladers, and cyclists near the Ward's Island ferry docks may be intrigued by the oversize rusted metal assemblages hanging from the fence of the Island tennis courts. Upon closer inspection, these will prove to be fantastical welded sculptures depicting strange creatures, like the winged toad that is the mascot of Island residents. Should they be so lucky as to visit the Island on certain dates of the year (like the Friday of the Simcoe Day weekend), these visitors will have a rare chance to see them in their full glory, when artist Bruce Smith connects them up to a gas feed line and sets them alight. His ornate fire sculptures are sometimes installed in the lake off the beach after dark, where the blazing images are reflected in rippling water. They have had winter outings on the ice of the lagoon, and they can be adapted to shower water instead of flame.

Photo: Min Sook Lee

Big Draw

Musicians do it, why not cartoonists? That was the thinking of Dave Howard when he founded the Toronto Comic Jam in 1996. Hoping to foster a comics community, Howard and an average of thirty others gather together at the Cameron House (*408 Queen St. W.*) on the last Tuesday of the month. The jam is simple: one cartoonist draws a panel and passes it on to the next cartoonist, who adds a panel; on and on it goes, until the story is finished and the group has drawn closer.

Missing Murals

Users of the Dufferin-St. Clair branch of the Toronto Public Library (*1625 Dufferin St.*) may be unaware that they're walking around under buried treasures. At the beginning of their careers, the now celebrated painters George Reid (pictured above) and Doris McCarthy were commissioned (in 1926 and 1932, respectively) to create murals for the upper level of the library walls; Reid's depicted themes like "Community Life," while McCarthy's showed fairytale characters. In a misguided renovation in 1964, the images were painted over, and now lie under seven layers of household paint.

The Regal Heights Residents' Association has been working with the library to raise funds to reveal and restore the work, section by section. At the time of writing only a small test patch – fortuitously showing a hand holding a book – had been uncovered. (Incidentally, McCarthy spent more than 40 years living and working in a scenic property at 1 Meadowcliffe Drive in Scarborough, which she named "Fool's Paradise." In 1999 she donated her land and home to the city, which in return has named a walking trail along the adjacent Bellamy Ravine for her.)

Galleries, Fresh & Unusual

Centre for Addiction and Mental Health often displays art done by patients.
1001 Queen St. W., 416-583-4339

Gallery 1313 is the hub of the thriving Parkdale arts scene.
1313 Queen St. W., 416-536-6778, g1313.org

Gladstone Hotel Art Bar is where you go for guzzlin' and gazin'.
1214 Queen St., W., 416-531-4635

Katharine Mulherin Contemporary Art Projects.
A trio of them, actually, that showcases some of the city's best young artists.
1040 Queen St. W.;
1080 Queen St. W.;
1086 Queen St. W., 416-537-8827

S.P.I.N. Gallery is one people always point to when they talk about the gallery boom.
156-158 Bathurst St.,
416-530-7656

Stephen Bulger Gallery specializes in photography.
700 Queen St. W., 416-504-0575

Hudson's Bay Company Gallery is media magnate Ken Thomson's private collection of Canadian art for public viewing.
104 Bay St., 9th Floor,
416-861-4571

YYZ Artists' Outlet is a long-standing artist-run centre.
401 Richmond St. W.,
416-598-4546

Look! Up in the Skyscraper!

Superman is the ultimate immigrant story. A young boy arrives from a strange land, grows up, and makes good in his adopted home. Much like the Man of Steel, comic artist Joe Shuster was a success. Born in Toronto in 1914, Shuster and his family moved to Cleveland, Ohio ten years later. There he met Jerry Siegel and the two young men created the comics world's most enduring character. Although resolutely American, Superman's adventures were clearly tinged by his creator's hometown. Clark Kent, the mild-mannered reporter, worked for a newspaper called *The Daily Star*. Eventually, the name was changed to *The Daily Planet*. The city of Metropolis was modelled on Toronto, so whenever Superman leapt over tall buildings in a single bound, he was hurdling a very familiar skyline.

The Performing Arts Scene

Photo: Ontario Tourism, 11198

Toronto is the third largest theatre production centre in the English-speaking world. Although the average person might recognize more famous names among the casts of London and New York shows, Toronto is home to a staggering number of original productions each year – certainly more than on Broadway (which is going through a period of Revival Hell at the moment). There are over 200 professional theatre and dance companies in Toronto, putting on about 10,000 live performances annually in some 90 venues. There are another 200-plus music presenters, including orchestras, chamber ensembles, opera companies, and choirs. Together, they perform at least 4,200 concerts a year.

Cheap Seats

Photo: Sarah B. Hood

Megamusicals aside, most Toronto tickets fall in the $10 to $25 range, but insiders know how to get even better deals. First off, the cheapest nights are Tuesdays and Wednesdays (most venues are "dark" on Mondays), and it's always worth asking about discounts for students, seniors, card-carrying members of arts organizations, or the "unwaged" (as it's often put). Many theatre productions and some dance or music events offer "PWYC" (Pay What You Can) tickets on Sunday matinees or other designated days. There's usually a suggested minimum. The T.O. TIX booth at Yonge-Dundas Square offers half-price tickets for a varying roster of theatre and dance productions on the day of performance (lots of actors shop there). When shows announce a sell-out, it's sometimes possible to get a "rush seat" by showing up at the box office one hour before performance. (This only works with larger venues.) Group rates are less expensive, and a group can be as few as 20 people ... sometimes even less.

Wired to the Scene

There's a trend to Internet ticket sales, and not just for rock concerts and big-ticket shows. The first one serving the independent theatre and dance community is the 24-hour Absolut Central Box Office at *torontoboxoffice.ca*. During the day and early evening, the phone line is also open at 416-504-PLAY.

QUICKIES

Walk through any major intersection and you're going to be blasted by images. Store signs, buses plastered with ads. Sale! Sale! All of it a blur. Into this scene comes Year Zero One, an online collective of digital artists. In the fall of 2002, founders Camille Turner and Michael Alstad booked time on a third-storey video billboard in the Yonge and Bloor area, cutting into regular commercial time with a series called Transmedia 2002. Each video in the series was 15 seconds long and provided sharp commentary on our celebrity-obsessed commercial culture. Alistair Gentry offered a mock ad called *Celebritoy*, with the caption that read "You're nothing until you're famous." Alstad's entry was slightly more notorious. His sampling of Andy Warhol's 1964 film *Blow Job* was called *Speed*, after the billboard owners rejected its original title: *15 Second Blow Job*. Sounds like a natural to us.

Philanthropists

You'd have to be pretty generous to top the largesse of local philanthropists. To date, the record is held by Senator Michael Meighen and his wife Kelly Meighen, who donated $5 million to the Stratford Festival a few years ago. (Kelly Meighen worked in the Stratford box office in her youth, and apparently had a *really* good time there.) Pioneering geneticist Lou Siminovich has created an important $100,000 annual award to go to a Canadian playwright, a designer, and a director in alternate years. Made permanent by an endowment fund of over $1 million, the Siminovich Prize honours his wife Elinore Siminovich, a playwright and lover of the arts. Though not phenomenally wealthy himself, the late Peter Sandor made a huge impact on the Baroque music community through a series of generous gifts to organizations like Opera in Concert and Opera Atelier. (As one awed company member remarked, "He'd given all his money away by the time he died.") Sandor was made an honorary graduate of York University for his contributions to the musical life of Toronto and Canada.

SPECIFIC IDEA

For over 20 years, AA Bronson, Felix Partz, and Jorge Zontal were the superstars of our art scene. Known as General Idea, their witty, pop culture critiques came in a wide array of media. *FILE* was a subversive send-up of *LIFE* magazine. The Miss General Idea pageant was surreal performance art. And even after the 1994 AIDS-related deaths of Partz and Zontal ended their collaboration, the idea of General Idea carries on at Art Metropole. Founded by G.I. in 1974, Art Metropole is a non-profit distribution centre that allows contemporary artists to bypass the common gallery system. Focusing on art in non-traditional formats such as books, multiples, and videos, Art Metropole represents almost 800 artists and 2,000 works at a time, including international art stars Yoko Ono, Christain Boltanski, and our own (transplanted) Canadian Janet Cardiff.

Gals' Night Out

Nightwood Theatre is Toronto's esteemed feminist theatre company. It's been responsible for developing some of the most important Canadian work by women playwrights. Formed in 1979 by Cynthia Grant, Kim Renders, Mary Vingoe, and Maureen White, Nightwood gave first productions to Djanet Sears's *Harlem Duet* and Ann-Marie MacDonald's *Good Night Desdemona (Good Morning Juliet)*. The annual sell-out fundraiser FemCab is a sensational lineup of famous and infamous women performing five-minute bits. In the comedy world, witty women come out to quip at the annual March of Dames comedy festival, originally a one-night stand, but now a full week of funny females. Alumnae Theatre, one of the oldest in town, is an amateur company of high calibre that stages full productions and develops new work by women at their New Ideas festival. And women who love women have an event all their own: *Strange Sisters*, Buddies in Bad Times' occasional "sexy lesbian cabaret."

Conducting Energy

Silver is the best conductor of heat and electricity, so we think there should be a silver medal for Alan Gasser (pronounced "gosser"). It would be our unofficial "best conductor" award for the funkiest choir director in town. He leads the spine-tingling, twelve-member Darbazi (pictured above, Gasser is far right) in the exciting polyphony of Georgia – the republic, not the state. He also codirects the Echo Women's Choir with his wife, Becca Whitla. The Echo repertoire is broadly multicultural and motivated by a spirit of social justice – it's also fun. Darbazi has a 2001 recording called *Darbazi & Friends: Music from Beyond the Black Sea* (*argosoft.com/darbazi*), and the Echo Choir's *Gonna Sing and Shout* (*deepdownproductions.com/artists/echo.htm*) can be found in an eclectic range of small shops around town. Some of this city's other offbeat choirs are the Chinese-Canadian Choir under Yan-Qiao Wang, which has performed seldom-heard work by important Chinese composers, Common Thread, a community chorus dedicated to diversity and social justice, and Singing Out!, the city's oldest and largest gay and lesbian chorus, under William Brown.

Other Opera

The Canadian Opera Company (*coc.ca*) may get the lion's share of the attention, but it's only one of about a dozen local opera companies. The standard rep is performed by Daniel Lipton's Opera Ontario (*operaontario.com*), Dwight Bennett's Opera Mississauga (*operamississauga.com*), and – sometimes rescored for treble voices – Canadian Children's Opera Chorus (*canadianchildrensopera.com*) under Ann Cooper Gay. Guiseppe Macina's Toronto Opera Repertoire is a finishing school for emerging vocal stars, Guillermo Silve Marin's Opera in Concert (*operainconcert.com*) performs

FOR THE RECORD

Wherever there's protest and political action, you can bet TVAC will be there. The Toronto Video Activist Collective is a loose-knit association of videographers formed in 1998 to monitor public demonstrations and other situations where the expression of popular opinion asserts itself, possibly at the risk of authoritarian disapproval. TVAC documents what the mainstream news media may not. (In one case, a few telling inches of tape were enough not only to clear a peaceful demonstrator charged with assaulting a police officer, but to bring him a generous settlement.) From time to time, TVAC creates compilation tapes with some of their best mini-documentaries. They can only be contacted via email through the website *lists.tao.ca*.

without sets or costumes, while Toronto Operetta Theatre (*torontooperetta.com*) focuses on operettas like *The Merry Widow*, *The Student Prince*, Gilbert & Sullivan, and so on. Opera Atelier (*operaatelier.com*), under Marshall Pynkoksi and Jeannette Zingg, has achieved an international reputation performing exquisitely authentic Baroque pieces. Experimental contemporary work comes from Wayne Strongman's Tapestry New Opera Works (*tapestrynewopera.com*), John Hess's Queen of Puddings (*queenofpuddingsmusictheatre.com*), and Thom Sokoloski's Autumn Leaf Performance (*autumnleaf.com*). Youngest of all is the newly formed Amphion Opera (416-962-7137) under Ian McAndrew.

SUPER 8 FOR THE NEW MILLENNIUM

Don't let anyone tell you Super 8 is dead! There's a thriving Super 8 film scene in this city, showcased at the annual Splice This festival in June (*splicethis.com*). Founded by Laura Cowell and Kelly O'Brien, the festival has shown work by such local artists as Sook-Yin Lee, Kika Thorne, Fiona Smyth, and John Porter. By the way, local filmmakers Rick Palidwor and Mitch Perkins bear the unique distinction of having created a new film process while working at a local lab. They call it "Super Duper 8" (it's like Super 8, but better), which they achieved by modifying the camera motor. Their first feature film shot in Super Duper 8 was called *Sleep Always*.

Wizard's Lair

In a comfortable but otherwise unassuming home in the Annex, north of Bloor, the secrets of ancient magic are carefully preserved. It's the home of David Ben, conjurer extraordinaire, who was apprenticed in his youth to a magician of international fame, from whom he learned the lore of the illusionist, along with considerable skills of sleight-of-hand. The charming and affable Ben initially embarked on a career in taxation law, but now lives mainly by the craft of wizardry. (One of his signature tricks is swallowing a handful of needles, then retrieving them, neatly threaded.) Over many years he has collected a thorough and fascinating library on the history of conjuring and illusion, including biographical material on figures like Houdini, professional journals of magic, and memorabilia like vaudeville posters of the turn of the last century. The archives are always growing; Ben recently came into possession of the world's largest collection of materials relating to magician Dai Vernon – a Canadian, and the man who taught Doug Henning. Among the gems: Vernon's own original silhouettes of celebrities like Cary Grant and silent film director D.W. Griffith, autographed by the subjects. Who could resist such treasures? Well, says Ben: "Something my wife would like is if I could make the books disappear."

Photo: Joan Berger

The Afrocentric voice is strong on Toronto stages. Gone are the seminal Black Theatre Canada and Theatre Fountainhead, but black playwrights find a biennial home at the **AfriCanadian Playwrights Festival** (*africanadian.com*). Rep company **Obsidian Theatre** (*obsidian-theatre.net*) assembles powerhouse performers of colour in theatre classics. ahdri zhina mandiela's **b current** devises dub-soaked wordplay. Nigerian-born Modupe Olagun stages contemporary African drama through her **AfriCan Theatre Ensemble** (*africantheatreensemble.com*). Under the direction of Brainerd Blyden-Taylor, the **Nathaniel Dett Chorale** (*nathanieldettchorale.org*) performs an eclectic range of Afrocentric music, while **Ensemble Noir** (*ensemblenoir.org*), under South African Bongani Ndodona, presents a strong annual contemporary music program. **Dance Immersion** (*416-203-0666*) showcases professional choreographers working in an Afrocentric idiom. **Groupe Bassan** (*francomu.org/groupe_bassan*) – originally from the Ivory Coast – explores African dance roots in a contemporary mode, and an assortment of other companies, like **COBA** (pictured above; *cobainc.com*), **Ballet Creole** (*balletcreole.org*), and **Canboulay Dance** (*416-737-7017*) – elucidate a Caribbean consciousness. Others – **Blaze**, **Hennessy Dance Team**, and **Bag of Trix** among them – explore the youthful vigour of hip-hop, break dance, and step dance forms, and the ballet world boasts accomplished choreographers like **John Alleyne** of the National Ballet … just to name a few.

MEET YOUR MAKER

Pleasure Dome (*416-656-5577, pdome.org*) is a collective that shows experimental films of every format, often with artists in attendance. Past happenings have included a live scratch soundtrack by New York DJs IXL and Excess to the Kung Fu classic *The Prodigal Son*, and many screenings of work by local artists. They don't have a dedicated space ("Pleasure Dome isn't really a space; it's a state of exhibitionism"), but they often screen films at Cinecycle, Martin Heath's famous, fugitive cinema down the laneway at 129 Spadina Avenue. You can become a Pleasure Dome member for $10.

PICKING A SHOW

For comprehensive listings in all disciplines, the *Toronto Star's* "What's On" section on Thursdays and the city website *Toronto.com* take the honours, but the best theatre and dance listings are in *NOW Magazine* weekly, and on the Toronto Theatre Alliance's *Torontoperforms.com* site. The best source for classical and new music, jazz, and opera listings is the free monthly *Wholenote* magazine (*thewholenote.com*). The local dance scene is discussed in detail monthly in *The Dance Current,* online at *danceinsider.com,* and on air weekly on CIUT 89.5 FM's vital "Evi-dance" (Sundays from 9 to 10 a.m.). The chatty and eclectic *edionysus.com* also hosts an interesting selection of performing arts groups' sites.

With so many theatre companies in operation, it's no wonder many of them specialize in some particular niche. Once known as Le Théâtre du P'tit Bonheur ("Theatre of Small Pleasures"), the **Théâtre français de Toronto** (*416-534-6604, theatrefrancais.com*) presents a season of French-language plays, usually including a European classic by somebody like Molière, along with Canadian plays. **Native Earth Performing Arts** (*416-973-4000, nativeearth.ca*), dedicated to First Nations stage artists, is the group that was responsible for getting Graham Greene (Supporting Actor Oscar nominee for 1990's *Dances With Wolves*), onstage for the first time. (Greene is pictured above, among the cast of Native Earth's *Dry Lips Outta Move to Kapuskasing*.) **Workman Theatre Project** (*416-583-4339, workmantheatre.com*), based at the Queen Street Mental Health Centre, creates work about mental illness and organizes an annual festival of Madness and the Arts. Probably their most famous collaborator has been "Papa" Denny Doherty, who spent some time with them before launching his own production about his years with the Mammas and the Papas. Alex Bulmer's **Sniff Inc.** is one of the most prominent companies in the field of disability arts; it's a powerful movement and a coming trend. **Brookstone Theatre** (*brookstonetheatre.com*), with their own space on Walmer Road, creates theatre work with a spiritual theme. **Ross Petty Productions** (*rosspetty.com*) is responsible for the annual Christmas Panto – the outrageously silly, traditional British slapstick musical fairy tale – at the Elgin Theatre.

The biggest commercial theatre producer in town is **Mirvish Productions** (*416-872-1212, mirvish.com*), which owns the Royal Alexandra Theatre (*260 King St. W.*) and the Princess of Wales (*300 King St. W.*) – more on them later. All the other commercial producers are smaller players who use rented spaces: most often the Elgin & Winter Garden (*189 Yonge St.*), the Canon Theatre – formerly the Pantages (*244 Victoria St.*), the Ford Centre in North York (*5040 Yonge St.*), the Hummingbird Centre (*1 Front St. E.*), the St. Lawrence Centre (*27 Front St. E.*), the Bathurst Street Theatre (*736 Bathurst St.*), or the little New Yorker Theatre (*651 Yonge St.*).

The biggest of the not-for profits is **CanStage** (*416-367-8243, canstage.com*), with two spaces of its own at 26 Berkeley. (CanStage also uses the St. Lawrence Centre for part of its subscription season.)

Buddies in Bad Times (*12 Alexander St., 416-975-8555, buddiesinbadtimestheatre.com*) is devoted to "queer" theatre – both in the sense of gay/lesbian/bi/trans, and in the sense of risky, edgy, and innovative. Its Alexander Street building was originally the home of George Luscombe's influential but now-defunct Toronto Workshop Productions, the first of the mid-size companies.

Tarragon Theatre (*30 Bridgman Ave., 416-536-5018, tarragontheatre.com*), until recently run by the late Urjo Kareda, specializes in developing and producing new Canadian plays. They've also been the first in many cases to stage English translations of Quebec playwright Michel Tremblay's work.

Theatre Passe Muraille (*16 Ryerson Ave., 416-504-PLAY, passmuraille.on.ca*), incubated in the heady atmosphere of Rochdale College, and founded by Jim Garrard and Paul Thompson, made its early reputation with collective creations like *Ten Lost Years* (about the Depression) and *The Farm Show*. The latter placed a troupe of actors in rural Clinton, Ontario to shadow members of the local farming community and build a play out of improvisations suggested by real life. (In an example of the self-referential nature of art, Michael Healey's recent hit *The Drawer Boy* was inspired by the story of the creation of *The Farm Show*.)

Factory Theatre (*125 Bathurst St., 416-504-9971, factorytheatre.ca*) has passed through many artistic

THE LEGACY OF ZHOU XUAN

One of the most famous Chinese singing stars of all time was Zhou Xuan. Born in 1920, she made over 200 recordings and appeared in a dozen popular films of the 1930s and '40s (notably 1937's S*treet Angel.*) She died far too young, at the age of 37, but her son Zhou Wei made his way to Toronto, where he spent some time as a busker in the TTC, performing on the *dizi,* or Chinese bamboo flute. (Current *dizi* busker Chun Jie Wang is no relation, although he studied with the same teacher as Zhou.)

directors and – perhaps as a result – has a less strongly focused personality than the previously mentioned companies. However, it has consistently scored with the development of new writers like George F. Walker and, more recently, Andrew Moodie.

Finally, **Lorraine Kimsa Theatre for Young People** (*165 Front St. E., 416-862-2222, lktyp.com*) produces great mainstage and touring work for kids, from toddlers to young adults.

A few smaller companies have their own spaces, but most rent venues like innovative theatre incubator The Theatre Centre (*1087 Queen St. W.*), our favourite Artword Theatre (*75 Portland Street*), the Poor Alex Theatre (*296 Brunswick*), Harbourfront Centre, or one of the spaces listed above. Prominent "homeless-by-choice" companies include the acclaimed repertory company Soulpepper Theatre, Necessary Angel, the GO7 group, Pleiades Theatre, Cahoots, Modern Times, a range of music theatre companies, and scores of little independents

TELLING TALES

For 25 years, the tellers of tall tales, anecdotes, fairy tales, and fables have gathered every Friday night to regale one another with the spoken word at 1,001 Friday Nights of Storytelling. Currently, the sessions take place at St. George the Martyr Church (*205 John St.*) at 8:30 p.m. It costs $4 to get in, and anyone who dares may tell a story. Those who don't dare yet can brush up their narrative skills at The Storytellers School of Toronto, which also programs special events. Their biggest annual do is Listen Up! The Toronto Festival of Storytelling (*416-656-2445, storytellingtoronto.org*), where, for two weeks each winter, Torontonians can listen to more storytellers than you could shake a talking stick at.

Small Spaces to Watch

Particularly on the music theatre scene, this city has seen an increasing number of shows over the past few years that have started out as small productions but have gone on to become major hits. Teresa Tova's *Still the Night*, a compilation of Yiddish songs that told the story of a pair of young women fleeing the Holocaust, went from its inception as an independent production on the stage of Theatre Passe Muraille right through to a New York success. At the 1994 Tarragon Spring Arts Fair, Richard Greenblatt and Ted Dykstra presented a 25-minute version of *2 Pianos, 4 Hands* (about growing up with music lessons). A full version appeared on the Tarragon Theatre Mainstage the following year, was subsequently picked up by Mirvish Productions for the Royal Alexandra Theatre, and toured around the world. Similarly, the comic musical *The Drowsy Chaperone* opened at the tiny Poor Alex Theatre, but enjoyed a full-blown run at the Winter Garden in 2001. If you want to catch small shows before they blossom into much bigger ones, keep an eye on the offerings at venues like the Poor Alex, CanStage's upstairs theatre at 26 Berkeley Street, and the "backspaces" at Passe Muraille, Tarragon, and Factory Theatre.

the world's a stage

Some of the most memorable performances are never produced anywhere near a theatre. Instead they're created in parks and train stations and even swimming pools, and they leave the strongest imaginative marks on the landscape when they're over.

Right of Passage (2000)

Shadowland Theatre, based on Ward's Island, is one of the companies that makes a specialty of outdoor performance; in this case, a story linking rebellious contemporary teenagers with the history of water rescuer William Ward, after whom the Island is named. *Right of Passage* used masks, music, shadow puppetry, lanterns, and stiltwalking along a roughly circular performance route that began right at the Ward's Island ferry docks. Best moment? Maybe the procession past the chip-munching, phone-monopolizing, rude, lazy, garish, and comical "Seven Deadly Teens."

Oedipus (1994)

In the early '90s, Die In Debt established a reputation for producing an acclaimed series of late-summer classics in the dust and weeds underneath the Gardiner Expressway and the Bathurst Street Bridge. This coproduction with Nightwood Theatre used the underside of the expressway as part of a monumental set. The audience was given the freedom to move around the action at will, and actors made their entrances from as far as 100 yards away. As with their *Romeo and Juliet* of the previous year, audiences gamely braved the inconveniences of the location to be carried away in the drama of the show.

Photo: Sarah B. Hood

The Coming (1992)

Caravan Stage Company brought its outdoor production *The Coming*, which had been a popular success in Kingston the previous year, to the prestigious World Stage festival. An ambitious musical odyssey about the dichotomy of technology and nature, it was staged over several hectares of the Leslie Spit, but it wasn't everyone's cup of tea. *eyeWeekly's* theatre editor Angela Baldassarre reported escaping with the caterers partway through the production, while Liam Lacey of the *Globe and Mail* called the company "a gang of humourless evangelistic eco-flakes" and wrote that "the experience seems designed to simulate what it's like to be kidnapped by a fundamentalist cult." (Strangely, the ticket reservation line started ringing off the hook as soon as the *Globe* article hit the streets.)

Medea on the Beach
(1989 & 1990)

Kensington Carnival won a Dora Award for the design of this breathtaking pageant production in Ashbridge's Bay Park. It retold the Greek legend of Medea at dusk along the beach, with net dancing, boats, and the fire effects so beloved of Artistic Director Ida Carnevali. One of the most evocative moments was the approach of real boats carrying live actors across the firelit water of the bay at nightfall.

Atlas Moves Watching
(1985, 1989, 1997)

Bill James, who specializes in choreography for unusual spaces, created a work that used multiple layers of the urban environment. In the 1989 presentation, it seated the audience in a then-vacant storefront on the southeast corner of Queen and Augusta, facing Queen Street. Dancers performed inside the space, but also out on the sidewalks and even from aboard passing streetcars.

hamburgers and pasta. After the stages are dark around Front and Berkeley, look to **The Jersey Giant** (*71 Front St. E., 416-368-4095*). But the Big Kahuna of schmooze ops has to be the annual **Dora Mavor Moore Awards** in June; not just the awards ceremony itself (to which anybody can buy a ticket for about $50), but the accompanying after-party, where you'll see every actor, director, and designer in town, as well as visiting celebs. The Doras are organized through the Toronto Theatre Alliance (*416-536-6468, thedoras.com*).

Ra (1983)

Another in R. Muray Schafer's Patria Cycle, this famous production by Comus Music Theatre borrowed themes from Egyptian mythology and initiated audience members into an ancient rite throughout an entire night, dusk to dawn, within various chambers of the Ontario Science Centre. The evening included several meals, dance, singing, and ancient Egyptian ritual performed by masked figures ... but not much sleep.

Tamara (1981)

A triumph of innovative theatre by Necessary Angel Theatre Company under the direction of Richard Rose, with a script by John Krizanc. Set in Fascist Italy, it imagined an encounter between artist Tamara de Lempicka and author Gabriele d'Annunzio. The thing that set it apart was its complex and creative staging. Using most of Strachan House in Trinity-Bellwoods Park, it invited audience members literally to follow the story; whenever a scene ended they were allowed to choose which character to follow to hear more of the tale. Attention to detail was a major factor; for instance, company members would throw bird seed around the entrance before the show so that a great cloud of pigeons would collect, to soar away at a dramatic moment later on. *Tamara* later had successful runs in New York, Hollywood, Portugal, and Poland.

Tempest on Snake Island (1981)

England's Welfare State are experts in celebratory outdoor theatre featuring splendid visual effects cobbled out of found materials. They joined forces with Toronto Island artists who were later to become the founders of Shadowland Theatre in a seminal environmental staging of Shakespeare's *The Tempest* on the wilderness of Snake Island. Paula Jardine was among the participants. "That's where I first saw torches and I thought 'Yah!'" she recalls. (Whereupon she went out and founded Vancouver's outrageously wonderful Public Dreams Society.)

STICK FIGURES

Not one but two stilt-dancing companies tower above prosceniums, parks, and parades. SwizzleStick Theatre (pictured above; *torontoisland.org/swizzlestick*), named for a Trinidadian whisk used to whirl together the multiple ingredients of Callalloo soup, enacts pageant and parties, from its scarecrow-themed *Harvest* in Dufferin Grove Park to its sublimely surreal *Dali Gala* at Bambu by the Lake. (They have delighted crowds at the Pride Parade as barely-dressed, flamingo-pink devils.) Performers with Ben Block's aptly named Higher Ground (*stiltdance.com*), formerly connected with Swizzlestick, now strut their own stuff in the guise of angels, devils, and fabulous winged spirits.

Immortal Harold

If you were asked to name the most illustrious audience member in Toronto theatre history, there'd be only one possible answer. Harold Kandel was a frequent theatre attender, and a particular fan of small theatre productions. Everyone knew him because he had a loud voice and lots of opinions, and no inhibitions whatsoever. Every actor who was performing in the 1980s has a Harold story. But anyone who ever had a chance to sit down over a drink with Harold knew him as a thoughtful, intelligent man, with a long history in left-wing politics, and – to the surprise of some – a wife. He died in 1994, and few have been so mourned in the theatre community, or remembered in so many ways. The newsletter of the Fringe of Toronto was named the *Fringe Harolds* in his honour, and there's an annual awards show called The Harolds, at which theatre artists working in the small, independent companies honour one another through a unique system. They were instituted in 1995, when a group of founding artists nominated thirteen recipients; each year the winners of the previous year are allowed to "Harold" a new artist of their choosing. Some of the members of the Illustrious House of Harold include Buddies in Bad Times founder Sky Gilbert, playwright M. Nourbese Philip, Fringe founder Gregory Nixon, and the entire Toronto Arts Council. (A final point: there were at least two other versions of Harold Awards before this one became established, a measure of the original Harold's reputation.)

PREPARE YE ...

There may never have been a more influential Toronto theatre production than the long-running 1972 *Godspell* at the Bayview Theatre; it was the first professional encounter of Martin Short, Eugene Levy, Andrea Martin, Gilda Radner, and Dave Thomas, among others. In the following year, Joe Flaherty and Brian Doyle Murray (brother of Bill) came to town to found The Second City, most of the cast simply transferred over, and the comedy world was never the same.

A Brief History of Shocking Moments on Stage

Photo: Alexandra Plada

In 1970, the "tribal love rock musical" *Hair* challenged Toronto as much by breaking down the actor/audience barrier as with its onstage nudity. One of Toronto theatre's first real controversies came in 1973 when playwright Michael Hollingsworth – who was only trying to stage the experience of being on acid – called down a firestorm of public opinion with his *Clear Light* at Toronto Free Theatre. It took the police 12 nights to arrive with an order to shut down the show; they contended it was immoral on the grounds of nudity and oral sex. (Granted, the semen was cooked and eaten – as was a baby later on in the show.) Hollingsworth himself points out that, "When that closed down, saying a four-letter word on stage was a big deal; if one did a recreation of that play, there would be a few jolting moments, but nobody would call the cops." (By the time Judith Thompson's esteemed *The Crackwalker* debuted at Theatre Passe Muraille in 1980, incidentally, a baby-cooking scene was no longer considered to be any impediment to acclaim.) *Clear Light* did no noticeable damage to the careers of its actors, like Nick Mancuso and Diane D'Aquila (who was playing Queen Elizabeth at Stratford last we noticed – and you don't get much more respectable than that).

In 1981, police attempted to lay a charge of indecency against the sexy musical *Let My People Come*, but it ran for months regardless. The following fall, they tried and failed again with the full-Monty musical *Oh! Calcutta!* Maybe earlier shows had paved

PRODUCE AND PRODUCERS

One Toronto neighbourhood has had a particularly catalytic effect on the theatre scene. Although there are no true theatre buildings in Kensington Market, it's spawned at least three important theatre companies in the modern era. Kensington Carnival, founded by Ida Carnevali (who arrived in Toronto in the early 1980s with a B.C. theatre company in a horse-drawn caravan), specializes in telling classic tales like Medea and Faust using carnival techniques like firebreathing, stiltwalking, and puppetry. It has nurtured a wide

Photo: Michael Vendruscolo

the way for this town's generally blasé reaction to naked actors and shocking scenes, like numerous episodes in the work of Hillar Liitoja's DNA Theatre. By 1991, no one seemed remotely appalled by his *Sick, A Chamber of Horrors* (surely the title would have tipped off the censors?). In *Sick*, the cast nailed the theatre doors shut and bound a well-known actor, naked, onto a crucifix with a vise on his penis. Similarly, Buddies in Bad Times's 1992 *An Investigation into the Strange Case of the Wild Boy* (pictured opposite) by Sky Gilbert – about sexual repression – elicited nary a raised eyebrow for all its cheerful frolicking in tiny loincloths. (For that matter, neither had his provocatively named *Ban This Show! … Robert Mapplethorpe Exposed*, two years earlier.)

These days, when *eyeWeekly* sex advice columnist Sasha van Bon Bon and her Dangerettes can perform widely publicized neo-burlesque strip shows at popular clubs to receptive audiences (and we won't even mention what's said and done on primetime TV), no theatre is going to get closed down for flashing some skin or talking dirty.

range of important artists, and its annual Kensington Festival of Lights has become an independent production. Ida Carnevali (her real name, by the way), also helped form KYTES (Kensington Youth Theatre Ensemble), another independent company, which produces challenging work with street youth and other young people at risk. The Augusta Company – named after Augusta Street in the Market – is one of this city's most important innovators, founded by the power-packed trio of Daniel Brooks, Don McKellar, and Tracy Wright. (McKellar (L) and Brooks are pictured, opposite, in the Augusta Company's *Red Tape*.)

Readings on Tap

We're not sure why – although there are a few theatres in the neighbourhood – but Bloor Street between Bathurst and Spadina is the hot spot for play readings – always in licensed locations, too. Most likely venues: the Victory Café (*581 Markham St., 416-516-5787*), Clinton's Tavern (*693 Bloor St. W., 416-535-9541*), and the Tranzac Club (*292 Brunswick Ave., 416-923-8137*).

If You Build It ...

The 1950s and '60s were tough on Toronto theatres; many older vaudeville houses and movie palaces were demolished in a possibly misguided drive towards modernism. However, the 20 years from 1985 to 2005 will go down in history as a remarkable era of theatre building and restoration, at a time when most other North American cities weren't doing anything at all in this department. The building boom coincided with the huge growth of an entirely new industry in megamusicals like *Les Miserables*, *Phantom of the Opera*, *Mamma Mia*, *The Lion King*, *Rent*, and locally-created products like *Kiss of the Spider Woman* and *Sunset Boulevard*.

• It really began back in 1963, when the **Royal Alexandra Theatre**, built in 1907 and named for King Edward VII's Queen Alexandra, was scheduled for demolition. Bargain king "Honest Ed" Mirvish saw its continuing potential, however, and – in what has turned out to be a great act of public benefaction – bought the building, refurbished it, and started to import touring dramas and musicals. Now, of course, Mirvish Productions (which has outgrown the Royal Alex, and uses several other venues as well) imports shows not only from the North American touring circuit, but also from the not-for-profit theatres around Toronto. The Royal Alex was filled with signed photos of the stars who've performed there, many of which now hang on the lobby walls. The rest, of course, adorn the interior of Ed's flashy bargain emporium at Bathurst and Bloor – making it likely that you'll encounter an Adolph Menjou, an Ethel Barrymore, a Claudette Colbert, or a Rex Harrison lurking behind a skid of cut-price baby food or bulk kitty litter. (If Ed's other ventures were ever to falter, he could probably set them all right with a well-timed venture onto e-Bay!)

• In 1981 the Ontario Heritage Foundation bought the **Elgin & Winter Garden Theatre** complex, a unique

double-decker theatre that had opened in 1913, but had lain closed since the '20s. The phenomenally successful 1985 production of

Cats was a catalyst for the restoration of the elegant venue, with its whimsical garden-theme upper level, complete with leafy branches and full moon. A collection of exquisite vaudeville backdrops was found during the renovation, some of which are displayed in the theatre's Cascading Lounges. (One of the seats — exactly which one is no longer known — was the one Public Enemy #1 John Dillinger sat in to see a movie at Chicago's Biograph Theater just before the feds gunned him down.)

• In 1988, Live Entertainment Corp. reopened the 1920 vaudeville house known as the **Pantages Theatre** for a production of *Phantom of the Opera* that would go on to employ eight Phantoms over the next ten years. Now renamed the Canon Theatre, the 2,200-seat building is absolutely sumptuous, and boasts the very best lobby in town; it allows audience members to make a grand descent down a curving staircase into the lower bar area.

Photo: Ontario Tourism, 13224

• In 1992, Follows-Latimer Productions opened the remodeled **New Yorker Theatre** (*651 Yonge*) with a hit production of *Forever Plaid* that ran for four years, sealing the venue's transition to live theatre from movies. (It was built in the 1930s as The Embassy, but was also known over the years as the Astor, the Tivoli, the Festival Cinema, and the Showcase Theatre, running variously westerns, porn, art, and action/horror films.)

Photo: Courtesy Tourism Toronto

• When Mirvish Productions decided to bring the musical *Miss Saigon* to Toronto, they realized its special-effects set piece (a realistic descending helicopter) would never fit inside the Royal Alex. Undaunted, they decided to build a whole new theatre, the sumptuous **Princess of Wales**. A complaint to the City (purportedly originating from the competition, LiveEnt) that the building lacked adequate parking didn't slow the Mirvishes down; they simply added underground parking to the plan and continued. Among its other attractions, the Princess of Wales features gorgeous woodwork, original murals by noted American artist Frank Stella, and – rarest of all – adequate bathrooms for women, so there isn't a nightmare line-up at intermission. When its namesake, Princess Diana, died, it became Toronto's memorial site, with ranks of bouquets appearing overnight in her memory.

• The $48,000,000 multi-venue **Ford Centre**, owned by the City of North York, opened in 1993 with a production of *Show Boat*.

Photo: Courtesy Tourism Toronto

• Mississauga's **Living Arts Centre** (*4141 Living Arts Drive*) opened in 1997. It houses two venues, Hammerson Hall and The Royal Bank Theatre.

• In April 2003, the Canadian Opera Company finally held the groundbreaking for the on-again, off-again "Ballet Opera House," now formally known as the **Four Seasons Centre for the Performing Arts**, a 2,000-seat venue at Queen and University.

SUMMER STAGES

The Stratford and Shaw Theatre Festivals pack in audiences from around the world, but they're certainly not the only summer theatres around Ontario. In fact, there are dozens, typically in pretty small-town venues, offering light comedies, musicals, and revues. The oldest of these is the **Red Barn Theatre** (*866-870-9911, redbarntheatre.com*) in the charming beach community of Jackson's Point, which has recently added air conditioning to its many advantages.

Photo: Ontario Tourism, 14163

Photo: Ontario Tourism, 197

The Blyth Festival (*877-TO-BLYTH, blythfestival.com*) has a high reputation for excellence in developing plays about rural Ontario. There are also summer seasons — many in historic buildings — in Cobourg, Meaford, Port Dover, Port Hope, Orillia, and Gravenhurst. The **Association of Summer Theatres Around Ontario**, a.k.a. "ASTRO" (*416-408-4556, summertheatre.org*), puts out a listings brochure every summer.

The musical *Show Boat* has engendered controversy since 1928 (when the word "niggers" was replaced with "darkies" in the libretto), but perhaps none more far-reaching than in 1992, when Garth Drabinsky's Live Entertainment Corp. announced plans to open the Ford Centre (then known as the North York Centre for the Performing Arts) with an $8 million production of Jerome Kern and Oscar Hammerstein's musical chestnut, under the direction of Broadway legend Harold Prince. LivEnt installed a four-storey replica of the "Cotton Blossom" paddle steamer as the *Show Boat* box office — complete with functioning smokestacks — outside the theatre; a move that soon proved redundant when the creation of The Coalition to Stop Show Boat began to give the production more publicity than it had ever desired.

The Coalition originally moved to stop the production because, they maintained, its racist character depictions made it inappropriate as the inaugural production in a $48 million, publicly-owned arts facility. The issue quickly grew clouded in early 1993 when a large-circulation black newspaper began to print stories that made a connection between Jews in general and the alleged anti-black sentiments of *Show Boat*. The Canadian Jewish Congress instantly objected. Then 19 of the 22 members of Toronto United Way's Black and Caribbean Fundraising Committee resigned over plans for a *Show Boat* benefit that had been expected to raise $100,000 for United Way and the CNIB, with damaging repercussions for United Way's community relations.

Throughout the spring of 1993, protests continued outside the theatre, public forums were packed, and newspaper editorials on the subject appeared almost daily. (Protests also sprang up outside the Princess of Wales Theatre, voicing displeasure with racial stereotyping in the megamusical *Miss Saigon*.) Despite huge public outcry, *Show Boat* opened in October 1993, but karma, it seems, will have its way. A decade later, LivEnt lay dead and buried, while the other players in the *Show Boat* drama — peace restored — are still going about their business as usual.

In the beginning was the **National Ballet of Canada** (*416-345-9686, national.ballet.ca*), and then came the Modernists: **Toronto Dance Theatre** (*416-967-1365, tdt.org*), founded in 1968 by Peter Randazzo, Patricia Beatty, and David Earle. As the dance scene started to come of age, professional companies in the contemporary idiom were born, like **Danny Grossman Dance Company** (*416-408-4543, dgdance.org*), the late and much-missed **Desrosiers Dance Theatre**, Serge Bennathan's **Dancemakers** (*416-535-8880, dancemakers.org*), Bengt Jörgen's **Ballet Jörgen** (*416-961-4725*), **Peggy Baker Dance Projects** (*416-516-4025*), Allen and Karen Kaeja's **Kaeja d'Dance** (*416-516-6030, kaeja.org*), Claudia Moore's **MOonhORsE Dance Theatre** (*c/o 416-504-6429*), and **Canadian Children's Dance Theatre** (*416-924-5657, ccdt.org*).

Over the same time, the always-bubbling cauldron of folk dance was spilling forth fully professional companies working in world traditions and fertile fusions, like the Afro-Caribbean expressions of Patrick Parson's **Ballet Creole** (*416-217-0966*) and Charmaine Headley and Eddison Lindsay's **COBA** (*416-658-3111, cobainc.com*). Our wealth of Spanish dance companies includes those of **Esmeralda Enrique** (*416-595-5753, flamencos.net*), **Paula Moreno** (*416-924-6991*), Carmen Romero of **Candela Flamenca**; **Ritmo Flamenco** (*416-435-4223, ritmoflamenco.com*), and **¡Arte Flamenco!** (*416-920-3774*). Among Middle Eastern specialists is Yasmina Ramzy of **Arabesque Dance Company** (*416-920-5593, arabesquedance.ca*), South Asian classical dance exponents include **Menaka Thakkar** (*416-222-4041*), and Lata Pada's **Sampradaya Dance Creations** (*905-608-2475, sampradaya-dance.com*), while Asian dance is represented by the likes of Xing Bang-Fu's **Xing Dance Theatre** (*416-603-9032, xingdancetheatre.com*), William Lau's **Little Pear Garden Collective** (*416-515-0683, littlepeargarden.com*), specializing in Peking Opera, and the butoh-tinged **Fujiwara Dance Inventions** (*c/o 416-504-6429*) of Denise Fujiwara.

FLOORS FOR FEET

Despite the wealth of theatres in this city, surprisingly few stages are designed for dance. For example, the National Ballet has its own floor, which it installs for every performance at the Hummingbird Centre. Among the handful of true dance stages are the Betty Oliphant Theatre (*105 Maitland*), the Winchester Street Theatre (*80 Winchester*), Buddies in Bad Times (*12 Alexander St.*), and Harbourfront Centre's Premiere Dance Theatre. The most recent is the new Dancemakers studio (*Distillery Historic Complex*), soon to be joined by the new Four Seasons Centre for the Performing Arts (*Queen and University*).

SPOTTING THE PROS

Even dance mecca Montreal has no equivalent to the weekday Teachers Collective held at 805 Dovercourt. It's where everyone in the contemporary dance community – including the most famous – goes in the morning to work on technique and share skills.

The cutting edge of dance is the world of independent choreographers – that is, dance makers who work without a permanent space, and in many cases with no office or staff. **DanceWorks** (*416-204-1082, danceworks.ca*), which began back in 1977 as an artists' collective, programs two annual series of independents in full mainstage productions. But it can be more fun to see the work in a rawer environment, like the orgiastic panoply of performance that is August's **fFIDA**, the Fringe Festival of Independent Dance Artists (*416-410-4291, ffida.org*), created by Michael Menegon and Allen Kaeja. Once a part of fFIDA is **Dusk Dances**, a park performance series organized in Toronto and Vancouver by Corpus (*corpus.ca*). Perhaps most intimate of all is **Series 8:08** (*series808.ca*), co-ordinated by dance artists Susan Lee, Yvonne Ng, and Jessica Runge. It's held at 8:08 p.m. on the last Saturday of every month at the Metro-Central YMCA (*20 Grosvenor St.*). For essential party chatting, some good names to know are Laura Taler (founder of long-running series Dances for a Small Stage), Roger Sinha, Marie-Josée Chartier, crossover visual artist Peter Chin, Darcey Callison, D.A. Hoskins, Kathleen Rea, Malgorzata Nowacka, and Holly Small. (Pictured above, clockwise from centre-front: Yvonne Ng, Nicole Fougère, Amy Hampton, Lisa Otto, and Karen Kaeja in Kathleen Rea's *Marrow*.)

We are inclined to argue that if you can't buy it in Kensington Market, you didn't need it in the first place. On the other hand, why miss out on exploring other tantalizing parts of the city?

Breath of Fresh Air

For just $501 you can buy part of a windmill, offset your own electricity costs, and contribute to the local development of the world's fastest-growing sustainable power source. In December 2002, Toronto became the first city in Canada with a wind turbine, located in Exhibition Place. (Although countries like Denmark already use lots of wind-generated electricity, Canada has yet to take big strides in this area.) Standing 98 metres – about the same height at the Royal York Hotel – the turbine is topped by three 29-metre blades that are capable of producing enough electricity for about 250 homes. A project of a community initiative named the **Toronto Renewable Energy Co-operative**, or TREC for short, the turbine is selling power to Toronto Hydro for at least its initial three years of production. Shareholders actually own part of the turbine through a co-op called WindShare, and are entitled to dividends from the sales to Hydro (estimated at about $8 per $100 share for 2004) or a proportional rebate on their own electricity bill. As electricity rates rise, so will profits. The turbine, powered by the wind rising off Lake Ontario, is silent, safe for birds, and emits no "greenhouse gases" as it generates power. A second TREC turbine is planned for the site of Ashbridge's Bay Sewage Treatment Plant. The minimum WindShare purchase is one membership share (at $1) plus five Preference Shares (at $100 each), and 16,000 Preference Shares are available to the public. In the first month, sales had already reached $400,000.
416-977-5093 ext. 1, trec.on.ca/windshare

ZENN and the Art of Automobile Maintenance

Why do we think you want a car with a top speed of 40 kph? Why, because it's electric, of course. The ZENN™ (for Zero Emission No Noise) is available from Toronto's own **Feel Good Cars Inc.** It has a range of about 50 kilometres between chargings and a classy Euro look. Even sexier is the planned reissue of the Dauphine Electric, which Feel Good will be producing in a limited edition. Why haven't you already seen them around the city? Well, at the moment of writing they're not street-legal in Ontario, although they can be used in 41 U.S. states (including New York). However, enabling legislation is on the verge. Meanwhile, they can be used off-road or under special permit. These electric cars plug in anywhere you can plug in a hair dryer. Now, the question you have to ask yourself is: will your windmill shares cover the cost of running your car?
836 Manning Ave., 416-535-8395, feelgoodcars.com

secret shopping districts

Liberty Village

Even with gentrification, the warehouse district south of King and east of Dufferin is still home to lots of interesting factory and import businesses. Some sell to the public all the time; you have to watch for others.

Maybe you can't cook like Susur Lee (who can?), but at least you can buy your plates from the same source. Ken Gangbar of **Ken Gangbar Studios** (*101-169 Liberty St., 416-532-4284*) holds one studio sale each year, in early December. (He also takes some private commissions.) The clean, minimalist lines of his hand-made, slab-constructed ceramics grace the very, very fine tables of restaurants Susur, Rain, Zoom, and Xacutti. In fact, should you be lucky enough to sample chef Lee's sensational tasting menu, 'round about course four your server will probably announce the ingredients of the delectable morsels on "the long Gangbar."

Home decor shop **Promised Land** (*416-531-4366*), which has snazzy outlets in the TD Centre and the Eaton Centre, offers warehouse sales on the second floor of 37 Hanna Avenue for about three days each month. It's a good bet for inexpensive bath bombs, candles, curtains, and decorations. Unit 2 of the same building houses the warehouse of upscale furniture, hardware, and decor boutique **Du Verre**. Call their Strachan outlet (*416-593-4784*) to find out about the next warehouse sale.

Rumah Inc., which has its retail outlet at 603 King West, sells furnishings from Indonesia, like wooden cabinets and tables. Every Saturday they open their warehouse at 27 Jefferson Avenue (*416-533-4859*) to the general public. The similarly luscious **Jalan** of Queen West welcomes shoppers to its 99 Atlantic Avenue warehouse on weekend afternoons – and at other times by appointment (*416-588-8354*).

For the past 80-plus years, the **Barrymore Furniture Co. Ltd.** has manufactured fine hand-built upholstered chairs and chesterfields at 1137 King Street West (*416-532-2891*). Their showroom is always open to the public, but they hold sales of showroom pieces every Boxing Day, and occasionally in the spring.

Niche Neighbourhoods

Like businesses tend to congregate; for example:

Antiques

Almost anywhere on Queen Street, but especially Leslie to Logan; Bathurst to Gore Vale, and Triller to Roncesvalles. (Most of these feature designer furniture outlets, too.) Also: Mount Pleasant south of Eglinton; Yonge from St. Clair to Roxborough, and Lakeshore Boulevard from Islington to Highway 10.

Photo: Sarah B. Hood

Computer hardware/ software

College from Spadina to Augusta.

Fabric and sewing supplies

Queen West from Spadina to Augusta.

Pawnshops

The east side of Church from Queen to Dundas.

From time to time there are also artists' studio sales in the Liberty neighbourhood. The best way to keep up with what's happening – apart from reading telephone poles – is to drop in to the **Liberty Village Market** (*65 Jefferson Ave., 416-630-0477*) or the **Liberty Street Cafe** (*25 Liberty St., 416-533-8828*) every once in a while to chat with locals, read notices, and pick up flyers.

The Junction

The Junction (*West Toronto Junction BIA: 416-767-6680, westtorontojunction.com*), named for its adjacent railway intersection, was one of the last holdouts among the "dry" neighbourhoods, which means that it's been very slow to develop the kind of restaurant scene that draws people into an area from outside. Partly for this reason – and partly because it's off the major east-west corridors – the strip of Dundas West from about Indian Grove to Runnymede has been preserved as if in a time capsule, with lots of original '50s, '60s, and '70s signs and storefronts. Its top draw is probably its enticing blend of antique shops, junk stores, and art galleries, but there are lots of other notable stores like **McBride Cycle** (*mcbridecycle.com*), which has been in business for just under 100 years. It's really half a bicycle shop (*2923 Dundas St. W., 416-763-5652*) and half a motorcycle shop (*2797 Dundas St. W., 416-767-0206*). Then there's **Kendrick Astro Instruments** (*2920 Dundas St. W., 416-762-7946, kendrick-ai.com*), which has everything for the amateur astronomer.

Pacific Mall

The largest Hong-Kong style shopping mall in North America, Markham's overwhelming Pacific Mall is crammed with video and electronics outlets, plus Hello Kitty merch galore, and a very popular arcade. The upstairs has been remodelled into "Heritage Town," a simulated old-fashioned marketplace, festooned with lucky fish and dragon sculptures. Their website is a wealth of information about traditional Chinese culture. *4300 Steeles Ave. E, 905-470-8785, pacificmalltoronto.com*

MI CASA ES SU CASA

Bring home a piece of somebody else's property from **The Door Store** (*43 Britain St., 416-863-1590*), where you'll find antique and unusual doors and all the fittings that go with them. **The Salvage Shop** (*1216 Queen St. E., 416-469-2557, salvageshop.ca*) sells second-hand stained glass windows and some doors, along with antique doorknobs, light fixtures, and fireplace mantels. They can also handle restoration of ironwork and lights. **Victorian Revival** (*1150 Castlefield Ave., 416-789-1704, hypersource.com/victorian*) deals in vintage lighting and other architectual antiques.

auction myths dispelled

1. *Ordinary people can't afford to buy at auctions.*
Actually, lots of auction houses sell rugs, furniture, and even art and jewelry at relative bargains.

2. *You might buy something by accident.*
"So wrong!" says one appraiser. And even if a misunderstanding did occur, you could simply say: "No, I didn't bid on that."

3. *In-the-know bidders give special, hidden signals to the auctioneer.*
Maybe the auctioneer knows some of the regulars and picks up on small gestures, but there's no special code.

4. *Auctioneers talk funny.*
Only in the movies.

Waddington's Auctioneers and Appraisers (*111 Bathurst St., 416-504-9100, waddingtonsauctions.com*) has been in business in Toronto since 1850, and they sell the widest range of items of any auction house. On the one hand, they handled the contents of Casa Loma and Maple Leaf Gardens, and have set records for sale prices of Inuit and other Canadian art. On the other hand, they hold "low-end" estate sales every week (china and silver on Wednesdays; furniture and rugs on Thursdays). There's no cost to get in. Usually you come early to look around, then come back later to bid on what you like. You're allowed to ask for the estimated value, and in many cases you can make an absentee bid.

Some auction houses specialize in one area, like stamps, rugs, or art. Here are a few around town:

Christie's Fine Art Auctioneers
170 Bloor St. W, 416-960-2063

Ritchies
288 King St. E., 416-364-1864

Dupuis Jewellery Auctioneers
908-94 Cumberland St., 416-968-7500

Empire Auctions
165 Tycos Dr., 416-784-4261

TURNING JAPANESE

When a customer leaves **Sanko** (*730 Queen St. W., 416-703-4550, toronto-sanko.com*), the door offers a polite electronic greeting in Japanese that translates roughly as "You're welcome." It's a culturally appropriate sendoff from a store that stocks everything Japanese, from a delightful assortment of Hello Kitty and Pocky snacks to exquisite ceramics, videos, magazines, and foodstuffs. The one thing they don't

Gallery Sixtyeight Auctions
3 Southvale Dr., 416-421-7614

Robert Deveau Galleries
297-299 Queen St. E., 416-364-6271

Sotheby's
9 Hazelton Ave., 416-926-1774

have much of is paper. For that you have to cross the street to the **Japanese Paper Place** (*887 Queen St. W., 416-703-0089, japanesepaperplace.com*), where you'll find handmade paper, cards, books, origami supplies, and rolls big enough to make your own shoji screens. They also run classes in papermaking. If you still have a yen for more Sanrio toys, there's also the amply-stocked **Dragon Seed** (*261B Spadina Ave., 416-596-7978*).

Photo: Sarah B. Hood

discount destinations

Dixie Outlet Mall

Over the years this once-modest shopping spot has grown to include more than 100 discount outlets. There are bargain shoes at shops like Aldo for Less; furniture and appliances at places like the Sears Outlet Store, and many unpredictable delights in the well named Fantastic Flea Market.
1250 S. Service Rd., Mississauga, 905-278-7492, dixieoutletmall.com

Orfus Road

A few blocks north of Lawrence between Dufferin and Caledonia Road lies a shopper's fantasyland of bargain outlets for women's fashions, men's suits, shoes, baby goods, kitchenware, and – our favourite – the Roots warehouse. The whole area used to be Barker Field, an airfield owned by the Leavens brothers (Clare, Art, and Walt), who had been in aviation since the barnstorming days. They offered pilot training, air delivery, crop dusting, and related services for several decades when the Dufferin and Lawrence neighbourhood was still outside the city proper (Leavens Aviation is still in existence). However, another family – the brothers Samuel and Morris Orfus – eventually bought the Barker Field land. When they redeveloped the area, they named several streets after the family, including Orfus Road and the nearby Samor Road (for Sam and Morris, of course). Orfus Realty has since passed into the hands of Morris's son Howard, who also runs the other family business: Playtime Bowl at 33 Samor, which has been in operation since 1954.

It's in the Bag

Bike messengers from all over the world look to Toronto for custom-made, waterproof bags from **Push The Envelope**, started by former messengers Reba Plummer and Pete Gray in the now-defunct shop known as The Bike Ranch. (Gray also specialized in a line of durable rubber kilts made from used inner tubes.) The original Push bag was a one-strap over-the-shoulder model designed to hold a courier's heavy load. Since then Push has branched out into a wider range of bags and pouches for "civilians." All models can be customized, with lots of colours and even complex appliqued images (from the Union Jack to the U.S.S. Enterprise). You can pick up ready-made bags or meet Reba herself at The Urbane Cyclist (*180 John St., 416-979-9733, ucycle.com*). Other outlets include Annie Thompson (*674 Queen St. W., 416-703-3843*) and The Bike Joint (*290½ Harbord St., 416-532-6392*). (By the way, the versatile Pete Gray now plays steel guitar at bars around town.)
Custom orders: 416-367-5974, pushtheenvelope.com

NOW YOU'RE COOKIN'

Forget the big mall outlets: the tiny **Fortune Housewares** (*388 Spadina Ave., 416-593-6999*) offers the best selection of home baking equipment of any we know, along with a wide range of other kitchenware. Check out the vast cookie cutter selection and the great supply of little glass bottles for gift portions of flavoured vinegars and oils. For pro quality restaurant supplies, there's **Dinetz** (*231 King St. E., 416-368-8657*) in the east and **Nikolaau Restaurant Supply** (*629 Queen St. W., 416-504-6411*) in the west.

Burning Desire

If you always thought a fireplace was out of the question because you live in an apartment, condo, loft, or trailer, think again! **In Flame** carries fireplaces and stoves that can be fitted to burn Sunjel, an ethanol fuel made from sugarcane. It carrries EcoLogo approval from Environment Canada and is not only odorless, but safe to burn indoors with no chimney or special ventilation. (And it humidifies the room at the same time.)
310-99 Atlantic Ave., 416-530-0555, inflame.ca

Kid Stuff

2 by 2

The Toronto-based online shop for twin-related T-shirts, with a handy links page. ("Multiples" are a trend, we hear.)
416-488-1038, 2by2multiples.com

Collectors Lane Hobbies

A giant warehouse filled with new and used model trains, boats, cars, rockets, ships, and planes for reasonable prices, along with vintage toys like Corgi and Matchbox cars.
1220 Markham Rd., Unit 1, 416-264-4941, collectorslanehobbies.com

George's Trains

Well-loved founder George Olieux is gone, but his model train shop lives on. A neighbourhood icon, it sells every scale of indoor and outdoor train, plus miniature bridges, trees, cows, people, buildings, and everything else you can think of.
510 Mt. Pleasant Rd., 416-489-9783, georgestrains.com

Hand Me Downs

The nearest local branch of the Ontario-wide new and used kids' clothing franchise operation.
5051 Hwy #7, Markham, 905-479-1869, handmedowns.com

For People Who Live in Glass Houses

When the sumptuous Elgin and Winter Garden theatre complex was being restored to its former glory, an important part of the project was the recreation of the extensive stained glasswork around the exterior box office. Enter **Serendipity**, specialists in custom stained glass, who even researched suppliers for unusual glass of the period. Do you want a portrait of your pet to grace your front door? They can do it. (In fact, they already have.) They also stock leaded glass panels and – although they don't make them any more – Tiffany lamps. Oh yes … the entrance to Ryerson's Neill-Wycik residence was another early Serendipity project.
894 Broadview Ave., 416-461-3339, serendipity.onthedanforth.com

For People Who Live in Grass Houses

Forget wood, tiles, linoleum, and stone; there's an entirely new floor covering material on the market. It's nice-looking, extremely durable, and – best of all – a sustainable resource that's easy on the environment. Bamboo, which is really a type of grass, can be harvested within five years of planting (as opposed to the 30 or 40 years it takes an oak or a maple to reach maturity). The stalk is peeled and cut into layers; almost all the plant is used, and the end result resembles a hardwood floor. (Oh, and they make sure not to harvest the type of bamboo that the pandas eat.) **Silkroad Bamboo Flooring** already carries bamboo flooring, plywood, and veneer, and they're expanding the line to include cork flooring and sustainably harvested maple.
K&M Bamboo Products Inc., 26-300 Esna Park Drive, Markham, 905-947-1688, silkroadflooring.com

occasional opportunities

Banff Designs

Banff is a premiere Canadian designer and manufacturer of hard-weather outerwear. Even though they've moved from their old warehouse digs, they still hold their blowout sale on the last Saturday of November. If you want to get the really good stuff, better buy a thermos ahead of time to hold the coffee that'll keep you alert as you wait in line overnight with bike couriers and other serious outdoorsfolk in the know.
610 Queen Street West, 588-4839, banffdesign.com

Cabbagetown Festival

On the first weekend after Labour Day, the Cabbagetown Festival takes over Parliament Street from Gerrard to Winchester, plus most of the residental neighbourhood east to the Don Valley, and some west to Sherbourne. It always includes a great outdoor craft sale at the entrance to Riverdale Farm, and sidewalk sales on Parliament itself, but the most entertaining shopping is to be found at the scores of household yard sales that spring up all over the neighbourhood.
Old Cabbagetown BIA, 416-921-0857

City of Toronto Auctions

Twice a year, usually in May and October, the City of Toronto auctions off its no-longer-needed vehicles, furniture, and equipment. In the past, items on the block have included parks maintenance vehicles, ambulances, desks, dividers, dentist chairs, and sundry items – like cameras, umbrellas, and watches – from the lost-and-found department at the Toronto Zoo. It's a free, one-day event, generally held on a Saturday at the Queen Elizabeth Building at Exhibition Place (although the location is expected to change).
Auction hotline: 416-392-1991. Voice: 416-338-5603, toronto.ca

Cowan Community Yard Sale

On weekends directly before or after the 24th of May holiday, neighbours on Cowan Avenue in the west end close off their entire street from Queen Street

Kidding Awound

Once there was The Last Wound-Up, a funky little place on Yonge Street. Then it expanded and moved into Yorkville. Now it's called Kidding Awound, but it still has the same sensational collection of wind-up toys, from inexpensive trinkets to antique collectors' items.
91 Cumberland St., 416-926-8996

Kol Kid

Pretty much the polar opposite of Toys 'R' Us, this tranquil, pretty little boutique conjures up a comfortable and secure Victorian childhood, with soft-toned hooked rugs, painted furniture, toys, and clothing.
670 Queen St. W., 416-681-0368

The Little Dollhouse Company

What this renowned shop has in doll sizes is probably more than you'll ever hope to own in a full-sized version.
612 Mount Pleasant Rd, 416-489-7180, thelittledollhousecompany.com

Merrily Around

Nice resale designer kids' clothes;
they also run an online toy store.
360 Montrose Ave., 416-531-7710,
merrilyaround.com

Misdemeanours

The great temptation for doting
aunties and fairy godmothers,
where you can buy ruby-coloured,
sequined slippers; maribou-bedecked
ballerina outifts, and *really cute* hats
with ears; it's the partner shop to
grownup designer Pam Chorley's
Fashion Crimes.
322 1/2 Queen St. W.,
416-351-8758

Samko Sales

For most of the year Samko operates
as a wholesaler only, but from
October to Christmas they're open to
the general public, selling
discontinued brand-name toys like
Fisher Price, Tonka, Lego, and Barbie
for prices in the range of 15% to
30% off.
11 Peel Ave., 416-532-1114

south to the railway tracks for a gigantic yard sale.
Usually it's scheduled for the Saturday, with Sunday as
the rain date.

Island Christmas Boutique

On the first Saturday in December, residents of Ward's
Island sell their creative wares to each other and select
city-side friends. Narrow aisles between tables set up
inside the Algonquin Island Clubhouse are crowded with
admirers of the Islanders' inimitable artwork, textiles,
crafts, preserves, home baking, herbal products, and
cards. There are always raffles for local good causes,
and absolutely the creamiest and best eggnog in the
known world.
416-203-0965, torontoisland.org

Mountain Equipment Co-op

Every April and October, MEC sells off its own rental
gear and invites members of the public to sell their used
outdoor sports and camping equipment on consignment
at the same time. The goods are limited to "self-
propelled, wilderness-oriented recreation." (So downhill
skis would be out, but cross-country would be in, get it?)
Items like MEC's rental snowshoes can be as much as
75% off; buyers are usually enthusiastic, to say the least.
In fact, one MEC staffer suggests going "just for the
entertainment value; it's a mad dash." Likely finds are
tents, camping items, canoe, kayak and bike gear, and,
increasingly, kids' stuff. For those interested in selling
their own equipment, MEC takes 10% of the
consignment price whether the goods sell or not. If they
do sell, MEC takes an additional 10%. If not, at least
you get your goods back. (Only MEC members can buy
or sell, but it's a mere $5 to join.)
400 King St. W., 416-340-2667, mec.ca

Toronto Hadassah-WIZO Bazaar

For more than 75 years the women of Toronto
Hadassah-WIZO have been putting together the ultimate
garment bazaar on the last Wednesday of October,
with mountains of every conceivable kind of clothing at
the Better Living Centre at Exhibition Place. Not for the
faint of heart! It's one of those events that you can only
"do" if you allow yourself several hours, and at that
you'll probably feel that you left some bargains behind.
Admission is a mere toonie, with children under 5 free.
416-630-8373, canadian-hadassah-wizo.org

Toronto Police Auctions

At one time Toronto Police auctioned goods that had passed through their "Property Evidence Unit" every month through a commercial auction house on Murray Road. These would include sports equipment, stereos, and other appliances, but the star attraction was often a batch of recovered bicycles that had not been matched with previous owners. At the time of writing the force is testing online auctioneering – through none other than e-Bay. If they decide to go back to the old system, you can find out about it at 416-808-7997.

Trinity Yard Sale

The annual community-wide yard sale in Trinity-Bellwoods Park (Queen West at Strachan) takes place on a Saturday in mid-June. It's one of the biggest of its kind, and a great venue for kids' clothes, toys, and small housewares.
c/o Trinity Community Recreation Centre, 416-392-0743

offbeat specialty stores

Photo: Sarah B. Hood

Balloon King of Canada

For anyone who is still secretly delighted by parties with themes, Balloon King is a garden of delights. Do you need flags of the world on toothpicks? A gross of plastic whistles? Tiny toys to fill a piñata or a grab bag? A bouquet of helium-filled balloons with a get-well message? The King has all that, plus inexpensive party favours, novelty hats, masks, and decorations for any holiday or occasion you might care to name.
374 Bathurst St., 416-603-4347

Binz

Storage solutions of all kinds, like trash cans, makeup tins, suction-mounted soap dishes, hangers, tubs, bags, and CD holders.
1934 Queen St. E., 416-690-4611

Safety Superstore

Now you can make every sharp corner round and soft; permanently seal every container holding a substance more toxic than apple juice, and render your baby UV-immune. (Don't worry. You'll be mostly over this stage by the time you have your second child.)
1600 Steeles Ave. W., Unit 25, 905-761-7233, babyproofingplus.com

Soda Pop

Reused children's clothing with labels like OshKosh and Baby Gap.
315 Roncesvalles Ave., 416-516-4200

Treasure Island Toys

With a "no war toys" policy and two wooden train sets in the store for kids to play with, Treasure Island is a winner among neighbourhood toy stores.
311 Danforth Ave, 416-778-4913

Birders Nature Stores

Toronto bird lovers snap up 34 tonnes of seed a year from these outlets, where you can buy a bird feeder for $6 or for $400, as well as a spectacular assortment of birdhouses, garden decor ... and lots of wild bird seed mix.
265 Eglinton Ave. W., 416-481-2431 & 2100 Bloor St. W., 416-604-9272, toronto.birdersnature.com

Feather Factory

Cathy Bull is an expert at making, cleaning, and refurbishing down and feather pillows and comforters, as well as cleaning duvets. How good is she? She's even been asked to make a pillow for the Pope!
1606 Queen St. W., 416-536-3391, featherfactory.com

Photo: Sarah B. Hood

House of 220

Appliances and fixtures that run on 220 volts (110 is standard in North America), so you can outfit yourself for long-term travel, or bear plug-in gifts to your friends in other countries.
1444 Gerrard St. E., 416-461-2602

Made You Look

An open-concept shop with natural brick walls that fronts a co-operative studio for jewellry makers. Lots of variety, and the work is beautifully displayed.
1338 Queen St. W., 416-463-2136

Mokuba

Ribbons of silk and satin and velvet; ribbons in all colours; metallic ribbons; ribbons of lace ... Who knew the humble ribbon could come in so many astonishing variations?
577 Queen Street West Phone: 416-504-5358

O2 Spa Bar

"All I need is the air that I breathe and to love you," the song goes. But if you feel the former isn't up to scratch, there's a solution. Since 1996, Shamila Hunter has been offering refreshing hits of medical-grade oxygen at her O2 Spa Bar, the world's first of its kind. You inhale it through something called a "nasal cannula," which might be considered sexy in a *Star Trek* kind of way. And the air can be flavoured, for example with orange essence.
2044 Yonge St., 416-322-7733, o2spabar.com

The Original Vermi Composter

Wanna produce great compost using worms, indoors? Find everything you need right here. Open Fridays, Saturdays, and by appointment.
2238 Queen St. E., 416-693-1027, vermitechsystems.com

Photo: Sarah B. Hood

Rana Gems

Whether you make your own jewellry or want to commission a custom-made piece, you'll enjoy these unimposing and friendly importers of a veritable pirates' hoard of corals, jades, pearls, and precious and semi-precious stones. (They also carry masses of strung seed beads in lots of colours.)
1151 Gerrard St. E., 416-466-7644

The Paper Bag Princess

The stars go shopping for vintage designer wear at the PBP's only other location, in Santa Monica, CA. That's where Julia Roberts bought the '70s black Jean Jourban Paris number that she wore to the 2003 Oscars. Fran Drescher got a 1956 Christian Dior beaded cocktail dress there. Christina Ricci found a great Halston outfit; Nicole Kidman did the cover of *Esquire* in a revealing '70s Giorgio top. What else do you need to know?
287 Davenport Rd., 416 925-2603, thepaperbagprincess.com

Shoppe D'Or

The ultimate in high-end second-hand, where you might well pick up last year's Chanel.
18 Cumberland St., 416-923-2384

Retail Bag Co. Ltd.

This is where you go to get paper, cellophane, or plastic bags by the hundreds or thousands. They also carry money-saving giant rolls of ribbon. For the Martha Stewarts among us, this is the place to go for bulk bargains that can shave big bucks off baking, crafting projects, and gift wrapping.
430 Adelaide St. W., 416-504-0280

Spy Tech

We're sure *King of the Hill*'s Dale Gribble would love this place, which stocks everything for the suspicious, the inquisitive, and the paranoid. Their specialty is video surveillance and miniature video transmitters, but you can also look to them for pinhole cameras, recording devices, bulletproof vests, and telephone voice changers.
2028 Yonge St., 416-482-8588, spytech.com

Photo: Sarah B. Hood

The Tin Taj

Ogre, the aptly named little dog, and his kittycat friends will greet you in the tiny Tin Taj where you can buy a quirky selection of toys and trinkets, mostly made of tin. But the best part is the custom framing. Proprietor Carol Anne Castray trained in Mexico in the art of decorative tinwork, and possesses a fine collection of rare and specialized tools for the job. She will craft a mirror to your specifications or mount artwork in a sculpted frame that incorporates images and text of your choosing.
913 Queen St. W., 416-703-7515

clothing

The Clothing Show

In 1977, a small-scale show and sale of vintage clothing was launched at the Palais Royale; it has grown to become Canada's largest show of vintage wear and work by new designers. The Clothing Show is a great way for people who aren't already involved with the fashion industry to make personal connections with designers and get onto their mailing lists for studio sales and fashion shows. It takes place each May and October at the Automotive Building at Exhibition Place. *416-657-2156, theclothingshow.com*

The DUDE Show

Twice a year, in December and June, about 30 independent designers get together for the Downtown Urban Design Event. Organized by two design companies – Ruckus and Spacegirl – it's just about this city's hottest one-stop shop for emerging fashion talent. It's usually held at Latvian House (*491 College St.*). *416-535-2468, ruckusdesigns.com*

Holt Renfrew Last Call

The location for end-of-line Karan, Prada, Versace and other finds that started out at Holt's main stores, for as little as 20% of the original price. *370 Steeles Ave. W., 905-886-7444*

Tom's Place

William Mihalik opened a garment shop called Williams' Bargain Second Hand Store at 54 Baldwin when he arrived from Hungary in 1958. William's son Tamas Mihalik worked with his dad from the age of 12, there and at 60 Kensington, then eventually bought the business in 1982, a couple of years after its move to the present location. Now Tom's Place is a Kensington Market legend, and a premiere spot for designer clothes at discount prices. He runs a sensational sale twice a year as a fundraiser for the Jewish Community Centre. *190 Baldwin St., 416-596-0297*

Photo: Ontario Tourism, 11784

Of course, any vintage shopper knows that Kensington Avenue north of Dundas is vintage heaven, with shops like Astro, Asylum, and the quintessential Courage My Love. But also check out the following:

Black Market

This is your destination of choice for '70s band T-shirts, leather jackets, and – if you're willing to pick around a bit – lots of amazing, unique stuff. The warehouse is rummage-sale style; the boutique has been more carefully selected ... and you'll pay a bit extra for that. *Warehouse: 256A Queen St. W., basement, 416-599-5858, blackmarkettoronto.com Boutique: 319 Queen St. W., 2nd floor, 416-591-7945, blackmarkettoronto.com*

out of the ordinary

Boudoir

One of the newest and most glam of the vintage stores, with a chic assortment of '50s and '60s cocktail frocks, hatboxes, Chanel accessories, and similar frou frou.
990 Queen St. W., 416-535-6600

Brava

Theatrical velvets and satins from the '30s and '40s, as well as more functional and contemporary coats, hats, and especially shoes.
483 Queen St. W., 416-504-8742

Cabaret Nostalgia

Wearable antiques for men and women, ranging from the '60s right back to the 19th century, with lots of items from the '20s and '30s. A serious collection of evening purses, ladies' hats, cigarette cases, and the like.
672 Queen St. W., 416-504-7126, cabaretvintage.com

Photo: Sarah B. Hood

If you're smaller than average, you tend to get stuck with childish styles (even actual kids' clothes). If you're bigger, retailers seem to think you like wearing polyster tents. And as for maternity…. here are some places that cater to sophisticated dressers of uncommon proportions.

The Answer

In the U.S. it wouldn't be so unusual to find top lines (Jones New York, Anne Klein, and so on), including sportswear, in sizes 12 to 24. But here, this is one of the few places that carries the upper size range.
2715 Yonge St., 416-483-5663

Easy Expressions

Like The Answer, but more in the business/casual end, with sizes 14 to 24.
Centerpoint Mall, 6332 Yonge St., 416-222-6166

Elegant Expectations

With opulently expectant women in the public eye (like Catherine Zeta-Jones, or Demi Moore before her), there's no reason for pregnant women to feel they have to dress for staying home. Elegant Expectations sells maternity clothes for people who go out to work and play, including Coccoli's classic Italian-inspired looks, the practical and great-looking Blissful Babes, and Lilith boutique's very funky Yummy Mummy line.
2 Toronto St, 416-368-5581, elegantexpectations.com

Melmira Swimsuits

When are we made to feel more body-conscious than while bathing-suit shopping? Melmira carries suits for women of all shapes, including those who are pregnant and those who've undergone mastectomies.
3404 Yonge St., 416-485-0576

Muskat & Brown

Good lines of day and evening wear for sizes 0 to 12.
2528 Yonge St., 416-489-4005

Price Roman

A husband-and-wife design team whose work will fit tiny petites with flair.
267 Queen St. W., 416-979-7363

Rubenesque

A designer consigment store with a mission! Nothing smaller than size 14, and their website makes it clear that they do not consider Kate Moss to be a style icon.
1751 Avenue Rd, 416-787-8893, rubenesque.ca

With Child

Sherry Leeder founded her Bravado Designs out of frustration with the existing clothing possibilities for nursing mothers. Her shop has recently passed into the hands of former manager Tina Martins, but it continues to sell Bravado nursing bras and other fashion items – but take note: not maternity clothes – as well as a full line of cloth diapers. (They also run a moms' group and "Lullabies and Lap Rhymes" classes.)
705 Pape Ave., 416-466-9693

Gadabout

About equally divided between clothing and housewares, Gadabout – which caters to the film industry – houses an almost bewildering supply of vintage textiles, table linens, aprons, and bedding. Plus toys, tools, silk flowers, buttons, china, gloves, and more, and even more!
1300 Queen St. E., 416-463-1254, gadabout.ca

Stella Luna

Genuine vintage from the '30s to the '70s, handpicked, with a nice sense of style.
1627 Queen St. W., 416-536-7300

The Toronto Vintage Clothing and Textile Show and Sale

This is the once-a-year source for original, museum-quality 19th-century clothing, handmade quilts, samplers, and similar treasures. It takes place every March at the historical Enoch Turner Schoolhouse; some of the proceeds go to the Multiple Sclerosis and Canadian Cancer Societies.
Enoch Turner Schoolhouse, 106 Trinity St., 905-666-0523 or 905-666-3277

When Does "Hidebound" Mean "Adventurous"?

A recent *NOW Magazine* survey found that BDSM is this city's most popular style of recreational deviance. Of course, you may just be looking for a nice leather jacket; either way, here are some of this city's top (so to speak) leather shops.

Acton Leather Co.

For years and years the venerable Olde Hide House — source of excellent leather, suede, and shearling coats — has advertised under the slogan "It's worth the drive to Acton." Well, they've opened a store one block west of Spadina on King, so we guess not enough people agreed.
522 King St. W., 416-203-7001, leathertown.com

local designers

Tip: If you don't happen to be a perfect size 4, you should feel free to ask at any designer shop whether you can order one of their existing pieces to fit you. Many will happily agree.

Annie Thompson

Annie Thompson designs artfully constructed, assymetrically cut clothing with a bold and sophisticated Bohemian style. Earth Mother meets Gaultier? Well, maybe. She also has a line of "Personal Baggage," including great yoga mat bags, and her shop hosts a well-chosen selection of independent lines. If you catch a peek through the curtain at the back you'll see her studio in action; some of her wildest creations for the Fashion Cares AIDS benefit adorn the west wall.
674 Queen St. W., 416-703-3843, anniethompson.ca

Any Direct Flight

Barbara Starr and Margot Allin share digs at this women's boutique, featuring interestingly textured classic day dresses, suits, and separates.
724 Queen St. W., 416-504-0017

Brian Bailey

Brian Bailey designs "real clothes for grownups," as one aficionado puts it. His softly tailored, sexy, and sophisticated woman's clothes have won lots of awards.
878 Queen St. W., 416-221-3355; Bayview Village Shopping Centre, 416-516-7188, brianbaileyfashion.com

Comrags

Joyce Gunhouse and Judy Cornish are among Toronto's most established local designers, having worked together for 20 years. Clean lines, solid earth tones, and a nice use of bias cutting in wearable, informal dresses, and separates characterize their recent work. And we love the linen.
654 Queen St. W., 416-360-7249; 3362 Yonge St., 416-485-6260, comrags.com

Damzels in this Dress

Although damsels Kelly Freeman and Rory Lindo met in Toronto, they sold their first clothes out of a Vancouver shop. Their work is edgy and contemporary; however, its has roots in earlier style eras. Their studio isn't open to the public, but they sell through retail stores around town, and they sometimes do studio sales.
416-598-0809, damzelsinthisdress.com

del.phic

A collection of young designers creating clubber gear and general streetwear for a youthful scene.
706 Queen St. W., 603-3334

Fashion Crimes

Pam Chorney was the first person in Toronto to offer excellent goth wedding gowns. Her clothes for women are heavily decorative, with big skirts and lots of exciting ornamentation. (She also runs scrumptious kids' boutique Misdemeanours.)
395 Queen St. W., 416-592-9001

Fresh Baked Goods/Fresh Collective

The self-styled "Laura-Jean the Knitting Queen" sits all day in her little shop with her doggies like the princess in Rumplestiltskin, but instead of spinning straw into gold she's making beautiful sweaters. (And she can knit her handiwork to any size, upon request.) No scrap of wool is wasted; if it's too small for a sleeve it becomes part of a multicoloured scarf. Laura-Jean has also recently opened Fresh Collective, which groups together whimsical and lovely work by independent clothing and jewellry designers – like Rosie Young of Beads for your Needs, Snoflake, Buttercup Days, Baby Ben (original quilts and baby buntings!), and Tart Bags.
Fresh Baked Goods: 274 Augusta Ave., 416-966-0123, freshbakedgoods.com
Fresh Collective: 692 Queen Street West, 416-594-1313, freshbakedgoods.com

Doc's Leathers

When you're into that biker thang, you want Doc's Leathers, whether you're craving boy/boy bondage, or you "just wanna ride your motorsickle."
726 Queen St. W., 416-504-8888, docsleathers.com

Metaleather

If you see yourself as a Celtic warrior or a swordmaiden of Rohan, Metaleather is just your style. How about a metal-inlaid bustier or a studded tunic? They've got you covered.
445 King St. E., 416-594-0171, metaleather.com

Northbound Leather

If you enter via Yonge Street, you'll find yourself in a fashion-forward designer leather shop. If you choose the back door (so to speak) on St. Nicholas, you'll have entered this city's premier palace of designer and custom fetish gear. Northbound holds an annual event on the third Saturday in October that's the fashion must-see for the leather set. They also run monthly parties known for the moment as "Fetish@5ive," because they take place at the club known as 5ive, at 5 St. Joseph Street.
586 Yonge St.; 7 St. Nicholas St., 416-972-1037, northbound.com

Hoax Couture

It now seems like a long time ago that the Hoax boys – Jim Searle and Chris Tyrell – moved uptown from Queen West to Yorkville; their men's and women's clothing has become a Toronto staple.
114 Cumberland, 416-929-4629, hoaxcouture.com

Kimina Fashion

Designer Kimin Zang uses natural fabrics and a minimalist approach to create easy, unstructured clothing for women and men, with simple lines that would suit both formal and leisure demands.
112 Yorkville Ave., 416-515-0999

Lilliput Hats

How lucky for Toronto that the tap-dancing class at the Board of Education was full when Karyn Gingras tried to register! She took a course in millinery instead, and that's why we now have Lilliput Hats. Using only antique lasts in her lively studio/boutique, she creates gorgeous, fanciful headgear for adults and kids out of felt and faux fur, silk and straw, and fabrics from denim to cashmere to velvet.
462 College St., 416-536-5933, lilliputhats.com

Modrobes

Somewhat attitudinal designer Saldebus got started selling directly to students in schools (catching their attention with a cry of "I want you in my pants!"). Eventually he decided Queen Street West would be a radical enough place to launch his storefront, which offers hoodies, shirts, and his signature lounge pants. (He now has outlets in several Ontario locations and one in Vancouver.)
239 Queen St. W., 416-597-9560, modrobes.com

Peach Berserk Cocktails

Peach Berserk founder Kingi Carpenter just wasn't satisfied with the state of the fabric industry, so she decided to silkscreen her own. Her look resembles something a creative nine-year-old girl might come up with at the back of her school copybook. (Think lipstick tubes, kitties, daisies, and pretty faces, all in vivid colours.) Peach Berserk specializes in fun items like prom dresses, and they'll custom design. They also offer popular silkscreen classes.
507 Queen St. W., 416-504-1711, peachberserk.com

Preloved

If you hadn't sent all those vintage sweats and Ts to Goodwill, you could have cut them up into interesting shapes, resewed them into great new clothes and opened a store. Wait … Preloved already did that!
613 Queen St. W., 416-504-8704, preloved.ca

Sim & Jones

The shop founded by Pui Sim and Alaryce Jones offers elegant urban women's and men's wear and home accessories, many with a hint of '70s flair. Perfect for the *Wallpaper* crowd.
388 College St., 416-920-2573, simandjones.com

Susan Harris Design

Susan Harris makes innovative sweaters and sleeves out of recycled wool, with little pieces of text worked into them. Her work is available at the One of A Kind Craft Show and Sale or at Annie Thompson (see above), as well as at her own studio, by appointment.
416-703-8537

Wenches & Rogues

Newfoundlander Jane Mifflin's cheeky and cheerful work shows a playful interest in texture and quirky little design details, while her staff is less attitudinal than some – maybe because she started off hiring Newfoundlanders familiar with her other outlet, in St. John's.
610 Queen St. W., 416-536-2172

I See England, I See France …

Bra Bar

Fancy and lovely bras in sizes from (guys, stop reading now!) 32AA to 52H.
118 Yorkville Ave., 416-921-4567

Chocky's

This old-school jobber's has brand-name underwear like Calvin Klein at deep discount – along with men's, women's and children's T-shirts, long underwear, and other essentials.
327 Spadina Ave., 416- 977-1831

Lingerie House

A good spot for discount lingerie.
2296 Bloor St. W., 416-766-5742

Super Sellers

Lots of undies (including Elita), bras and lingerie items at great prices and in a wide range of sizes. They have a frequent shopper card, too.
474 Yonge St., 416-925-5031

Thrift Shops

Tip: With any thrift shopping, the wealthier the neighbourhood, the better the pickings.

St. Vincent de Paul Society

This 150-year-old Roman Catholic charity for the relief of poverty runs a number of modest little shops that are great for traditional baby clothes and suchlike.

66 Bond St., 416-203-9631
253 Broadview Ave., 416-461-8602
391 Drfitwood Ave., 416-661-3126
265 Lakeshore Rd. E., 905-278-0437
60 Newcastle Rd., 416-503-2403
ssvp.on.ca

Salvation Army Family Thrift Stores

Run by the Salvation Army, of course, these are perhaps the most threadbare of the thrift outlets – but that makes it all the more fun when you find something great.

1219 Bloor St. W., 416-533-9553
1675 Jane St, 416-247-0505
2291 Kipling Ave. 416-746-3500
974 Pape Ave., 416-425-9625
1147 Queen St. W., 416-536-3361
252 Parliament St., 416-955-0362
665 St. Clair Ave. W., 416-651-2825
2360 S. Service Rd., Oakville, 905-825-9208
salvationarmy.ca

Make Me Sew Saree

Photo: Sarah B. Hood

You can buy ready-made Indian garments at outlets like **Sonu Saree Palace** (*1420 Gerrard St. E., 416-469-2800; 991 Albion Rd., 416-742-2800, sonusaree.com*). More fun would be to choose a length of fabric and have a saree with its accompanying tight blouse, or the loose trousers, tunic, and scarf known as *salwar-kameez*, made just for you. (Sonu can take your measurements and send the material to a tailor on your behalf.) Depending on your tastes and requirements, you can buy a saree length for as little as $10 to $20, with the price going up from there according to fabric and decoration. You'll want an armful of bangles to go with that; the nicest selection is at **Maharani Fashions** (*1417 Gerrard St. E., 416-466-8400*), and the marked price – between $5 and $40 – is not for the individual bangle, but for the set. Men's outfits and suiting fabrics are also available.

Photo: Ontario Tourism, 11951

shopping with a conscience

Tip: Oddly, Danforth at Chester is the epicentre for ethical gift shopping.

Blue Moon

A not-for-profit shop that supports craftspeople in developing countries through sales of fair trade goods.
375 Danforth Ave., 416-778-6991, bluemoon.org

Calico

You can only shop at this "urban village market" on Saturdays. It features goods produced by people from at-risk, low income, or marginalized backgrounds. You'll find clothes, crafts, art, and the gorgeous beeswax candles of Christopher's Hive.
St. Lawrence Market, lower level, 416-203-7885, calicomarket.com

Photo: Sarah B. Hood

El Pipil

Cheerful and colourful, El Pipil sells fair-trade South American crafts.
267 Danforth Ave., 416-465-9625

The Garbage Palace

You never know what you'll find at The Garbage Palace. They only sell garbage and things they can make out of it. It's a favourite with film set decorators – for instance, the contents of Meg Ryan's apartment in the 2003 film *Against the Ropes* mostly came from there. Count on unusual cards, small home furnishings, and very peculiar found-object clocks. They also offer classes in such skills as clock-making and mosaic mirror-making.
970 Queen St. W., 416-530-5850

Goodwill

Goodwill creates social opportunities through the operation of its stores and the revenue they generate. At the Main Store you'll find furniture, sporting goods, and other large items, as well as the Buy-The-Pound outlet where, yes, the goods are priced by weight. (Don't miss the Main Store Annex!) Also, watch for auction items at every branch; these are picked out from the incoming donations and displayed through the week, then auctioned off on Thursday or Friday. Typically you'd find odd pieces of fine china, jewellry, collectibles like Beanie Babies, and occasional musical instruments or antiques.
Main Store: 234 Adelaide St. E, 416-366-2083
Buy The Pound: 234 Adelaide St. E, 416-362-4710
720 Burnamthorpe Rd. W., Mississauga, 905-949-8660,
469 Carlaw Ave., 416-461-3559
299 Coxwell Ave., 416-465-8569,
3003 Danforth Ave., 416-686-9815,
3302 Dufferin St., 416-782-3913
1224 Dundas St. E., Mississauga, 905-276-6879

4975 Dundas St. W., 416-207-9691

2642 Eglinton Ave. E.,
416-265-4106

306 Gerrard St. E., 416-921-3396

4568 Kingston Rd., 416-284-0146

2075 Lawrence Ave. E.,
416-755-1248

60 Overlea Blvd., 416-422-0998

28 Roncesvalles Ave.,
416-534-1686

585 St. Clair Ave. W.,
416-656-5550

5010 Steeles Ave. W.,
416-745-6329

2625-C Weston Rd., 416-241-2020

1030-A Wilson Ave., 416-398-0174

goodwill.on.ca

Value Village

A North-America-wide chain (called Savers in the U.S.). Each outlet has a relationship with a charity serving its own commnity. The draw of Value Village is that every single store is supposed to receive two new truckloads of goods every single day.

1319 Bloor St. W., 416-539-0585

2119 Danforth Ave., 416-698-0621

2345 Keele St., 416-247-7372

924 Queen St. E., 416-778-4818

valuevillage.com

Grassroots Environmental Products

Everything for living lightly on the earth, from composting supplies to cleaning products.
408 Bloor St. W., 416-944-1993; 372 Danforth Ave., 416-466-2841, grassrootsstore.com

Planet Aid Canada

Affiliated with the International Humana People to People Movement, Planet Aid is a registered charity that sells new and recycled vintage, designer, retro, and remade men's and women's clothing and accessories to benefit Children's Town (for street kids and orphans), and HOPE (which fights AIDS), both in Zambia. They can also connect people with development work in Africa.
480 Parliament St., 416-504-5332; 546 Yonge St., 416-924-8928; 160 Baldwin St., 416-597-1743, planetaidcanada.org

Ten Thousand Villages

Carefully and thoughtfully run by the North American Mennonite communities, Ten Thousand Villages sells wares produced by people in developing areas who would otherwise be unemployed or underemployed. (They also organize a gift sale at Harbourfront every December.)
2599 Yonge St., 416 932-1673; 362 Danforth Ave., 416 462-9779 (Also: The Mennonite Centre Store, 2701 St Clair Ave. E., 416 757-9242), torontoareamennonites.ca or tenthousandvillages.com

YWCA International Boutique

This volunteer-run shop just behind the corner of Bloor and Yonge offers crafts and other products that support social justice causes.
14 Roy's Square, 416-924-4762, ywcator.org

naughty necessities

Come As You Are
Straightforward, matter-of-fact information and a browser-friendly atmosphere make Come As You Are a classic, with a good selection of toys, books, lubricants, and related products.
701 Queen St. W., 416-504-7934, comeasyouare.com

Good For Her
A sex shop for women, with a full roster of ongoing practical workshops ranging from "Giving Head" to "Flirtation" to "Belly Dance." The classes are open to women only – including transsexual/transgendered women and sometimes trans men – but men are welcome in the shop.
175 Harbord St., 416-588-0900, goodforher.com

He and She Clothing Gallery
Leather and PVC garb (always stylishly displayed on the ladder-mounted mannequins outside the door), plus lots of fetish gear in this east-end shop that promises "more of everything."
263-265 Queen St. E., 416-594-0171, heandsheclothing.com

Photo: Sarah B. Hood

Music

Bad Lad Music
Run by DJ Bad Lad himself, the premiere outlet for Caribbean sounds: soca, reggae, hip-hop, R&B, and dance.
4417 Sheppard Ave. E., 416-335-5292

Cosmos Records
Vinyl, vinyl, vinyl!
607 Queen St. W, 416-603-0254

Dundas & Spadina
Look for street vendors to stock up on Asian pop (also discount phone cards).

Greek City Video
Maybe the sound of the bouzouki is an acquired taste, but if you like powerful vocalist Haris Alexiou as much as we do, here's where you'll find her. (Lots of Greek movies, too.)
452 Danforth Ave., 416-461-6244, greekcity.com

Neurotica
Second-hand CDs and lots of unusual vinyl.
642 Queen St. W., 416-603-7796

MissBehav'n

This boutique has a charmingly naughty air about it, and a real live parrot inside. On pleasant Saturday afternoons, strolling pedestrians do the double take when they notice the live lingerie models in the window. The shop especially caters to women, with its stock of stillettos; sparkly, sexy garb (including choices for plus-size gals), and lots of equipment for love bondage. There's even complimentary cappuccino.
650 Queen St. W., 416-866-7979, missbehavn.com

Priape

The self-styled "emporium of gay erotica" has the usual array of insertable toys and lubricants, but their claim to fame is their video/DVD collection. Lots of lit too, and a longstanding relationship with the leather community built upon their popular Montreal-made house line of partywear and other leather fashions. And, yes, they do have leather cleaner.
465 Church St., 416-586-9914, priape.com

Take a Walk on the Wild Side

As its name (after the classic song) suggests, Take A Walk On The Wild Side stocks everything for the she-male, including shoes, lingerie, wigs and eyelashes, plus-size pantihose, and "Jayne belts," the must-have for eliminating telltale boy bulges. On the serious side, TWWS offers a supportive environment for members of the transvestite/transsexual/transgendered community.
161 Gerrard St. E., 416-921-6112, wildside.org

Play de Record

Import soul-jazz, jungle, hip hop, techno, soca, reggae, and house, including lots on vinyl.
357A Yonge St., 416-586-0380, playderecord.com

Photo: Sarah B. Hood

Rotate This

One of the greats, since the days when vinyl was the only option. Particularly good for acid jazz.
620 Queen St. W., 416-504-8447

Song Bird Music

A nice place to buy second-hand instruments, so you can make some music of your own.
801 Queen St. W., 416-504-7664

Soundscapes

Unlike so many music shops, this one is tranquil and sunny, and as at home with jazz, classical and world music as with rock, pop, or hip-hop.
572 College St., 416-537-1620

In the Family

Dave Snider Music (*3225 Yonge St., 416-483-5825, snidermusic.com*) doesn't sell music to listen to, but it does have a fabulous trove of sheet music and fake books. By the way, founder Dave Snider is one of three musical brothers, of whom the others are Lou and Art; Art being the best known. A member of the Canadian Country Music Hall of Fame, he ran his own dance bands before spending a decade as conductor for the television show *Country Hoedown* (later *The Tommy Hunter Show*). He also founded Chateau/Canatal records (Gordon Lightfoot's first label) and Sound Canada studios.

Joe Sealy (piano) and Paul Novotny (bass), 1999 Toronto Downtown Jazz Festival, Montreal Bistro. Photo: Paul Hoeffler

Photo: Sarah B. Hood

The Vision in Tele-vision

He started out in 1972 with a weak signal and an aggressive idea. His TV station would feature young, hip, and good-looking anchors. No longer chained to a desk, literally or figuratively, the on-air personalities wandered around the studio while reading the news. In the background, the newsroom was in full, frantic view. Moses Znaimer and Citytv were a hit, even more so after he started airing his infamous, soft-core *Baby Blue* movies on late-night television. In the 30-odd years since then, Moses has led viewers to his on-screen promised land. Citytv was followed by the hit channels MuchMusic and then Bravo! The medium clearly has been the message.

But now that message is mixed. In April 2003, Znaimer stepped down from his influential post to become executive producer of Learning & Skills Television, a little-known CHUM Ltd. property in Alberta. Rumours persisted that Znaimer was forced out, but media moguls always have plenty of options. Like in front of the camera.

He's done it before. His biggest role came in *Atlantic City*, legendary director Louis Malle's 1981 crime drama, in which he played Felix, a thug hunting for a stolen stash of cocaine. He talks tough to Susan Sarandon and waves a gun around before being shot to death by Burt Lancaster. No wonder Burt's flicks seldom air on late-night TV.

Old News

The first newspaper in town was the *Upper Canada Gazette*. Hitting the streets on October 4, 1798, the *Gazette* was resolutely pro-government and, despite a small blip during the American Invasion of 1813, published unimpeded for 20 years.

Then there was the *Colonial Advocate*. Publisher William Lyon Mackenzie had a serious hate-on for the ruling class and, from November 25, 1824 onward, he roused rabble with the best of them. His printed attacks were pointed but hardly profitable and his paper was losing money before long. Respite came from a most unlikely source. On June 8, 1826, while Mackenzie was out of town, a group of angry young Tories broke into the *Advocate* offices and threw the printing press into Toronto Bay. Mackenzie sued successfully and was awarded enough money to keep publishing another eight years before he quit journalism and entered politics. He was the first mayor of Toronto.

Busy-Body

Born in an era of activism, *The Body Politic* was Canada's best-known gay newspaper. The first issue hit the streets in October 1977 and it quickly became an early voice of the gay movement. A collective of roughly 15 people met every week until 1987, when the paper finally folded after 135 issues. Along the way there were notorious police busts (one after an April 1982 article on fistfucking) and plenty of pre-Pride pride. The collective also founded its own publisher, Pink Triangle Press, which to this day continues to produce *The Body Politic's* successor, *Xtra!*

THE BARE FACTS

Fans of television news know what they want: a quick hit and visual flash. And no show offers more of it than *Naked News TV*, where on-air personalities read the news and casually disrobe. Created by Fernando Pereira and Kirby Stasyna, the show, which is broadcast from a secret studio in the east end, first aired over the internet in December 1999. Ratings quickly soared to the point where *Naked News* now hits over six million screens around the world. Now that's coverage.

It's a little known fact now, but Toronto was once the tabloid capital of this country; five rags were running in town during the first half of the 20th century. Their names were notably sensational: *Hush, Flash, Thunder, Justice Weekly,* and *Jack Canuck.* Some, like *Thunder,* were haphazardly published and outrageously idiosyncratic. *Thunder*'s driving force was an ex-Alberta provincial policeman named Patrick Sullivan, who was obsessed with the disappearance of theatre owner Ambrose Small and connected that mystery to a conspiracy within the Catholic Church. After making less-than-veiled references to the widow Small and a church minister, Sullivan was charged with obscenity.

Hush, in comparison, was a model of journalism. The most resilient of the tabloids, *Hush* was founded in November 25, 1927, by an antagonistic horse-breeder named Strathearn Boyd Thomson, and ran in various incarnations all the way until 1973. With peak sales of 50,000 at five cents a copy in the 1940s, *Hush* dished out high society gossip and low life drama with equal aplomb. A classic *Hush* story, published April 12, 1941, was titled "Sissy Wants Mama Back": "For only five months out of 15 years, Carry Nitkin, an ultra-smart type of young woman, lived with her lawful husband, Morris Nitkin. Then she went her separate way, praying to heaven that she could undo the marital chains that bound her; she found other gentleman friends, enjoyed the pleasures of other company, and Morris was left with an aching void in his heart." Seems Morris punched out one of his wife's male friends and ended up in court.

"She refused to go to the fights with me," he complained. "Do you think it's right? I love her."

"There is nothing I can do about it," replied Justice. "All you can do is just keep away. You may have some grounds for anger, but you have got to keep the peace."

"There is something deeper than anger," replied Morris. "It is love. Can I make phone calls to her?"

"What kind of sissy are you?" asked Justice scornfully....

BUT NO MOSHING

Rock 'n' roll first came to town on April 30, 1956. Bill Haley and the Comets, who shared the bill with The Platters and Joe Turner, drove 13,000 teens at Maple Leaf Gardens into an orgiastic display never before seen in the city. "Like natives at a voodoo ritual," the *Toronto Star* reported, "the crowd writhed and reeled until their pent-up emotions burst the dam of reason."

Beatlemania, Part One

With the British Invasion growing louder by the day in the 1960s, local boy Dave Marden decided to join the troops. He changed his name to Jack London and claimed his birthplace was Liverpool. He sang in a British accent and, along with his backing band The Sparrows, became one of the hottest acts in Yorkville's music scene. London's Liverpudlian "roots" were enough for Capitol Records, which signed Jack London and the Sparrows to a major label deal, the first ever for a Canadian band.

Super Freaky

Yorkville was once our Haight-Ashbury, with over 40 music clubs and coffee shops crammed into five small blocks. **The Riverboat**, **Purple Onion**, **Gate of Cleve**, and **The Flick** were just some of the names. But the most notorious of all might've been the **Mynah Bird**. Owner Colin Kerr, who started in business with a bird shop on Bloor Street, tried every promotional trick in the book to get the Mynah going: go-go dancers, body painting, even a nude male chef. But his best idea was to manage his own band. The Mynah Birds were fronted by Ricky James Matthews, an American hiding out in Yorkville from the U.S. Naval Reserve. Soon, the Mynahs added a local guitarist named Neil Young and a big-time investor, department store heir John Craig Eaton, who bought the band new equipment. Things looked really rosy when Motown Records signed the Mynahs to a record deal. The band cut 16 tracks before Motown began to fret over having an AWOL sailor as lead singer, so the record was never released. Matthews eventually turned himself in and the Mynah Birds broke up. Fed up, Young hocked Eaton's equipment and found rock stardom in California, beginning with Buffalo Springfield. And Matthews? He got out of the brig, changed his name to Rick James, and scored with the funky hit "Superfreak."

TRIED, TESTED, AND TRUE

She's perhaps our truest cult heroine. Mary Margaret O'Hara is everywhere and nowhere in this town; everywhere because she is often spotted in the Queen West or Annex areas, or hanging out in some club, and nowhere because fans have been waiting since 1988 for a follow-up to *Miss America*, her album of off-kilter torch songs. She has refused all offers so far, recording only scattered songs, back-up vocals, film soundtracks, and, strangest of all, a car commercial for General Motors.

Beatlemania, Part Two

The Beatles played Maple Leaf Gardens in 1965. They had signed for one show only, but Gardens owner Harold Ballard sold tickets for two. Warning the band not to disappoint their fans, Ballard forced the Fab Four into doing both shows. And he didn't stop there. He had Gardens staff shut off the water fountains and turn up the heat for the summer concert, then delayed both shows for over an hour and waited for the big concession sales to roll in. Almost 300 fans fainted and had to be carried out.

ADDING INSULT TO INJURY

In 1968, upon his second visit to the O'Keefe Centre (as the Hummingbird Centre was then called), song-and-dance man Sammy Davis Jr. was reviewed by Patrick Scott in the *Toronto Star* under the headline "This One-eyed Negro-Jew Lacks Class." Understandably the irate Rat-Packer vowed never to return. (He did eventually, but not until 1977.)

Knowing How to Blow

Fifty years ago, on May 15, 1953, legendary be-bopper Charlie Parker joined Dizzy Gillespie, Bud Powell, Charles Mingus, and Max Roach onstage at Massey Hall: the only time all five men played on the same stage at the same time. Dubbed "The Greatest Jazz Concert Ever," the show nonetheless had problems. Parker, who had to be billed as Charlie Chan because of contractual obligations, had recently hocked his sax for quick money and had to play on a plastic instrument. Money was actually a source of irritation for everybody since the entire quintet was being paid only $1,450. That same night, there was a big Rocky Marciano-Jersey Joe Walcott title fight; during intermission, Bird and Diz went to the nearby Silver Rail to catch a few rounds, and ended up 45 minutes late for the second half of the show. Roach had to take the stage alone, buying time until the rest of the band returned. Jersey Joe, by the way, lasted only two minutes and 25 seconds. All of the songs that evening were more than double that length.

Old Toronto Bands

• **The Ugly Ducklings** were the best of the old 1960s Yorkville bands. Their pre-punk garage sound has aged reasonably well. Singles like "Nothin'" and "Gaslight" made them Mick Jagger's favourite Canadian band.

• **Rough Trade** was true 1980s raunch 'n' roll. Teenagers from that time had their already-unstable glands extra-confused by the androgynous Carole Pope's crotch-grabbing antics during "High School Confidential."

• Boston. Kansas. Chicago. Why not **Toronto**? Lead singer Holly Woods worked the 1980s era of Spandex and hair to perfection on a hit like "Your Daddy Don't Know."

• Another '80s band, **Platinum Blonde**, was Toronto's great glam rock entry. "Doesn't Really Matter" could have been a song about singer Mark Holmes' big pout and bigger hair.

• Originally from Hamilton, **Teenage Head** gave tired old Toronto a much-needed taste of punk with teen anthems like "Let's Shake." Although one taste might have been enough after the summer of 1981, when a Head concert at the Ontario Place Forum started a full-scale riot.

BAD CALL OVERTURNED

Most people remember the famous incident from 1992 when — in a classic case of getting hold of the wrong end of the stick — then-Toronto Mayor June Rowlands banned up-and-coming songsters Barenaked Ladies from a Nathan Phillips Square performance on the grounds that the band's name was sexist. Far fewer are those who noticed or recall that, when Barbara Hall became Mayor in 1994, the band played the City's official New Year's Eve bash.

Photo: Kirk MacGregor

DRUMMING UP BUSINESS

Graeme Kirkland has been drumming around town for a long, long time. The street musician and bucket player (yes, he plays overturned buckets) has worked with everyone from Mary Margaret O'Hara to Jane Bunnett to the National Ballet of Canada. But a few years back he started playing a new tune: investment counselor. So the next time you hear him beating the skins in the Annex, you can also get answers to a few quick questions about your stock portfolio.

Five New Toronto Bands

Photo: V.S. Dobbs

• **The Constantines** came from Guelph, Ontario, but have taken Toronto by storm. "Incite"-ful lyrics and a big, soul-punk sound on a song like "Young Offenders" are only amplified during their energetic live shows.

• **Danko Jones** is made for rock 'n' roll: cool name, big tongue. The charismatic front man for his eponymous band can also sing a little, as his searing "Sound of Love" suggests.

• **FemBots** are the duo of Dave MacKinnon and Brian Poirier. Their songs are often built around found sounds, whether coming from a plunger, a balloon, or an answering machine message. The results, which some call honky-tonk dub, are weird but they work. Check out "Mom's Ether Blues."

• **The Hidden Cameras** made their name on the strength of their outrageous live shows, which would feature a pair of nearly naked men in balaclavas dancing. But the band is more than a gimmick. Front man Joel Gibb seems to channel The Smiths, and "Golden Streams" is just about the loveliest pop song about urine you could ever imagine.

• **Royal City** shares a hometown and a label, Three Gut Records, with The Constantines, but the similarities end there. Their songs, like "Blood and Faeces," are lo-fi tunes of sin and not-quite salvation.

Since its inception, *NOW Magazine* has had a close relation with the local indie music scene. How close? Well, if you spot a cube van delivering bundles of the weekly tabloid on any given Thursday, chances are good that the driver and "hoppers" are up-and-coming musicians. The one-day-a-week job suits many a struggling music maker, since it pays just about enough to cover basic rent. The *NOW*-truck hall of fame includes members of Daddy's of Eden, Brule Sound Pharmacy, Fifth Column, It's Patrick, Random Order, Morgan le Faye, Wyrd Sisters, Mother Tongue, Swamperella (pictured above), Courage of Lassie, Drastic Measure, The Garbagemen, Roach Motel, Laura Repo, Change of Heart, Pigfarm, Peepshow, Rheostatics, The Mercurymen, The Lost Dakotas, The Snowdogs, and Growl, not to mention Cyrus, Scott B. Sympathy, Lorrina Belluz, Brother Different, Dean Crawford, Ron Reid, Steve Rhodes, and Jalynn Ridley.

MAKING TRACKS

On January 30, 1938, a small group of model railroaders, including Borden Lilley and Harry Ebert, met in Ebert's basement, and thus was born the **Model Railroad Club of Toronto**. Since 1946, club members have been meeting every Wednesday night in a former munitions plant to construct and run the O-scale marvel that is the fictional "Central Ontario Railway," running between Lilleyburg in the south and Ebertville in the north. For only two weekends each February, the public is invited to view this marvelous miniature world, and the usually deserted industrial laneway gets as crowded as the midway at the Ex.

8-37 Hanna Ave., 416-536-8927

TORONTO ICONS IN THE MOVIES

The Gooderham and Worts distillery complex is possibly the most often used facility for location shooting in Toronto, although it's often unrecognizable to the average person. However, many of our landmarks have starring roles in the movies. Here are some of the most prominent:

1. In its most notable of several film appearances, **Casa Loma** is the training ground for the mutant *X-Men* (2000).

2. **Yonge Street**, including the Zanzibar strip club, Sunrise Records, Future Shop, and Sam the Record Man, is the turf over which Jean Claude Van Damme battles the Russian Mafia in *Maximum Risk* (1996).

3. *Cocktail* (1988), starring Tom Cruise as a NYC bartender, featured **Stoopy's Tavern** (then known as Soupy's) at 376 Dundas Street East. Then, in the 1993 comedy *The Ref*, set in small-town Connecticut, burglar Denis Leary asks, "What's the worst dive bar around here?" He's directed to Stoopy's.)

Trinidad isn't the only wellspring of soca and calypso. (After all, it was Toronto's own Anslem Douglas who originated the all-too-catchy "Who Let the Dogs Out?") Local calypsonians compete annually for the title of Calypso Monarch through the Organization of Calypso Performing Artistes (OCPA). In June and July, competing calypso "tents" (really weekly club nights) showcase their roster of performers, culminating in a gala showdown. Each performer must bring forth two new songs, usually comic, satirical, filled with wordplay, and based on local issues – whether these be lofty (politics, policing) or light (TV talk shows). Among the local stars are 1991 Juno winner Jayson, Beginner, Crooner, King Cosmos, Macomere Fifi, and Harold "De Hurricane" Hosein, more widely known as the popular Citytv and 680 News weather guy. It's tricky to track down the Calypso Tent schedules in the daily and weekly entertainment listings, but they're faithfully featured on the websites *fetenet.com* and *toronto-lime.com*, as well as in free weekly community papers like *Share* (available in all Coffee Times locations), *Caribbean Camera*, and *Pride*.

Pining for parang? Begging for bhangra? It can take a little effort to track down the rich world music scene in this town, still inexplicably sidelined by mainstream media. That having been said, Billy Bryans' *mundialmusic.com* is a sensational one-stop shop for Toronto lovers of Latin, Asian, and African music, with concert listings, CD release info, and links to independent distributors, artists, media, and promoters. Toronto World Arts Scene, a.k.a. *'twas magazine* (*twas.ca*) is the insider's newsletter for world music and dance. For $25 you can subscribe for two years (*P.O. Box 133, Station P, 704 Spadina Ave., M5S 2S6*). Incomparable *Kala* is a glossy 48-page quarterly that gets deep into all aspects of South Asian culture around Toronto. You can subscribe for $20 per year (*Kala Group, P.O. Box 18253, 250 Wincott Dr., M9R 2R0, 416-248-9896*). Cheeky *MyBindi.com* takes a lighter look at the same community, with a definite – though not exclusive – penchant for Bollywood gossip. The monthly *Word Magazine* (*wordmag.com*) focuses on the urban scene, but also carries strong coverage of reggae, dub poetry, African music, jazz, and blues. The lineups on the community radio stations (CHRY 105.5 FM, CIUT 89.5 FM, and CKLN 88.1 FM) are also packed with world sounds – alongside every other format that doesn't get enough mainstream airplay. Among the many standouts are CKLN's **"Reggaemania"** (Thursday nights at 9), **"Masala Mixx"** (Saturdays at 4, followed by **"Sounds of Africa"** at 6), and **"The Musical Triangle"** (Sundays at 4). Jowi Taylor hosts CBC 94.1 FM 's **"Global Village"** on Saturdays at 7. To get deeper into the Caribbean scene, listen to Jai Ojah Maharaj's **"Caribbean Connection"** on late-night on CHIN 101.3.FM, or take a dose of FLOW 93.5's **"Soca Therapy"** with Dr. Jay on Sundays at 6.

4. Much of *The Killing Fields* (1984) was shot in Thailand, but the **Royal York Hotel** was also used as a location.

5. *A Christmas Story* (1983) was voted the No. 1 holiday movie by *TV Guide* in 2000. This sleeper hit about the boy who wants a Red Ryder BB Range Rifle for Christmas was largely shot here, although the family home is in Cleveland and the kids attend Victoria School in St. Catharines. But any Torontonian would recognize our **Red Rocket streetcars**, highly visible in the early Christmas shopping scenes.

6. The Canadian film *Silent Partner* (1978) used the then brand-new **Eaton Centre** as its major location. Especially memorable is the scene where an armed Santa Claus elbows shoppers out of the way on the escalator.

Bacchanal Time

Photo: Sarah B. Hood

7. In *Silver Streak* (1977), Gene Wilder and Richard Pryor ride a train into **Union Station**; in fact, they crash right through its walls.

8. *The Black Stallion* (1977) used the old **Woodbine Racetrack** for night scenes, and also staged an invitational race at Fort Erie Racetrack to draw a convincing crowd. (It was, sadly, rained out.) Crews also had a hard time arranging permits for the scene where the panicked racehorse gallops through real Toronto streets.

9. The television studio in *Network* (1976), the multiple Oscar winner about media manipulation, was really **CFTO TV** in Scarborough.

10. The **University of Toronto** stood in for Harvard in the ultimate campus drama *The Paper Chase* (1973). It later appeared as MIT in Matt Damon and Ben Affleck's *Good Will Hunting* (1997).

Photo: Sarah B. Hood

Caribana brings more tourists to town than any other event or attraction. Founded in 1967 as the Caribbean community's Centennial gift to Toronto, the early August event is one of North America's most famous street festivals. Still, many locals don't know that the world-famous parade of 4,000-plus brilliantly-costumed dancers is actually a competition between rival camps of costume builders, who get together months ahead to build the spectacular finery on a theme of – for example – nature, ancient history, fantasy, or political satire. Each participant pays about $50 to $100 for their costume and the right to win' their waist down Lakeshore Boulevard. Every single mas' camp welcomes visitors to view the costumes from about mid-June onwards, and all are eager to indoctrinate newcomers into the carnival tradition. The easiest ways to find them are to pick up Caribbean papers like *Share*, *Caribbean Camera*, and *Pride*, or to visit websites like *toronto-lime.com* and *fetenet.com*. (Some of the biggest mas' producers maintain their own sites, like *saldenah.com*, *mastoronto.com*, *callaloo.net*, and *borokeetecanada.com*.)

Also, many people don't realize that Caribana is a two-week festival with a host of ancillary events. One of the best parties is the Junior Carnival on Eglinton, when all the kids, from about 3 to 18, parade in their own costumes. It's usually held on the weekend before the big parade (which in turn is always the Saturday of the Simcoe Day long weekend). On the Thursday night before the parade, it's the King and Queen of the Bands competition at Lamport Stadium, when the biggest and flashiest costumes get their moment under the lights in a spectacular grandstand show. On the Friday night, Yonge Street from College to King becomes the unofficial parade preview: no costumes, but thousands of Caribana revellers out to party and be seen. And for the two days following the parade, Caribana takes over

Olympic Island for an idyllic family picnic with two stages of Caribbean dance, music, and comedy, and an outdoor market of crafts and food.

Occasionally, the big-league stars make their appearances. Sean Coombs (a.k.a. "Puffy" and "P-Diddy") has been a parade guest, and Billy Dee Williams (a.k.a. *The Empire Strikes Back*'s Lando Calrissian) was spotted at the island music festival a few years back. Most outrageous celeb showing would have to be Wesley Snipes, who turned up on the parade route one year with a retinue of followers, who circulated at the shade-sporting action star's command to invite the prettiest girls to party with him later.

Staying in the Festive Spirit

Photo: Ontario Tourism, 13009

• Caribana isn't the only time to get into a costume and parade in the streets. The annual late-June Lesbian, Gay, Bisexual, Transsexual, Transgendered **Pride Parade**, for example (*416-927-7433, pridetoronto.com/parade*) is open to any group that wants to enter, or to compete for prizes like "Most Fabulous Float," "Most Fabulous Choreography," and "Most Fabulous Hat." And best of all, you don't even need a costume!

• The exuberantly political Clay and Paper Theatre (*416-537-9105, clayandpapertheatre.org*) animates plays and processions around Dufferin Grove Park (at Dufferin below Bloor) throughout the year, but their

TEN CLASSIC CANADIAN FILMS SHOT (AT LEAST PARTLY) IN TORONTO

1. *Bollywood/Hollywood*
(Deepa Mehta, 2002)

2. *The Sweet Hereafter*
(Atom Egoyan, 1997)

3. *Rude* (Clement Virgo, 1995)

4. *Highway 61*
(Bruce McDonald, 1991)

5. *Perfectly Normal*
(Yves Simoneau, 1990)

6. *I've Heard the Mermaids Singing*
(Patricia Rozema, 1987)

7. *Strange Brew*
(Rick Moranis & Dave Thomas, 1983)

8. *Ticket to Heaven*
(Ralph L. Thomas, 1981)

9. *Outrageous!*
(Richard Benner, 1977)

10. *Goin' Down the Road*
(Don Shebib, 1970)

FREQUENT FILMERS

To the best of our knowledge, the director who has made the largest number of prominent feature films in the Toronto area is — none too surprisingly — hometown horror hero David Cronenberg (pictured above).

His total is nine so far: *Spider* (2002), *eXistenZ* (1999), *Crash* (1996), *M. Butterfly* (1993), *Dead Ringers* (1988), *The Fly* (1986), *Videodrome* (1983), *The Brood* (1979), and *Crimes of the Future* (1970). Next in line would be Atom Egoyan (pictured below), with seven: *Ararat* (2002), *The Sweet Hereafter* (1997), *Exotica* (1994), *Calendar* (1993), *The Adjuster* (1991), *Speaking Parts* (1989), and *Family Viewing* (1987).

strongest community festival is the **Night of Dread**, held on the Saturday closest to Hallowe'en. It's a night of street parading, bonfires, live music, and a feast, designed to give people a chance to exhibit their fears and laugh at them. In the weeks leading up to the festival, volunteers can attend mask- and puppet-building sessions, learn stiltwalking, or make their own cardboard "fear" to burn on the night. Dress code is black-and-white.

• Later, in the very darkest time of the year, Kensington Market glows and glitters with the lanterns, masquerade, and magic of the **Kensington Festival of Lights**, which culminates in the burning of a giant figure representing the old year. Anyone can get involved, whether that means performing in one of the streetside *scenarios*, attending a lantern-making workshop, or just turning up to St. Stephen's-in-the-Fields Church at 365 College Street at dusk on the Winter Solstice, December 21. It's produced by Red Pepper Spectacle Arts (416-598-3729), who usually invite all comers to their Market workshop (160 Baldwin, Unit 36) to build spectacular masks and costumes and become otherwise involved throughout December.

Photo: Nir Bareket Photography

Exhibitions of Curiosity

Some might say you could never get tired of the Royal Ontario Museum, but if you've had enough of mummies, bats, and dinosaur bones – not to mention shoes, ceramics, and textiles – here are some alternatives:

• Recognizing that "There are fewer prewar TVs left in the world than Stradivarius violins," Moses Znaimer of the Citytv empire decided to found the modestly named **MZTV Museum of Television** (*277 Queen St. W., 416-599-7339*). Conveniently located inside the CHUMCityStore building, it presents a rotating selection from a collection of more than 300 vintage television sets, along with related memorabilia.

• The **Toronto Police Museum and Discovery Centre** (*40 College St., 416-808-7020*) includes crime-stopping artifacts like police vehicles, uniforms, confiscated weapons and evidence, displays about notorious local crimes, and an exhibit on Elmer the Safety Elephant. There's also a gift shop called – what else? – the Cop Shop.

• Did you know that Arnold Palmer's first professional victory was in Canada, or that North America's oldest golf club is in this country? If not, you haven't been spending enough time at the **Canadian Golf Hall of Fame and Museum** (*2070 Hadwen Rd., Mississauga, 905-849-9700*). Structured to mirror an 18-hole course, the Museum offers an historical overview of the game and its rules, tools, and champions.

• If you have a hankering to view an ornithopter, then the **Toronto Aerospace Museum** (*Downsview Park, 65 Carl Hall Rd., 416-638-6078*) is for you. Commemorating Canadian aviation history, the recently opened facility owns a number of historical aircraft, including the Lancaster bomber that was for many years displayed on a pedestal on Lakeshore Boulevard near Exhibition Place, causing the occasional fatigued driver to swerve to avoid an imagined collision with the apparently incoming plane.

• You can really get to the heart of your sweet tooth at the **Redpath Sugar Museum** (*95 Queens Quay E., 416-366-3561*), which documents the production of sugar from the cane to the grain. (And it's free!)

LIFE IMITATES ART

Sometimes it's just not clear where the real world ends and the movies begin.

• After September 11, 2001, City of Toronto officials decided to limit access to film crews wishing to shoot on the grounds of the R.C. Harris water filtration plant, in order to safeguard the city's water supply. At the time they made their decision, the film that was in production on the site was *The Tuxedo*, in which Jackie Chan battles a criminal mastermind who's trying to poison the world's drinking water.

• Think the pill was the first big breakthrough in birth control? Think again. And then head over to the **History of Contraception Museum** (*19 Green Belt Dr., in the Janssen-Ortho building, 416-449-9444*), where you'll see over 600 baby-preventing devices. IUDs, sponges, and early Egyptian condoms made of animal membranes. Inconceivable!

• When the 2000 Molson Indy took over Toronto, Sylvester Stallone took over the Indy to get realistic footage for *Driven*. Producers of the racing-car drama also staged a car chase on University Avenue.

• Steven Seagal is known for his run-ins with gangsters, but not just onscreen, it seems. The tough-guy star has made several films with producer Julius R. Nasso, whom U.S. courts have linked with John Gotti's Gambino crime family. According to U.S. federal prosecutors, Nasso and friends have made attempts to extort very large sums of money from Soagal, including in 2001, while Seagal was in Toronto during the making of *Exit Wounds*.

• Beginning in 1984, the silly but popular *Police Academy* movies used the former psychiatric hospital grounds on Lakeshore Boulevard in Etobicoke as the Academy campus. At the time of writing, Toronto Police were moving their real-life training academy to the same site.

Early Days

Before 1970, the Toronto moviemaking industry was somewhat leaner than it is today. In 1900, some short documentaries were made here (*Soldiers of Britain, Steeplechase Toronto, Toronto Mounted Rifles*), and a few obscure features were shot during the silent era. Most notably, on April 19, 1904, George Scott & Co. filmed a very short documentary entitled *The Great Toronto Fire*, showing the streets before the conflagration, the fire trucks racing to the scene, and the fire itself. A copy is kept at the National Archives. Prolific director Sam Newfield (with over 250 films to his credit, mainly cowboy movies) came to Canada in 1935 to shoot the low-budget *Thoroughbred* – a.k.a. *The King's Plate* – an improbable romance about a chronic gambler who wins a horse in a dice game. In 1958, William Davidson directed a collection of Morley Callaghan stories under the title *Now That April's Here*, with Canadian stalwarts John Drainie and Raymond Massey among the cast. Sydney J. Furie, who directed *The Ipcress File* and *Lady Sings the Blues*, was born in Toronto and made his first films here: *A Dangerous Age* (1958) and *A Cool Sound From Hell* (1959). In 1959, Montrealer Julian Roffman shot T*he Bloody Brood*, starring Peter (*Columbo*) Falk as a sinister drug dealer on the beatnik scene; Roffman also made *The Mask* here in 1961 (reissued as T*he Eyes from Hell* and *Face of Fire*). It's a 3D horror flick about an archaeologist cursed by an evil artifact. In *Nobody Waved Good-bye* (1964), Peter Kastner and Julie Biggs star as teenagers coping with her pregnancy. An 81-minute student film directed by David Secter called *Winter Kept Us Warm* (1965) was the first Canadian film to be invited to Cannes. Leslie Neilsen has a role in the 1969 *Change of Mind*, about a white man whose brain is transplanted into a black body. Barbara Hale (*Perry Mason's* Della Street) and Robert Cummings were a comic married couple in *The First Time* (1969), directed by Frank Tashlin (*Will*

Success Spoil Rock Hunter?, *Cinderfella*, *Geisha Boy*). That same year, TV director Alan King (*Kung Fu: the Legend Continues*, *Road to Avonlea*) anticipated the reality TV craze with *A Married Couple*, a 90-minute film that turns the camera onto a husband and wife and simply films the fireworks. (Lest you doubt, no less a personage than the *New York Times'* Clive Barnes called it "quite simply one of the greatest movies I have ever seen," by the way.)

And to the best of our knowledge, the first movie shot somewhere else but set in Toronto was the 1933 British film *The Man From Toronto*, starring Jessie Matthews, Ian Hunter and Frederick Kerr.

North York, North York

Toronto is most often shot as New York City. Among dozens of examples:

• *Where the Heart Is* (1990) is a little-known but evocative film with Dabney Coleman as a rich Manhattan real estate developer who decides to teach his almost-adult children – including Uma Thurman – some life lessons by making them support themselves in an antique house they want to save from the wrecker's ball. The house itself (if it wasn't a set) would have stood on Oxley Street, near the intersection of Adelaide and Spadina. Other scenes take place at the Royal Bank Plaza, the TD Centre, the Toronto Stock Exchange, and St. Lawrence Town Hall.

• There's a myth about *Three Men and a Baby* (1987), the lukewarm remake of a popular French feel-good comedy, starring Tom Selleck, Steve Guttenberg, and Ted Danson. In one scene an extra figure appears in a doorway; the rumour is that it's the ghost of a little boy who supposedly died in the apartment where the film was shot. However, it's really just a prop carboard cutout, and it appears in other scenes as well. (The interiors were all shot on a sound stage anyway.) Some of its exteriors were shot on Duncan Street at Pearl, and at the Gooderham and Worts complex, the John Innes Community Centre on Sherbourne Street, Scotia Plaza, and the Royal Alexandra Theatre.

OOOPS!

Generally people think it's advantageous when their neighbourhood is used as a film location, but that's not always the case.

• *The Long Kiss Goodnight*, with Geena Davis and Samuel L. Jackson, was largely filmed in Toronto (Honest Ed's blazing sign is prominent in one scene), but shooting also took place in February 1996 at an historic, century-old hotel in Muskoka called Windermere House. Somehow, during filming, the hotel caught fire and burned to the ground. (The film lighting was blamed, but the cause was never proved.)

• In 1999, when the Jamie Foxx adventure *Bait* was being filmed, a special effects explosion at the King Edward Hotel came close to becoming an adventure in itself, breaking windows in an ambulance and the coffee shop, and causing a spike in 911 calls.

• In October of 2000, while Bruce McDonald was filming *Picture Claire* in Kensington Market, a woman named Mary Fish wandered into the shoot, whistling. She was asked to be quiet, but objected. Next thing she knew, she had been clapped into handcuffs and taken away to spend the night in a 14 Division cell. The case of the so-called "whistling grandmother" actually came to trial in March of 2003, but charges of causing a disturbance were thrown out because it took so long to get to court.

• There were public complaints about the decision to film *American Psycho* (2000) in the first place, since the Bret Easton Ellis novel was cited as a favourite of convicted rapist and murderer Paul Bernardo. However, it was shot in Toronto, using – among other sites – The Senator (*249 Victoria St.*), Monsoon (*100 Simcoe St.*), The Phoenix (*410 Sherbourne St.*), Montana (*145 John St.*), Shark City (*117 Eglinton Ave, E.*), and the Boston Club (*4 Front St. E.*).

• The plot of the supernatural thriller *Bless the Child* (2000) with Kim Basinger and Christina Ricci originally involved an incident in which someone is pushed off a subway platform. However, the TTC would only sanction use of the Lower Bay Station for filming if the murder was changed to an accidental fall. There's also a car accident scene on a bridge; since the Blue Water Bridge between Sarnia, Ontario and Port Huron, Michigan was under construction, it was available for shooting, and New York City scenery was later added into the background.

• In the children's movie *Harriet the Spy* (1996), Harriet attends Lord Dufferin Public School, while the Capitol Theatre and the historic George Brown House make recognizable appearances. In the film Harriet and her friends use a customized, oversized tricycle with a big, flat, cargo-carrying platform. It passed into private hands after the filming, and can sometimes be seen in transit on the streets around Augusta Avenue between Queen Street and Kensington Market.

After NYC, Toronto is most often made to look like Washington D.C. in the movies. In fact, the 1998 pilot for TV's *The West Wing* was shot here, using the Native Women's Centre (*191 Gerrard St. E.*), St. Francis of Assisi Church, and the Ontario Legislative Buildings at Queen's Park. What other cities has Toronto been dressed as? *Mrs. Winterbourne* (1995) – with Ricki Lake, Brendan Fraser, and Shirley MacLaine – counterfeited upper-crust Boston with locations like Hazelton Lanes, St. James Cathedral, and Queen Street West. *Never Talk To Strangers* (1995) was a should-have-been-sultrier suspense film with Rebecca de Mornay and Antonio Banderas, set in Philadelphia. Identifiable Toronto locations include High Park, Toronto Island Airport, and St. Patrick's Market Square near Queen and John Streets.

It's not clear exactly where in America *Bulletproof Monk* (2003) is supposed to take place; it's probably set in NYC, but the charmingly comic Chow Yun-Fat action thriller is a Toronto location-spotter's dream. It features a fight-scene-with-helicopter atop an industrial building at Bathurst and Lakeshore, a chase across Nathan Phillips Square, an endangered child in the Bloor/Yonge subway, and baddies holed up under a scaffolded Old City Hall, to name just a few choice moments.

Johnny Mnemonic (1994) was the film Keanu Reeves made that wasn't quite *The Matrix*. It's set in Newark, New Jersey in 2021, but Keanu/Johnny flees the Yakuza through the closed lower levels of the Bay TTC station. When he's led up a flight of marble stairs into a guerrilla medical outpost, he asks: "Where are we?" At the screening we attended, one wag called out (correctly): "Union Station!" Some of the other settings include Allan Gardens, Casa Loma, Metro Hall, the tiny O'Keefe Lane, Riverdale Presbyterian Church, Spadina House, and Villiers Street. However, the VW-dropping-from-a-bridge scene took place in Montreal, under the Jacques Cartier Bridge.

OUR TOP TEN TV SHOWS SHOT IN TORONTO (THE MODERN ERA)

1. *Sue Thomas: F.B. Eye* (2003 on). We're waiting to see where this one goes. Will it have a long and happy life, or will it go the way of such series as *Katts and Dog*?

2. *Blue Murder* (2001 on). Maria Del Mar (*Street Legal*) returned to the mean streets of Toronto (shot as itself!) to investigate homicides, the more gruesome the better.

Then there's Chicago, which is the theoretical setting of the phenomenally popular *My Big Fat Greek Wedding.*

3. *La Femme Nikita* (1997-2001). With Aussie Peta Wilson as Nikita (and Toronto Island resident Matthew Ferguson as Birkoff), this series successfully extended the storyline of Luc Besson's stylish French thriller.

4. *Psi Factor: Chronicles of the Paranormal* (1996-2000). Having Dan Aykroyd introduce a show doesn't necessarily make it good, but this spooky series eventually managed to become more than just an *X-Files* clone.

5. *Relic Hunter* (1999-2002). Tia Carrere stars as a (blatant) cross between Indiana Jones and Lara Croft in a show that ingeniously manages to make Toronto look like various parts of Asia and South America.

However, Nia Vardalos's travel agency is situated at 439 Danforth. She goes to classes and meets her husband at Ryerson's East Kerr Hall, and the actual wedding takes place at St. Nicholas Ukrainian Catholic Church (*770 Queen St. W.*). In *Adventures in Babysitting* (1987), also set in Chi-town, Elisabeth Shue and the gang pour out of a blues bar. The interior is in Illinois, but the exterior clearly shows the sign for the Silver Dollar on Spadina just north of College. *The Santa Clause* (1994) also filmed Toronto as Chicago, including a visit to the Toronto Zoo. So did (wait for it) 2002's multiple Oscar winner *Chicago*, in which Old City Hall on Queen Street was used for the courthouse. The only one

displeased with the latter arrangement was apparently real-life Chicago Mayor Richard M. Daley, who was quoted as saying (with a questionable grasp of geography): "I don't see why we have to go overseas."

We might give Norman Jewison (pictured above with Denzel Washington) the prize for most memorable scenes in Toronto locations. Think of his film *Moonstruck*; the 1987 Cher/Nicholas Cage hit offers a convincing picture of Italian New York, using locations like Colborne and Victoria Streets, Dufferin and St. Clair, and Little Trinity Church. It also has a notable scene at the Keg Restaurant, the former Jarvis family mansion, on Jarvis Street. For the Metropolitan Opera scene, Jewison set up cameras at a theatre in Markham and recruited Canadian opera singer John Fanning and soprano Martha Collins, who were rehearsing in town, to appear "onstage" as *La Boheme*'s Rodolpho and Mimi. Although they would have been perfectly capable of doing their own singing, the opera stars lip-synched their roles: that's how Fanning, a baritone, got to portray one of opera's most famous tenor roles. (Fanning's explanation is that the director simply "needed someone with a beard.")

Jewison also produced (but didn't direct) 1988's *The January Man*, in which Kevin Kline, Alan Rickman, and Mary Elizabeth Mastrantonio gaze at the stars at the (now closed) McLaughlin Planetarium while trying to solve a murder. In the same film, Kline and Mastrantonio enjoy a quickie at the Sutton Place Hotel after attending a funeral at Metropolitan United Church. (And National Ballet stars Kimberly Glassco and Rex Harrington appear briefly onstage when the unhappily married Susan Sarandon is stood up by her husband at the ballet.)

Just for the record, Jewison also shot *The Hurricane* (1999) with Denzel Washington here, as well as *Bogus*, with Gérard Depardieu and Whoopi Goldberg (1996), and *Agnes of God* (1985), with Jane Fonda.

6. *RoboCop* (1994, reprised as the miniseries *RoboCop: Prime Directives* in 2001). Like *Nikita*, an extended riff on a successful film. Where else can you watch a futuristic gun battle at Metro Hall? (The Skywalk from Union station to the SkyDome also features as Delta City Shopping Centre.)

7. *Twitch City* (1998-00) is Don McKellar's idiosyncratic revisiting of *Three's Company*, with a little *King of Kensington* homage thrown in. It was filmed on Augusta Avenue and one year, during the Kensington Festival, the shop Bikes On Wheels (*309 Augusta*) achieved a truly surreal effect by offering continuous showings in their window, directly across from the apartment featured in the series.

The University of Toronto successfully sued Paramount Pictures over the 1999 movie *Varsity Blues*, because the team in the movie used the same name as Toronto's teams (to which the university holds trademark rights). Furthermore, the school thought the film's depiction of college sports was kind of offensive. (The *University of Toronto Bulletin* quoted Blues football coach Bob Laycoe at the time as saying that the movie "makes a mockery of everything the real Varsity Blues are trying to convey to our alumni, fans, and potential recruits.") In the spring of 1999, Paramount settled with the university for an undisclosed amount and agreed to print a disclaimer on the video and the book disassociating the fictional Texas team from the real Toronto one. Some of the money was used for scholarships.

In a similar – but weirder – case, twin Toronto-area kickboxers Michael and Martin McNamara filed a $37 million lawsuit against Miramax, Alliance Atlantis, and Front Row Entertainment over the name of the Jackie Chan movie *Twin Dragons*. They claim that they have been using the Twin Dragons name professionally for over 25 years. (They even have two films to their credit: *Twin Dragon Encounter* and *Dragon Hunt*.) The Chan film was originally released in 1992 as *Shuang long hui*, and was much later issued in North America under the English title. At time of writing there was no word on the suit's outcome.

8. *Traders* (1996-00) featured more of Sonja Smits from *Street Legal* in a generally satisfying Bay Street brokers series. Of course, it went down when the market did. (We still can't get our heads around Patrick McKenna playing both the charismatic Marty Stevens on this show and Red Green's doofus nephew. *Tour de force* or what?)

9. *Due South* (1994-98). It started as a TV movie, but eventually caught on big with audiences, due in part to Paul Gross's likeable and convincing performance as the manly yet soft-spoken Mountie Benton Fraser.

10. *Forever Knight* (1992-96) is the cult hit with Geraint Wyn-Davies as a vampire cop seeking redemption that long preceded *Buffy's* Angel.

Star Gazing

September's annual **Toronto International Film Festival** has grown from rough-and-ready beginnings (under its original name of The Festival of Festivals) to a lofty international status that places it second only to Cannes in the hierarchy of world film fests. TIFF has generated a plethora of legends both hair-raising and heartwarming.

For instance, the first Canadian film to open the Festival was *In Praise of Older Women*, which was also the solo producing debut of later-to-be media mogul Robert Lantos. A sexual coming-of-age story, it starred Tom Berenger opposite Karen Black *and* Susan Strasberg *and* Helen Shaver *and* Marilyn Lightstone – among several others. The film was to open on September 14, 1978, but with only a week to go the Ontario Censor Board declared that it couldn't be screened unless two minutes of footage were cut – specifically, a scene involving Berenger and Lightstone behind a couch. A torrent of national debate began, almost matched in intensity by a drenching rainstorm on opening night. The event was further complicated by the fact that 4,000 people had been invited to the Elgin Theatre, which at the time couldn't accommodate more than 1,600. Festival staff had to stage-manage a wild scrum with anxious fire marshalls and soaked patrons in evening attire. A second screening was hastily negotiated at the New Yorker just up the street, with each reel being hurried between buildings as soon as it had been seen at the Elgin. In all the confusion, it seems almost anticlimactic that the *uncut* version was shown, deviously substituted for the stamped and sealed official edition by Martin Heath, now proprietor of the back-alley film venue Cinecycle. (The official version was also in the projection booth, just in case, labelled *Wild Strawberries*.) A quarter century later, all has been forgiven, and *In Praise of Older Women* has taken its place in history as one of the first Canadian commercial successes.

For all its seat-of-the-pants style in the early days, the Festival didn't cancel a single screening in its first 25 years. That achievement came to an end on September 11, 2001, when activities were all called off in response to the terrorist attacks on the U.S. In the sorrowful aftermath, parties, red carpets, and celebrity interviews were canceled, along with the Awards Luncheon (winners were announced via media release). Dozens of stars were stranded in the city with the downing of all air

OUR TOP TEN TV SHOWS SHOT IN TORONTO (THE PIONEER ERA)

1. *Maniac Mansion* (1990-93). The quirky scientist dad was Joe Flaherty, and the theme was sung by Jane Siberry.

2 & 3. *Degrassi Junior High* (1986-88) and *Degrassi High* (1989-91). Those confused kids are so popular that they've actually generated four series so far – counting *Kids of Degrassi Street* and *Degrassi: The Next Generation*. (There isn't really a Degrassi High, but Degrassi Street is just east of Broadview and Gerrard.)

4. *Street Legal* (1986-94). Sonja Smits, Eric Peterson, Cynthia Dale, and the rest made 124 episodes plus a TV movie of this grown-up but good-hearted courtroom drama series.

5. *Night Heat* (1985-91). A gritty, '80s-flavoured crime drama. The *Night Heat* tech crew once carefully strewed garbage around the Toronto location to simulate a U.S. urban streetscape; when they came back from a break, overzealous city cleaners had cleaned it all up.

6. *Seeing Things* (1981-87) starred Louis Del Grande as a psychic detective in one of Canadian TV's longest-running series.

7. *King of Kensington* (1975-80). The classic of all classics, starring the late, beloved Al Waxman, who really *was* the King.

Photo: Courtesy CBC

8. *Coming Up Rosie* (1975-76). A little-remembered after-school comedy series about a group of neighbours that starred Rosemary Radcliffe in the title role, with a sensational roster of co-stars, including Fiona Reid, Catherine O'Hara, Dan Aykroyd, and John Candy.

9. *Wojeck* (1967-68) cast John Vernon effectively, as a crusading Chief Coroner.

10. *The Forest Rangers* (1964-66). Who can forget Sgt. Scott, Joe Two Rivers, and the Junior Rangers Chub, Pete, Mike, Cathy, and Gaby from this popular adventure series? (It was actually shot just north of Kleinburg, Ontario.)

traffic over North America — although some household names chose to hightail it to the border in rented limos. TIFF marked the anniversary the following year by closing until 11 a.m. and by presenting gala screenings of two films inspired by the tragedy.

Over the years, the partying has been just as legendary as the films themselves. These days things are a little quieter than in the beginning, but they can still get pretty outrageous. Take the celebrations for 1998's *Very Bad Things*. At the official Polygram party, security was so overzealous that *Toronto Star* film writer Rob Salem was manhandled on his way in, and even one of the hosts, Polygram exec Judy Holm, was blocked from the VIP section. Meanwhile, the film's director Peter Berg and star Cameron Diaz — along with a few friends like Janeane Garafolo, Vince Vaughn, Ben Stiller, and vocal vixens Medieval Babes — indulged in a dizzyingly round of partying at various venues, resulting in scrambled interview rosters the next morning. (The film's other big name, Christian Slater, was comparatively well behaved.)

But access to the stars isn't always so exclusive; in fact, some of them are a real breath of fresh air. During the 2001 Festival, moviegoer Janice Flisfeder was waiting in line to see the flick *Thirteen Conversations About One Thing*, when she felt faint. The next thing she knew, she was lying on the sidewalk and being resuscitated by the film's star, Matthew McConaughey. Would-be celeb spotters who aren't willing to trust to such serendipity can always try dining at the well-known hot spots like Sotto Sotto, Bistro 990, The Rosewater Supper Club, and The Courthouse. But word is that Sassafraz has become *so* well known as a Hollywood hangout that the herd is moving to fresher pastures.

Nightlife

Back in the 1800s, taverns outnumbered churches in this city by a ratio of six-to-one. Not much has changed over the years because a night on the town in Toronto offers ample opportunity to drink, dance, and even disrobe (for charity, no less).

Injunction Junction

In 1903, the Reverend T.E.E. Shore was not a happy man. All around him, beverage rooms were booming; hotels, he claimed, were cesspools of harlotry and vice. From his pulpit at the Annette Street Methodist Church, the pastor railed against the demon rum, and voters in the election of 1904 agreed: the Toronto Junction (then a municipality, now only a neighbourhood) would go dry. On April 30, 1904, the last legal day for liquor, 10,000 drinkers flooded the Junction's six small hotels. Fights broke out. The police were called in. One souse, stumbling out of the old Peacock Hotel, brandished an empty glass and yelled, "I don't care for the police or anybody!" Order, eventually, was restored and the taps were turned off. And they stayed off for the next 90 years. The wets failed to win plebiscites in 1966, 1972, and 1984. Folks finally got a little service in 1994.

Still Hopping

One of the more heartening stories in recent years is the revival of the **Palais Royale Ballroom**. With concerts and raves becoming popular at the old lakeside dancehall, revelers past and present have become connected. In the 1930s and 1940s, the stucco-and-clapboard venue was the hottest joint in town. Every Saturday night, an average of 900 people would show up to cut a rug. And think the bouncers are tough today? Back then, there were endless restrictions: no lushes, no mashers, no pros. And for Pete's sake, hang on to your girl! Jitterbuggers who lost their grip were considered too wild and were quickly shown the door.
1601 Lakeshore Blvd. W., 416-532-6210

Taking it to the Streets

From about 1914 to 1920, a Yiddish cabaret called The People's Theatre entertained crowds at 332 Queen Street West near the shmata strip on Spadina. In the '20s, it was transformed into a vaudeville house known as **The Rivoli**, and that's the name that owners David Stearn, Andre Rosenbaum, and Jeffrey Strasbourg (also of the Queen Mother) reverted to when they acquired the restaurant and club in 1982. In those days, Queen West was just beginning to be known as a trendy destination, and The Riv proprietors saw the potential for a people-watching sidewalk spot outside their doors. However, although city bylaws technically allowed for the creation of something called a licensed "boulevard patio," none in fact existed anywhere in town. It took a persistent lobbying campaign for The Riv to become the very first, so, next time you're sipping a cool one in some delightful sidewalk location, you might consider raising your glass to Toronto's patio pioneers.

I Remember You Well in the Drake Hotel

The Drake Hotel has a long history. Built in 1890 (one year after its neighbour, the Gladstone, which is the oldest hotel in town), it has been called the Cecil, the Stardust, and D.A. Small's. But no matter what name, the Drake has always been just a beer-swilling joint. Until now. New owner Jeff Stober, who paid $860,000 for the place, has transformed the old down-and-outer into a boutique hotel, albeit one with a difference. He wants the Drake to be part of the 'hood. It offers everything for the Queen Street scenester. Yoga studio, music venue and, of course, a well-stocked bar. Stober has said he's influenced by New York's famous Chelsea Hotel.
1150 Queen St. W., 416-531-5042, thedrakehotel.ca

BIG SPENDERS

Heading out on the town but hard up for dough? Try the **Done Right Inn**. The cozy neighbourhood bar on Queen Street West accepts Canadian Tire money as well as the real thing. Owners Michele Menard and Lisa Sevazlian, who opened the bar in 1999, wanted something to distinguish themselves from every other joint in the area. Still, when customers come in, they don't always believe their ears. Menard says a six-month haul netted only 200 Canadian Tire dollars.
861 Queen St. W., 416-703-0405

Photo: Sarah B. Hood

DANCE TILL DAWN
The Matador Club Country
Music is the oldest after-hours club
in town. It was opened in 1964
by Anne Dunn, a single mother of
five who wanted a business that
wouldn't interfere with her main job
of child-rearing. Her odd schedule
(open Friday and Saturday, from
1:30 a.m. to 5:30 a.m.) keeps this
country and western joint twangy
well into the wee hours. It also made
The Matador popular with anyone
looking for one last dance. So that
means old-time hoofers share the
floor with the downtown chic in
their Doc Martens. And even an old
poet-singer like Leonard Cohen, who
sang about The Matador in "Closing
Time," isn't out of place.
466 Dovercourt Rd., 416-533-9311

It's a white sign with her name in red letters: Czehoski.
Jean Czehoski first moved into this building at 678
Queen West in 1922. She lived upstairs and worked
downstairs in the family deli, run first by her father and
then by her brother, Stanley. When Stanley died in
1990, the deli closed. But Jean stayed. For the next
12 years, she could often be seen sitting in the old deli
window, so often in fact, she was even dubbed a piece
of minimalist performance art. The old street changed
before her eyes and, inevitably, change came for her
too. She sold the building in 2002, moved to a nearby
apartment and watched as the old window was papered
up. **Czehoski's Bar**, slated for a fall 2003 opening, was
on its way. Run by Brad Denton and partners, the front
parlour of Czehoski's will have a take-out counter in the
style of the original deli and a lounge in the back room.
The sign will stay the same. And Jean? She has an open
bar tab and a reservation for life.
678 Queen St. W.

• The **Cadillac Lounge** is easy to spot. It's the joint with half a Caddy sticking out of the front. Inside, car mementos take a back seat to The King. Everyone loves Elvis, right? Certainly long-time drinkers here do and hopefully, so do some of the upscale types that have been frequenting the place since Parkdale's faux-dive renaissance. Similar vibe, same owner at **Graffiti's**, in Kensington Market.
1296 Queen St. W., 416-536-7717

• Far away from anything even remotely funky, **The Gem** has that claim all to itself. Great jukebox and friendly staff make this a worthy destination for far-away types, much to the chagrin of folks who live just blocks away.
1159 Davenport Rd., 416-654-1182

Photo: Howard Akler

• Next time you're wandering around the west end, stop in at **Intersteer Restaurant**. Besides the beer, the traditional Polish food is worth the visit.
361 Roncesvalles Ave., 416-588-4705

• Folks on the Danforth know the only café for them is, well, **The Only Café**. The place is packed on weeknights, but even busier for weekend brunch. We're told the waffles are one reason why.
972 Danforth Ave., 416-463-7843

Photo: Sarah B. Hood

Lounges

• The trip starts at **Airport Lounge**, with its psychedelic bright red walls and pink shag carpet. Slink into a comfy chaise (it's Philippe Starck, doncha' know) and let all the cocktail chatter swirl around you.
492 College St., 416-921-3047

• More shag carpet awaits you at **Ciao Edie**, a below-street-level spot that has long been a favourite for the kitschy klatch.
489 College St., 416-927-7774

Photo: Sarah B. Hood

• **Cobalt** is another on the seemingly endless strip of College Street lounges. This one takes cobalt blue as its signature hue. Is anyone else amazed at all the things you can do with cranberry juice?
426 College St., 416-923-4456

• Downstairs from the divey Monarch Tavern is the upscale piano bar, **Lounge 88**. This place was an It spot for at least a few weeks. *12 Clinton St., at College St., 416-531-5833*

• Smack dab in the middle of clubland, **Red Drink Boutique** is the swishest of the swish. A back alley entrance emphasizes the exclusiveness of the place. We'd like to comment on the décor, but we weren't glamourous enough to get in. Give it a try. *225 Richmond St. W., 416-351-0408*

• The perfect place for an assignation, **Souz Dal** has an exotic name and intimate setting. If the blood red walls don't stir the passions, just sit back and quietly sip your cocktail. *636 College St., 416-537-1883*

• On the hunt for something uptown? **Safari Bar & Grill** serves food on the first floor and has an upstairs lounge with billiards. Live jazz on Tuesdays. *1749 Avenue Rd., 416-787-6584*

• Okay, maybe College Street has become too slick to be called a 'hood, but **Sneaky Dee's** has been around a lot longer than any of those other poseurs on the strip. Long after last call, the place still serves heapings of greasy goodness. Which may be why locals call it Sneaky Disease. *431 College St., 416-603-3090*

Not Your Granny's Bingo

Wholesome meets lewd every Monday night at the **Living Well Café**. The name of the game is Dirty Bingo, with all the proceeds going to charity. At two dollars per play, that's come to $75,000 over the last four years. That's the wholesome part. The lewdness isn't just the sex toy prizes, but the naked players. Every time a bingo ball rolls an "N," a volunteer sheds one article of clothing. By the end of the game, the charitable soul has bared all and passes through the café with a well-placed bag in order to gather further contributions. *692 Yonge St., 416-922-6770*

• At the end of a long alleyway is the **Betty Ford Temple**, a paean to all things pleasurable. Dance up a storm or sink into one of their soft, velvet couches and enjoy your drink. You're home.
469 King St. W., at Spadina Ave., 416-598-4050

• So secret we don't even know when it's open, **Club 56**, in Kensington Market, is a dank underground dance space that was once a punk club.
56 Kensington Ave., at Baldwin St., no phone

Photo: Howard Akler

• It can be tough to find **The Green Room**. The entrance is in an alley behind the Poor Alex Theatre. Once you're in, it's also tough to find your friends, because the two-floor space is dark and packed. Once you find your friends, it's tough to find a waiter. But not as tough as at sister bar, **The Red Room**, on Spadina.
296 Brunswick Ave., at Bloor St. W., 416-929-3253

• Speakeasies, that Prohibition phenomenon, are back in vogue. Take **Ting**, a place so hush-hush, we can't even offer an address. Let's just say it's in the Queen and Dufferin area. No sign outside and no alcohol license inside, so you'll just have to make do with fancy organic eats and, ahem, something to drink. After-hours joints like this aren't usually around for long, but hey, tings change.

Clubs

Comfort Zone
Where the party keeps going. Ravers head here early Sunday morning and sometimes don't emerge until Monday.
486 Spadina Ave., 416-763-9139, comfortzone.to.com

Element Bar
Deep house, big shoes, and skimpy outfits.
553 Queen St. W., 416-359-1919, elementbar.com

Mad Bar
Venerable spot for hip-hop.
230 Richmond St. W., 416-340-0089, mad-bar.com

Revival

Formally the Polish Leisure Hall, this house is packed on Saturdays, when former Platinum Blonde singer Mark Holmes hosts his Mod Club and spins 1960s Brit pop.

783 College St., 416-535-7888

Roxy Blu

While the reputations of other clubs rise and fall, this place keeps its cool with rare grooves and deep funk.

12 Brant St., at King St. W., 416-504-3222, roxyblu.com

Una Mas

For a surprisingly long time, this has been the place for funk and hip-hop.

422 Adelaide St. W., 416-703-4862, unamas.net

All Dressed Up and Nowhere To Go?

There's no more joyously unbridled expression of drag delight than gay Latin dance club **El Convento Rico** (*750 College St., 416-588-7800, elconventorico.com*), where the dress code ranges from Ricky-Martin-with-Mascara to full-blown Carmen Miranda. On Havana Night (Thursdays), the club offers free salsa lessons and a generous Cuban buffet, while the weekend drag shows are legendary. It's one of the few spots where you might find the dance floor packed with couples of every gender arrangement. Over on Church Street, the open-window drag shows at **Bar 501** (*501 Church St., 416-944-3272*) are so popular that they attract tour buses, while **Zelda's** (*542 Church St., 416-922-2526*), with its waiters in drag on the patio, attracts lineups. But the boys who'd just like to have a quiet dinner in ladies' clothes prefer the much more subdued **PJ Mellons Wine Restaurant** (*489 Church St., 416-966-3241*). A little further east at **Pimblett's** (*263 Gerrard St. E., 416-929-9525*), Geoffrey Pimblett serves up British-style roasts, chops, and other comfort food on charmingly mismatched, rosebud-sprigged china from Goodwill. Menus are glued inside back issues of *The Tattler* and other Britophile mags, and indeed, Geoffrey himself has been know to don a pair of sensible pumps and a picture hat for a royal outing à la Queen Mum at the annual Pride parade. Meanwhile, his neighbouring **Pimblett's Rest B&B** (a.k.a. The End House, *242 Gerrard St. E., 416-921-6898*) is a self-styled Fawlty Towers. Its Agatha Christie Room is furnished with dozens of the great mystery writer's books – and a secret passage to the "Queen Mothers' Bedroom."

dark desires

You'd need a fine-toothed comb to sort the overlapping goth and fetish scenes into entirely separate strands; however, some clubs and events are clearly goth venues, while others are more focused on fetishism. In either case (visitors take note!), dress code *counts*. Fetish possibilities might or might not include leather, rubber, PVC, bondage gear, cowboy, French maid, military, or schoolgirl. When it comes to fetish play, trust and respect are key elements, so one shouldn't even *think* of joining a hot-wax dripping or bondage scenario before being clearly invited to do so. This is particularly important because any game that could involve physical or psychological discomfort is normally set up with mutually understood safe words or signals for stopping the action, and no one should be participating unless they're clear on the rules. (Also, as the informative *toronto-goth.com* primly advises, "There's no point in introducing yourself as Mistress Supreme So-and-So The Almighty Dominant Bitch Goddess From Hell, if the first time you play it becomes clear that you're really Jane Doe The Waitress Who Picked Up a Riding Crop For The First Time Last Week And Still Isn't Sure Which End Is Which.")

Genuine Goth

Photo: Sarah B. Hood

Vatikan (*1032 Queen St. W., 416-533-9166*) is run by the owners of the former Sanctuary, which – in what must be one of the most tellingly ironic developments in this city's history – is now a Starbucks. **Savage Garden** (*550 Queen St. W., 416-504-2178, savagegarden.ca*) is also a goth-friendly spot, most particularly on the first Thursday of each month, known as **New Scream**. Popular with goths, but not exclusive, is **Dark Rave**, which takes over all four floors of the Big Bop (*651 Queen St. W., 416-504-6699*) on first Saturdays of the month.

Gay and Lesbian

The Barn is not a place for horsing around. This is a serious party, with three floors of pick-up prospects. *418 Church St., 416-977-4702*

Pope Joan is the oldest lesbian bar in town. *547 Parliament St., 416-925-6662*

Photo: Sarah B. Hood

The Toolbox is a pillar of the gay leather, denim, and bear (think heavy and hairy) scene. Thursdays are "Underwear Night," when the briefs may be very brief indeed. *508 Eastern Ave., 416-466-8616, toolboxtoronto.com*

Woody's, a Church Street staple with regular events like Best Chest night, has gained extra fame after being featured on the television show *Queer as Folk*. *465-467 Church St., 416-972-0887, woodystoronto.com*

Karaoke

The Bovine Sex Club
hosts Kickass Karaoke, called
"the real imitation."
542 Queen St W., 416-504-4239

Clinton's Tavern, a veteran
joint in Little Korea, has log-cabin
wallpaper and regular karaoke.
Quite a combo, but it works.
693 Bloor St. W., 416-535-9541

Gladstone Hotel has a long
history of boozin' and beltin' it
out, country-style.
1214 Queen St. W., 416-531-4635

**Manila By Night Karaoke Bar
& Restaurant** is a true Filipino
hangout. Great noodles too.
4949 Bathurst St., 416-225-1078

XO Karaoke offers songs in
English, Korean, Japanese, and
Chinese. Private rooms are available.
693 Bloor St. W., 416-535-3734

Full-blown Fetish

The Reverb's **Fetish Nights** are "kinky glamour parties" held on third Saturdays (651 Queen St. W., 416-504-6699, fetishmasquerade.com); they offer three rooms of pleasure and a dark play dungeon. Last Tuesdays see **Madame X's Fetish Night** at the Limelight (250 Adelaide St. W., 416-593-6126). Then there are queer-positive **Sin Sundays** at Dance Cave atop Lee's Palace (592 Bloor St. W., 416-532-1598). Northbound Leather hosts the monthly **Fetish@5ive** at 5ive (5 St. Joseph St., 416-972-1037, northbound.com). The **Black Eagle** (457 Church St., 416-413-1219, blackeagletoronto.com) runs an Underwear Night on Tuesdays, plus "Jock-and-Boot Sundays." (At all times they frown, however, upon clubwear, cologne, drag, sandals, sneakers, and sportswear — except head-to-toe uniforms.) Among their facilities are a dentist's chair and a crucifixion area for tie-up games and other inventive fun.

Hankie Pankie

Straight folks hear rumours from time to time about the ornate communication systems devised by gay men to communicate their inclinations and desires by non-verbal means. We're here to assure you with confidence that it's all true. In specialized bars where people are openly cruising for S&M or bondage partners, it's still common to speed up the process and cut down on potential misunderstandings by making use of elaborate hankie codes. In general, a hankie worn in the left pocket indicates dominance, while the right is submissive or receptive. Some of the easier ones to remember are: black for S&M, yellow for "water sports," and grey for bondage. But the list (which varies slightly from establishment to establishment and city to city) is extremely long, and gets down to oddities like mosquito netting for outdoor sex. Novices need to exercise caution here: unless the seeker can confidently distinguish teal from robin's egg blue in a dim light, for example, they risk mixing up the hankie that means mutual oral stimulation with the one for genital torture!

Top Hops Stops

The year 1986 was important to Ontario beer drinkers (and that would be most of us). That's the date when the very first Ontario brewpub license was granted, in Welland. The first in Toronto was the Amsterdam, which opened on John Street in August 1986, later merging with its cousin, The Rotterdam, to become the **Amsterdam Brewing Co.** (*600 King St. W., 416-504-1040*). It's now the only place in town to buy bottled beer when the beer stores are closed. Master brewer Joel Manning enjoys a lot of creative freedom; he originated the strong, raspberry-flavoured Framboise for his own wedding in August of 1991 and used to reissue it on his anniversary. (Now it's a year-round seller with its own specially imported German ceramic bottles.) Like Steam Whistle, Amsterdam gives away all the spent malt from the brewing process to a Mennonite farmer in Acton, who, though he doesn't drink alcohol himself, is pleased to feed the protein-rich leftovers to his – presumably very contented – dairy cows.

In 1991, Ron Keefe opened the **Granite Brewery** (*245 Eglinton Ave. E., 416-322-0723, granitebrewery.ca*), modelled after his brother Kevin's successful Halifax pub of the same name. Both brothers use a rare open-top fermenting method that they learned at England's Ringwood Breweries. In fact, Granite Brewery's most popular beer is called Ringwood, followed closely by the 5.6% Peculiar. Like Manning at the Amsterdam, Keefe is a lobbyist for less strict brewpub rules; for instance, he'd like to retail beer for customers to take away. We'd drink to that.

For many years the John Street Roundhouse – opened in 1932 to service railway locomotives – stood empty, its fate undecided, until Cam Heaps and Greg Taylor started looking for a place to put their brewery. The former Upper Canada Brewing Company colleagues

Live Music

The Cameron House, a Queen West institution, hosts acoustic country Sundays, with suitable-sounding bands like The Foggy Hogtown Boys and The Hokey Jeremiahs.
408 Queen St. W., 416-703-0811, thecameron.com

Cutty's Hideaway is a Caribbean dance hall deep in Greektown, with great calypso acts like the legendary Mighty Sparrow.
538 Danforth Ave., 416-463-5380

Photo: Sarah B. Hood

had two criteria for their new business: they wanted to open it in a heritage building, and they wanted to call it "Steam Whistle," to conjure up that blissful feeling of a Fred Flintstone-style quitting time. It was only *after* they decided upon these requirements that they heard the

City was calling for occupants of the antique steam-powered roundhouse property. **Steam Whistle Brewing** (*255 Bremner Blvd., 416-362-BEER, steamwhistle.ca*) now occupies bays 1 through 11 of the building, and they conduct daily tours. (Bays 12 through 32, which still contain railway equipment, are closed to the public except on the annual Doors Open Toronto weekend.)

The Feathers (*962 Kingston Rd., 416-694-0443, home.primus.ca/~eastleaf*) is a cheery, traditional English-style pub that brews its own house beers and carries a dizzying selection of single-malt scotches – just about one for each day of the year. Once a month or so they hold a whiskey challenge, where contestants try to match eight superb samples with descriptions, and guess the malts. (They'll organize private challenges for small groups of at least eight people.)

C'est What? (*67 Front Street East, 416-867-9499, cestwhat.com*) also maintains a righteous collection of whiskies, but their fame has been made on their international beer selection – including lots of local craft ales and their own in-house Cask Ale, Coffee Porter, Hemp Ale, and so on. They're also a premiere venue for indie music, in what seems like a separate space, but is actually their own music room, **nia** (*19 Church*), host to the likes of Barenaked Ladies, Rufus Wainwright, Ron Sexsmith, Sarah Harmer, and Hawksley Workman.

The Horseshoe, which opened in 1947, has been the launching pad for big-name Canadian bands like Blue Rodeo and The Tragically Hip. *370 Queen St. W., 416-598-4753, horseshoetavern.com*

Hugh's Room is the place for folks who like folk. *2261 Dundas St. W., 416-531-6604, hughsroom.com*

Lee's Palace, which began life as a movie theatre, still has great sightlines and the most garishly-painted storefront in town. Also home to The Dance Cave, which has a mod night called Bif Bang Pow, and Vazaleen, a popular gay party held the last Friday of the month. *529 Bloor St. W., 416-532-1590, leespalace.com*

this is the place for ...

Beer: Belgian wanna-bes can head over to the **Esplanade Bier Markt**, which has 100 brands of beer to choose from.
70 The Esplanade, 416-862-7575

Bourbon: Although it's better known as a restaurant, you can get a true taste of New Orleans at the **Southern Accent** bar. With brands like Old Rip Van Winkle, who could resist?
595 Markham St., 416-536-3211

Champagne: Bubbly connoisseurs swear by **Café Brussel**. And why not? With a selection of over 60 champagnes, you can sample non-vintage stuff by the glass or splurge on a $400 bottle of Salon.
143 Danforth Ave., 416-465-7363

Martinis: The best place to swizzle your stick is **Babylon Café**. The menu lists over 160 kinds, so you'll likely be amazed at all the things you can sip.
553 Church St., 416-923-2626

Rum: Appleton Estates tastes better than ever at **Tropical Nights**. This east end restaurant brings the Caribbean close to home with palm trees and tropical birds.
3114 Danforth Ave., 416-693-9000

Scotch: With almost 200 single malts behind the bar, **Allen's** is where to go when you want to learn what "peaty" means.
143 Danforth Ave., 416-463-3086

Photo: Sarah B. Hood

Wine: **Crush** is the perfect place to acquire a sophisticated palate, with 30 wines by the glass and weekly tastings.
455 King St. W., at Spadina Ave., 416-977-1234

Lula Lounge only opened in 2002, but it has quickly gained a reputation for great Latin music. Learn to salsa or just sit back, sip your drink and listen to Afro-Cuban jazz.
1585 Dundas St. W., 416-588-0307, lula.ca

The Rex Hotel has jazz seven nights a week, plus matinees on Saturday and Sunday.
194 Queen St. W., 416-598-2475

Tequila Lounge, plopped on top of a Pizza Pizza franchise, has managed to compete with the more established Lee's Palace.
794 Bathurst St., 416-536-0346

The House on Parliament (*456 Parliament St., 416-925-4074*) — a hangout for Cabbagetown neighbourhood folks (especially sports dykes) — is a dependable destination for classic pub grub. The pub in the University of Toronto's Graduate Student Union building, simply known as the **GSU Pub** (*16 Bancroft Ave., 416-978-8466, gsu.utoronto.ca/pubcafe.html#cafe*), surely rates the prize for most laid-back drinking establishment in the city. It boasts nutritious Mediterranean-inspired food and a smoke-free space in the upstairs Sylvester's Café (named after an accomplished mouser who used to live in the building). Since the University built its Earth Sciences Complex around the building in the late '80s, it's been strangely hidden away. You reach it via an archway on Huron Street south of Wilcocks. Last time we checked, they were still serving extremely inexpensive pitchers of intriguing drafts like Robinson's Lager, GSU Cream Ale, and Buzz Hemp Lager, to be consumed in comfortably dilapidated couches or on what may be this city's only patio on a car-free street. Important tip: it's not open on weekends. Housed in a former Canadian Imperial Bank of Commerce, **Pauper's** (*539 Bloor St. W., 416-530-1331, madisonavenuepub.com/paupers*) has a fine range of pub fare, including vegetarian choices and a tasty daily soup-and-sandwich special. Its other amenities include a sidewalk patio, a dim main floor with an almost-Art Nouveau ambiance, darts and dancing in the second-story lounge, and a rooftop patio. Erudite diners may win a prize for identifying the author of the daily quotation on the chalkboard. As their URL suggests, it's owned by the same people who run the also-pleasant **Madison** (on *Madison Ave.*). Other standouts are **The Artful Dodger** (*10 Isabella St., 416-964-9511*), which follows the classic British model, with worthy fish and chips and weekend brunches replete with giant sausages, and the **Ben Wicks Restaurant & Pub** (*425 Parliament St., 416-961-9425*), named after the well-known cartoonist.

LOUD AND CLEAR

These are boom times for local bands. Want proof? Tune into **Wavelength**. The live music showcase, held every Sunday night at Sneaky Dee's on College Street, has built a huge following since opening night in February 2000. Almost any group with a guitar has hit the mic here: Precious Little, Pony Da Look, Atomic 7. And with a website and monthly zine, Wavelength keeps all the bits and pieces of the scene well-connected. "They've built a community of friends who give a damn," says Tyler Clark Burke, co-founder of Three Gut Records, whose bands Royal City and Cuff the Duke are Wavelength regulars. "There's nothing egomaniacal about it. It's all just a good way for everyone to fit in."

431 College St., wavelengthtoronto.com

Photo: Sarah B. Hood

In a class all its own is the Irish pub. With elegant woodwork and genial regulars, the **Dora Keogh** (*141 Danforth Ave., 416-463-3086, allens.to/dora*) is an outstanding representative of the genre, and a favourite with music lovers for its Sunday-afternoon Celtic jam sessions. Officially they're both called "Tara Inn," but aficionados know that the original is the **Wee Tara** (*2609 Eglinton Ave., 416-264-2723*), while the newcomer – which is bigger – is simply the **Tara** (*2365 Kingston Rd., Scarborough 416-266-6200*). Most of the staff at both locations are straight from Ireland, and the Tara lays out a much more elaborate menu than you might expect, serving its mains – like stuffed pork filet, baked salmon, and the meaty "Big Fella" platter – with sunflower bread on the side. The **Irish Embassy Pub & Grill**, in its lofty 1873-vintage bank building (*49 Yonge St., 416-866-8282, irishembassypub.com*), is upscale and downtown. Also highly recommended, despite the nasty names, are **Scruffy Murphy's** (*150 Eglinton Ave. East, 416- 484-6637*) and **Dirty Nelly's** (*1522 Bayview Ave., 416-485-0955*).

LET THE RUDDER GUIDE YOU

Since the BamBoo has closed up shop on Queen West and morphed into **Bambu By The Lake** right next to Harbourfront Centre (*245 Queen's Quay W., 416-214-6000, bambubythelake.com*), the waterfront has definitely become world music central – especially when you consider that **The Guvernment** (*132 Queen's Quay E., 416-869-0045*) and **The Docks** (*11 Polson St., 416-469-5655*) are just a bit further down the way. For the quintessential BamBoo/Bambu experience, track the movements of one King David Michael Rudder, premiere Trinidad calypsonian. Rudder usually plays a couple of gigs just before the Caribana/Simcoe Day long weekend (the closer to that weekend, the pricier the cover). He invariably brings out his expat Trini rooting section, along with a goodly few Canadian converts, who will sing along with David's every word while winin' down. If you want to join in, but have a limited capacity for song lyrics, at least make sure you know the chorus to "The Hammer" ("Laventille, here we come, we're singing praises to your son...") and maybe "High Mas" ("Oh-ah-ah, Oh-ah-ah, I love my country; oh-ah-ah, Oh-ah-ah, I feelin' irie"). Just those will carry you pretty far into the vibe.

Trivial Accomplishments

About 15 years ago, a company called NTN started broadcasting live, interactive trivia games into bars across North America. With the spread of the Internet, NTN isn't quite so popular as it once was, but you'll still find avid players in Toronto locations like the Firkin pubs, Shoeless Joe's, Gabby's, Scotland Yard, and the Spotted Dick. But the most popular location is **Joe Mercury's** (*2345B Dundas St. W., 416-535-1324, toronto.com/joemercurys*), and it's always packed on Tuesdays when the big game comes on. That's where "NAGROM" (that's "Morgan" spelled backwards) racked up enough lifetime points to rank officially among the top ten Canadian players. But since NTN trivia was first introduced, no other player has evoked more admiration, speculation, and controversy than the legendary DAVETV, whose signature has regularly appeared at the top of this continent's scoreboards for more than a decade. From personal acquaintance, we can verify the existence of this mythic Torontonian, known in everyday life as Dave Hallett. He's been banned from several spots – including Joe Mercury's – for his hot temper, but those who do admit him know that he'll put them in the top rankings. He routinely plays with five boards at a time, drinks very little, and is soft-spoken and friendly with new players, often sharing correct answers. Most evenings, the way to find him is to go into any NTN bar and watch the lists of Canadian winners. It'll be hard to know if he ever stops competing, though, because players across the continent have taken to using the famous moniker, so DAVETV will probably prevail as long as NTN trivia is still being played.

24-7

We're still not a city that never sleeps, but there's a lot you can accomplish between dusk and dawn in this town.

Noshing

Most kitchens close between 10 and midnight, but comfort food may be found 24 hours a day at the last remaining **Fran's** (20 College St., 416-923-9867) and at **Vesta Lunch** (474 Dupont St., 416-537-4318), where Aris claims they don't even own a key for the front door. Lighter fare and a coffee-house atmosphere prevail at **7 West Café** (7 Charles St. W., 416-928-9041). Those who are still peckish can buy fresh Italian bread and pastries in the wee hours at the **Golden Wheat Bakery** (652 College St., 416 534-1107) or **Commisso Brothers & Racco Italian Bakery** (33 Eddystone Ave., 416-743-6600; 8 Kincort St., 416-651-7671). Monday to Friday, it's never too late for full grocery shopping at **Dominion** (425 Bloor St. W., 416- 923-9099; 3090 Bathurst St., 416-783-1227; 89 Gould St., 416-862-7171; 656 Eglinton Ave. E., 416-482-7422). On weekend nights, late-night shoppers may have to resort to a pricier deli selection from **Rabba Fine Foods** (37 Charles St. W., 416- 964-3409; 256 Jarvis St., 416- 595-9679; 9 Isabella Ave., 416-928-2300; several other locations).

Sports Bars

La Cervejaria might not seem like a real sports bar because of the blaring Latin pop songs, but try getting a seat here during the World Cup.
842 College St., 416-588-0162

Monarch Tavern has become a gathering place for Leaf fans. That means beers, cheers, and wait-till-next-years.
14 Clinton St., 416-531-5833

Sports Centre Café has 75 TV screens, so you can watch everything from hockey to hurling, and soccer to sumo wrestling.
49 St. Clair Ave. W., 416-928-9525

Billiards

The **Academy of Spherical Arts** is housed in the old Brunswick Billiards factory building. True to that spirit, the place is vast and classy. Antique tables and high ceilings harken back to the time when this was just a gentleman's game.
38 Hanna Ave., 416-532-1501, sphericalarts.com

Another classy place to shoot some stick is the **Charlotte Room**. Snooker tournaments and scotch-drinking are equally common here.
19 Charlotte St., 416-598-2882

A more down-and-dirty spot is **Central Billiards**. Ignore the Members Only sign and take a deep breath before heading in. It's a real, smoke-filled pool hall.
468 Queen St. W., 416-504-9494

Fun

Insomniacs can pick an all-night lane at **Bowlerama** (*5429 Dundas St. W., 416-239-3536; 5837 Yonge St., 416-239-3536; 115 Rexdale Ave, 416-743-8388*), chalk up a cue at **Central Billiards** (*468 Queen St. W., 416-504-9494*), work out the kinks at **World Gym** (*675 Yonge St., 416-966-4967*), or surf the Net at **Iklick** (*1453 Queen St. W., 416-538-3317*). However, the misleadingly named **Insomnia Internet Bar/Café** (*563 Bloor St. W.*) is only open until 2 a.m. on weekdays and 4 a.m. on weekends, and the **Café Never Kloses** (*187 Queen St. E.*) actually does, and fairly early at that!

Emergencies

No clean clothes for the big day tomorrow? Time for **24 Hour Coin Laundry** (*566 Mount Pleasant, 416-487-0233*). School or business crunches can probably be solved at **Kinko's** (*505 University Ave., 416-979-8447; 2430 Yonge St., 416-322-3455; 459 Bloor St. W., 416-928-0110; other locations*), which offers 24-hour photocopying, computer access, and printing. For 2 a.m. toothaches, your only hope will be the 24-hour **Shoppers Drug Marts** (*700 Bay St., 416-979-2424; 1630 Danforth Ave., 416-461-2453; 3089 Dufferin St., 416-787-0238; 523 St. Clair Ave. W., 416-538-1155*). If you forget your key on your way out the door, call **A Perfect Pick Locksmiths'** 24-hour emergency mobile service (*905-616-2565*). If the pipes burst, call **Lampert Plumbing Services** (*25 Wingold Ave., 416-787-4921*). And if – heaven forbid – your kitty is ailing, call **Annex Animal Hospital** (*716 Bathurst St., 416-537-3128*), *Veterinary Emergency Clinic (280 Sheppard Ave. E., 416-226-3663; 1180 Danforth Ave., 416-465-3501*), or **Willowdale Animal Hospital** (*256 Sheppard Ave. W., 416-222-5409*).

Toronto the Good has always been a bit of a misnomer. Sure, our infamous blue laws once shut the city down on Sundays, but any kind of suppression is bound to push the shenanigans that much further underground. So we've dug it all up for you: the bootleggers, bank robbers, and a bevy of mysteries from the great beyond.

Photo: Sarah B. Hood

A Slight, a Fight, a Blight

Bad blood between blue bloods led to the last fatal duel in Toronto. John Ridout, the 18-year-old son of Ontario's surveyor-general, was a law student in the family firm. One July day in 1817, he called on Samuel Jarvis, another lawyer, to discuss a civil suit between the two families. Words were exchanged and Jarvis, whose family name would later find its way onto a city street, gave his antagonist the heave-ho. Literally. Not one to be slighted, Ridout returned later and assaulted Jarvis with a cane. Jarvis again knocked the boy down, setting the stage for the final duel. Three days later, the two men and their seconds gathered before dawn at old Elmsley Field, near the corner of today's Yonge and College Streets. Pistols were chosen. Each one had a single bullet. The men were to stand back to back, walk eight paces and turn around. Jarvis's second would call out "one, two, three, fire!" and that would be that. But at the count of two, Ridout fired and missed. He claimed he could not hear the count properly. The men huddled together to discuss proper etiquette. After several minutes of deliberation, it was deemed proper that Jarvis should have his shot. So he did. Ridout, unarmed now, stood there and was killed instantly. A memorial stone, embedded in the west wall of the porch at St. James Cathedral, makes no mention of the duel: "A blight came and he was consigned to an early grave."

what have we done to deserve this?

For a town so often accused of being goody-goody, Toronto has seen its share of bad times. And not plain old bad, but bad of biblical proportions.

April 19, 1904: Around 8 p.m., a small fire had broken out near the top of the Currie Neckwear factory at 58 Wellington Street West. It was a windy night and before long, the flames had whipped across the buildings of Bay Street. Soon, some of the Front Street buildings were on fire too. Then, the wind changed direction, taking the fire east to Yonge. Employees of the *Evening Telegram*, at Bay and Melinda Streets, managed to save their building, but others weren't so lucky. By 5 a.m. the next day, almost 100 buildings had been either destroyed or damaged. The Great Toronto Fire had left 5,000 people out of work.

Photo: City of Toronto Archives, Fonds 1244, 2

February 12, 1926: Several days of heavy snowfall left the city covered. Inconvenient but not awful, until all that white stuff sent thousands of rats scurrying for food and warmth. They found both, often in the basements of downtown homes and cellars of shops. The rodents had become such a problem that one newspaper ad asked for "cats, good rat-catchers." The frustrated advertiser had tried all forms of extermination, from poison to traps, and had been outclassed every time. He now turned to "the domesticated pussy" in hopes of having the day saved.

RIOT!

One of the most appalling events in the city's history started with a softball game. On August 16, 1933, teams from the Harbord Playground and St. Peter's Church were playing at Christie Pits, a park at the corner of Bloor and Christie Streets. Several thousand were in attendance. Taunting the mostly-Jewish Harbord team, some of the fans unfurled a large white sheet with a painted swastika, then shouted, "Heil Hitler!" Jewish fans, already on edge because of the news in Europe and the formation of the Swastika Club in the eastern beaches earlier that summer, became enraged and charged the crowd. Fights broke out. There were only two police at the Pits that day and they were easily outnumbered. With no one to control the violence, the fighters quickly grew in number; reinforcements for both sides came from nearby neighbourhoods, armed with clubs, chains, bats, and broom handles. The Christie Pits Riot lasted four hours before order was restored. An estimated 10,000 people were involved.

TOO SMART FOR HER OWN GOOD

In 1912, Bessie Starkman was a poor housewife who lived at 63 Chestnut Avenue with her husband and two daughters. Needing money, she took in a boarder named Rocco Perri. Three months later, Bessie and Rocco ran off together in search of a better life. They found it in Hamilton, becoming the biggest bootleggers in Southern Ontario; by the mid-1920s, the couple grossed over $1 million. Rocco, officially a salesman for the Superior Macaroni Company, oversaw the shipments, while Bessie kept the books. Acknowledged as the first (and probably only) Jewish woman to command an Italian mob, Bessie was indeed the brains behind the operation. Unfortunately, she wasn't smart enough to steer clear of the American mobs. After welshing on a drug deal, Bessie was shot to death in her Hamilton home on August 13, 1930.

October 15, 1954: Hurricane Hazel blew into town on this day, dumping over seven inches of rain onto the streets and 40 billion gallons of water into the rivers. The Humber, Don, Rouge, and Credit Rivers all were in flood, sweeping away bridges and eroding their banks. An entire street, Raymore Drive, south of Lawrence Avenue, was washed away, taking 14 houses and 36 people with it. All told, 81 people died and over 4,000 families were left homeless. And then there's the story of Harry de Peuter. Living on the Holland Marsh, just north of the city, de Peuter, his wife, and 12 children were in their house when it uprooted and went sailing down the flooded marsh. The house would tilt in the swirling water and all 14 de Peuters would race from side to side, trying to balance it out. One of the kids even got seasick before their two-mile trip ended in a field of carrots.

August 2, 2001: A stretch of unusually hot weather gave rise to an attack of aphids. The little green bugs, which migrate from plant to plant during the seasons, got their calendar all messed up and started to swarm the eyes, noses, and mouths of an aghast populace. Cyclists were driven to distraction. Pedestrians hid their faces in hands and shirts. Perhaps no one was bugged more than the baseball players at SkyDome. The game was constantly delayed so players could wipe their eyes clean. "I think it's a plague coming down on the city," pedestrian Rosetta Powell told reporters, as she picked the critters out of her hair. "It's because we're too sinful."

Shady Side of the Street

York Street is pretty respectable these days, but it was once the worst stretch in town. Packed into three small blocks were ten brothels, eight blind pigs, and a handful of pawn shops that fenced stolen goods. And since York was a main road connecting the train station to the downtown core, there was never a shortage of suckers passing by. In the late 1800s, theft, prostitution, and drunkenness were so common that extra constables were required just to patrol this small street.

Cold Cases

Among all the files still under investigation by Toronto Homicide detectives, three stand out.

1. This city's most puzzling cold case is the 1973 murder of 17-year-olds Donna Stearne and Wendy Ann Tedford. On the night of April 27, the two teens took a bus from their homes to Yorkdale Mall and spent a couple of hours shopping. Then they took another bus to the Sit 'n Eat Restaurant at Keele north of Wilson, had a couple of Cokes, and left at about 11 p.m. Several people around the neighbourhood reported hearing loud bangs around midnight, and early the next morning a young student found the bodies of the two girls, fully clothed, lying in a nearby vacant lot, where they had both been shot in the head. Several months later, a .38 Colt revolver turned up in the Windsor area. It had been reported stolen in a break-and-enter several months before the two girls were killed, and was quickly proved to have been the murder weapon, but investigations around Windsor failed to provide any more useful clues.

2. The longest resident of Toronto Police Service's Most Wanted list is Dennis Melvyn Howe – also known as Michael Burns, Wayne King, Ralph Ferguson, and Jim Myers. Since 1983, he's been sought for the heartbreaking murder of then-nine-year-old Sharin Morningstar Keenan, who was abducted from Jean Sibelius Park in the Annex. The case was featured on TV's *America's Most Wanted* several times, most recently in 2000. Some believe that Howe, who would now be over 60, has died in the interim, but police frequently receive tips from as far away as Florida from people who think they may have seen him.

3. Most of us develop a bad back from time to time, but few of us develop a solution. However, that's just what Torontonian Frank Roberts did when tennis laid him up with back pain. In 1980, he started Obus Forme Ltd. to manufacture and market his own highly effective design for a pain-relieving back support. Soon the Obus Forme was being sold in 26 countries, with annual sales in the tens of millions of dollars. But Roberts was never given the chance to rest on his therapeutic laurels. One morning in August 1998, when Roberts was 68, he drove to his Hopewell Avenue business, parked his car neatly in the parking lot, and went to get some bagels that he'd bought from the trunk of his car. That's when a gunman – "not a big man," and wearing dark clothes –

NO NEWS IS BAD NEWS

In November 1935, the body of 20-year-old Ruth Taylor was found in Fairmount Park, off Gerrard Street East. Not long after, garage mechanic Harry O'Donnell was arrested for the murder. The case was both big news and a small problem. O'Donnell's wife, a dedicated *Toronto Star* reader, was in serious condition in hospital after giving birth. Doctors feared the news of her husband's arrest would make her take a turn for the worse. So, on November 8, the *Star* printed a phony edition, carrying everything but news of the arrest, and delivered it to the hospital. The real edition carried stories of the arrest and the fake paper. Later on, when she heard the truth, Mrs. O'Donnell fainted. Mr. O'Donnell was hanged.

shot and killed him with a handgun in broad daylight. There has never been an arrest. "Somebody saw something and they're afraid to come forward," is the opinion of investigating Detective Ray Zarb, who says he's still hopeful.

When the police are looking for information from the public, they post details of their investigations at *torontopolice.on.ca/homicide*. They also invite people with useful information to give them a call at 416-808-7400.

THE BEARER OF BAD NOOSE

Toronto has an inglorious history of capital punishment. On October 11, 1798, an illiterate tailor named John Sullivan became the first person to hang. His crime? Buying whiskey with a forged three shilling, ninepence note (worth about 84 cents today).

The last hanging took place at the Don Jail on December 11, 1962. Ronald Turpin and Arthur Lucas were tied back-to-back, hooded, and then hanged. Turpin had killed Constable Frederick Nash, while Lucas was a hitman who murdered Theland Carter, a witness in an American drug trial, and an unfortunate bystander named Carol Newman.

Cut to the Chase

Ever since Bonnie and Clyde took their show on the road, there has been a fascination with lawless couples on the lam. The most recent Toronto version involves Ron and Loren Koval. The Kovals were co-founders and majority owners of King's Health Centre, a private medical facility at the corner of Queen and University. Established in 1996, King's offered elite clients everything from podiatry to an in-house golf clinic. However, despite several big-name doctors and patients, the centre did not have a healthy bottom line. Financing was hard to come by and the Kovals became an increasingly stressed-out, chain-smoking pair of health care providers. Then, on Friday, October 13, 2000, they didn't show up for work. They spent that weekend in New York City, with their daughter Amy, and then disappeared. The cops, led by Detective Steve Burnham of 52 Division, were called in and a quick look at the books revealed dummy accounts, shell companies, and a case of million-dollar fraud. With a five-day jump on the cops, the Kovals were rumoured to be anywhere from Costa Rica to Panama. The cops questioned every one of their associates and then the press was hot on their tail too, with the *Globe and Mail* sending reporters all over the map in search of a scoop. When Detective Burnham discovered that some of the money had moved through Amy's bank account, word leaked out that the cops were ready to arrest the daughter. Like any good parents, the Kovals came to their child's rescue. They emerged from their hiding place in Myrtle Beach and turned themselves in at the Canadian border. A team of cops needed six hours to count the US$1,230,898.62 that the couple had with them. Ron, who said he was tired of running, was dying for a smoke.

The Peculiar Departure of Ambrose Small

Ambrose J. Small, missing millionaire, whose fate is still an unsolved mystery.

On December 1, 1919, 53-year-old self-made millionaire Ambrose Small sold his interests in a profitable chain of live theatres for a tidy $1.7 million. The following day he deposited the cheque, finished his afternoon at the office, and then seemingly vanished from the face of the earth. With the money safely in the bank, it's always been assumed that Small was murdered, and as recently as 1965, Toronto Police followed up a purported lead as to the whereabouts of a body, but none has ever been found. The case was internationally famous in its day; a $50,000 reward was posted. The flames of public interest were fiercely fanned when it was discovered that Small – a married man – had kept a succession of mistresses, sometimes entertaining them in a lavish boudoir hidden away inside Toronto's Grand Theatre. Furthermore, Small's personal assistant disappeared too, and was discovered living a new life under an assumed name, but nothing could be proved against him beyond the theft of some bonds. The provincial government carried out a Special Inquiry in 1936, but to this day Small's disappearance is as great a mystery as it was 90 years ago. Although the case was officially closed in 1960, its ripples are still occasionally felt. Small plays a part in Michael Ondaatje's *In the Skin of a Lion*, and many believe that his ghost still frequents his favourite theatre, The Grand in London, Ontario.

OFF TARGET

Bank employees always seem like a sedate bunch; busy with paperwork and unfailingly polite. But for many years, they had a secret edge. Managers and tellers routinely kept loaded pistols on hand and, in the event of a robbery, were expected to start shooting. Bank staff from all over town took target practice at the police firing range. Rumours even circulated that the old Bank of Toronto had its own firing range in a basement downtown. Employees packed heat until 1957, when a robbery occurred at a Toronto-Dominion branch at Dundas and McCaul. The bank manager fired and accidentally killed one of his own employees.

DRIVING HIM CRAZY

Anthony O'Toole was a man on a mission. On the night of January 3, 1989, he stole a car and drove down Ossington Avenue. Picking up speed, he hurtled across Queen Street, cutting off a bus, and smashed through the front doors of the Queen Street Mental Health Centre. The car continued down a glass corridor, stopping 91 metres later because of two flat tires. Miraculously, no one was hurt. O'Toole said he was trying to rescue his mother, who was being poisoned by hospital staff. There was no record of his mother being there, which was a good thing since that left room to hold O'Toole for psychiatric assessment.

Busy Day at the Banks

Mondays are brisk business for the banks. After the weekend, people come to get some more cash. On January 23, 1983, those withdrawals came fast and furious. That morning, the Bank of Montreal on downtown Yonge Street was knocked over for $1,200. Sergeant Paul Byer was soon examining the crime scene. On his way back to 52 Division, he passed the Toronto Dominion Bank at Church and Wellesley Streets, where he saw a man bolt out of the bank and into a cab. Byer calmly tailed the taxi and eventually arrested the man with $1,300 worth of ill-gotten gain in his pockets. Good news for the bank, right? Wrong. Not 90 minutes later, another hold-up man walked into the same bank and got away unmolested. And that was only the morning.

After lunch, two men in ski masks entered the Canadian Imperial Bank of Commerce at Dixon Road and Carlingview Drive in Etobicoke. They flashed handguns, hopped the counter and cleaned out the teller's cages to the tune of $4,300. And lastly, there was the lone bandit who cashed out $1,800 from the Royal Bank at Bloor Street and Lansdowne Avenue. "Five banks in one day," Staff Sergeant Bert Novis told reporters. "I'm afraid to come to work tomorrow."

The Midnight Dumping Bandit

These days, bank robbers and bootleggers aren't the worst crooks around. Environmental criminals are a bigger concern. Take Tony Lopes. For 20 years, he illegally dumped construction site waste all over town: city streets, private property, even a vacant lot across from the Strachan Avenue police station. Lopes rang up 22 convictions and $460,000 in unpaid fines, but the man investigators called "the midnight dumping bandit" continued with his dirty work, until November 1997, when he was caught at a west end site *in flagrante dumpo*. The cops and two local reporters gave chase along the banks of Black Creek until Lopes, choosing the lesser of two pursuers, threw himself upon the mercy of the press. Case closed. Still, there are many more enviro-crooks out there. The city, we're told, sends garbage spies into many suspect areas. These snoops get down and dirty. Arriving at an illegal dump, they courageously sift through the trash and look for an address that connects to an offender.

Stranger Fugitive

The story of Red Ryan is the stuff of fiction. A career criminal who escaped from Kingston Penitentiary in 1923, Ryan spent several months in the U.S., robbing banks, before his recapture. Back in the pen, he fell in with the local chaplain and eventually got work as a prison nurse. Word of his rehabilitation spread. Prime Minister R.B. Bennett even came to visit and, after 11 years, Ryan was released. He returned to Toronto as the toast of the town, got a job as a greeter at a downtown tavern, and signed his name to a series of "Crime Doesn't Pay" articles for the *Toronto Star*. Of course, this was all a ruse, as Ryan was still knocking off banks in his spare time. Several cops knew he was hanging out with his old crowd, but because Ryan was lionized in the press, they felt he was hands off, until the inevitable happened: in 1936, ten months after his parole, Ryan was shot and killed during a hold-up at a Sarnia liquor store. One year later, the shock of the story spilled into Morley Callaghan's novel, *More Joy in Heaven*. The fictionalized version features Kip Caley, who tries to go straight until the conflicting pressures of high and low society leave him with no choice but to return to a life of crime. Poetic license or what?

Oprah's Pick

Which Toronto politician has appeared on *Oprah*? Not the media-savvy Jack Layton, nor the oft-quoted Mel Lastman, but North Toronto councillor Anne Johnston. A cozy, diminutive lady whose looks may cloak to some her strength and drive, Johnston was called up by the TV show's producers in 1993 when she was championing the cause of streetside scavenging. At the time, "garbage-picking" was actually illegal in Toronto, whereas Johnston wanted to encourage it through a once-a-year recycling day. Well-known for her own lucky finds – bicycles, a vintage rocking horse, and much of the furniture at her farmhouse retreat – Johnston enjoyed the chance to spread the word to some 40 million viewers. But she wasn't pleased when her decorative cane (a practical accessory while she was recuperating from a broken hip) was confiscated on the set.

HALF BAKED

In March 1992, an unarmed robber tried to make off with the cash box from Steeles Bakery & Appetizer, but he was promptly shot in the leg by owner Norm Gardner. This small news item became a bigger one because Gardner, who also happened to be Vice-Chair of the Metro Police Services Board, was one of a handful of citizens licensed to carry a firearm. However, the pistol-packing politician refused to explain how or why he had a permit. After a short internal investigation, Gardner was cleared of all charges and went back to baking bread.

STICK-INTO-IT-IVENESS

He lives in his studio and can talk passionately about his craft. He chooses his materials with the utmost care and concern for the finished product and is sincere in trying to bring his high-value goods to customers at a reasonable price. Johnny Cameron, also known as the Kinky Cobbler, is a local dildo artisan. Since 2001, he has handcrafted his sex toys out of silicone, rather than rubber, because it is safer and easier to sterilize. Safety concerns also led him to design a hold-firm ring at the base of the dildo, which will keep a condom from rolling up the shaft. Cameron (*kinkycobbler.com*) has three dildos in his line, the most popular being the well-proportioned Epicurian Rose. You can even get your choice of six colours. And Cameron donates a portion of his proceeds to Hepatitis C research.

Two Top Cops

In 1928, Dennis C. Draper became Chief Constable without ever having worn a badge. A retired brigadier general with deep political connections in Tory Toronto, Draper may be the only police chief ever with a criminal record. On September 30, 1941, Draper was returning from a visit with the Peterborough police chief when he crashed into another car near Newtonville. One man died and three others were injured. Draper, drunk, was charged with dangerous driving. Somehow, he managed to keep his job for five more years.

His successor, John Chisholm, was the exact opposite. A long-time cop and detective of renown, Chisholm often seemed ill-prepared for the political aspects of the job. He quarreled with his boss, Charles Bick, chair of the Toronto Police Commission, and was taken to task for an unauthorized $25,000 stool pigeon fund. By 1958, Chisholm was in poor health and some thought he would resign. On July 4 of that year, officers responded to a call in High Park and found the body of their chief, slumped in the front seat of his car – dead of a self-inflicted gunshot.

Raid or Wrong?

On September 15, 2000, cops busted the Pussy Palace, a women's bathhouse night that was being held at Club Toronto (*231 Mutual St.*). Allegedly looking for liquor violations, five male officers spent over an hour inspecting the premises. They took the names of 10 women, but all charges were dropped after the negative press that followed.

Cops also kicked in the doors of the Toronto Compassion Centre, on August 13, 2002. The TCC is a non-profit medical marijuana dispensary near Bathurst Street and St. Clair Avenue. With over 1,200 members suffering from AIDS, Hepatitis C, and bipolar disorder, the Toronto Compassion Centre has been a necessary, controlled, and inexpensive source for pot since 1997. Since the raid, they have moved deeper underground. The office has moved and the address is known only to members, who must have photo ID. Four of the six people arrested in the raid have seen their charges dropped.

Fit to be Tied

In the early 1800s, Stephen Ellis and his wife were the first locals charged with running a brothel. For reasons lost to history, Mr. Ellis was released while the missus was put in the stocks. All of which shows that the law can be a little confusing in these matters. Even today. Take the case of Terri-Jean Bedford. In 1993, as Madame de Sade, she opened her Bondage Bungalow up in Thornhill, a suburb in north Toronto. Police raided the joint one year later, slapping Bedford with the anachronistic-sounding charge of running a common bawdy house. She explained that there was no sex for sale at her place, only cross-dressing, bondage, and infantilism. This legal loophole became a knot and, five separate trials later, Bedford was convicted and fined by the Ontario Court of Appeal in 1998.

But she wasn't whipped yet. She continued to be an outspoken critic of the courts, saying the ruling gave her no clear indication of what a dominatrix was legally allowed to do and not do. In the meantime, she moved downtown and opened Madame de Sade's Bondage Hotel. Formerly known as the Millicent Farnsworth Sissy Maid Academy and Charm School, the hotel had an adult baby nursery, medieval dungeon, and a sissy dorm for those gentlemen in need of a little forced feminization. Plus, she offered a continental breakfast for weekend guests. In 2003, Bedford took a breather. The hotel was put on hiatus while she worked on a book (*madamedesade.com*) that documented her lifestyle and legal concerns.

COURT INTRIGUE

We've seen it occupy four grown men throughout an entire Sunday brunch: gossip about the potential rising and falling fortunes of the principal players in TICOT, the Imperial Court of Toronto, formerly known as the Trillium Monarchist League (*npconsultants.com/ticot/ticot_intro.htm*). TICOT is several things, of which the most vital is a fundraising body that supports charities like Casey House, AIDS Tijuana, The Canadian Lesbian and Gay Archives, Sick Children's Hospital, and Gilda's Club. It's also a sensational social circle for the drag

Naked Ambition

For those who may not have been following them, the adventures of lawyer and nudist Peter Simm and the TNT!MEN make a revealing chapter in the legal history of this city. Simm and his group, whose name is an acronym for Totally Naked Toronto Men Enjoying Nudity, are at the centre of a number of cases designed to expose the issue of public nakedness. In the late '90s, Simm and friends laid bare their plans for a nude beach section of Hanlan's Point, a campaign that found success soon after it was unveiled. In the spring of 2000, Simm defended the Church Street dance club The Barn, which had been charged with permitting disorderly conduct after TNT!MEN celebrated a naked night there. The case was dropped due to misplaced paperwork; a plus for The Barn, but a setback for TNT!MEN, who lost a chance to bring the debate out into the open. However, the group was delighted in June 2002 when Provincial Court Judge Robert Bigelow ruled that simply allowing people to be naked in a club doesn't violate Ontario liquor laws. Later that year, they won another round in the ongoing drive to disrobe when seven men charged at Pride festivities were cleared; since every one of them had at least worn footwear, the onus was on the Crown to prove indecency – something it failed to do. So it seems that Simms and TNT!MEN are gradually winning their point – barely.

community, and organizer of a series of glitzy, glam events, of which the glitziest and glammiest is the Coronation Ball to honour the winners of the annual campaign for the highest court honours. At the time of writing, the imperial crowns grace the heads of His Most Imperial and Sovereign Majesty The Golden Winged Sapphire Lion Emperor XVI Nelson Jeronimo and Her Most Imperial and Sovereign Majesty The Delicious & Nutritious, Crystal Fyed Pucci Peacock, Protector of Feathers, Flare and Fancy, Ethereal Erte Empress XVI Plum Vicious.

Come One, Come All

Charitable folk are always quick to offer a helping hand. Never more so than during the annual Masturbate-A-Thon, held every May. Participants are sponsored for every minute they stroke, finger, or feel themselves on the appointed day. And no timekeepers are necessary since the whole process operates on the honour system. The event, co-sponsored by **Come As You Are** (*701 Queen St. W., 416-504-7034, comeasyouare.com*) and three American sex shops, has raised US$20,000 for sexual health organizations since 1998. In 2003, the proceeds went to Voices of Positive Women, an advocacy group for HIV-positive women.

who has a bigger mouth? nooooo-body!

Photo: Nestor Ponce

He is the longest-serving mayor of any major city on record. Beginning with his first term in North York in 1973 and ending (after the 1997 amalgamation of six municipalities into a megacity) in downtown Toronto in 2003, Mel Lastman has been front and centre for a long, long time. This is not always a good thing. He's raised taxes, cut services, admitted to an adulterous affair that produced two sons, and has seen his administration embroiled in an ugly computer-leasing scandal. But, hey, he always gives good quote.

December 1969: After being elected to North York Board of Control. "Now all I want to know is, what does a controller do?"

March 1983: Explaining his suggestion that North York switch to Daylight Savings Time in March rather than April with the rest of the province. "Well, there are more car accidents at night."

May 1996: After calling Edmonton a "dull, flat town" and comparing it to a "clapboard outhouse," he flew there to have his ass literally kicked by a city councillor in the photo-op of all photo-ops. Humbled, Mel said "for me to say they live in outhouses is wrong and bad."

June 2001: Before flying to Africa to drum up support for Toronto's Olympic bid. "What the hell do I want to go to a place like Mombasa for ... I just see myself in a pot of boiling water with all these natives dancing around me."

Five Bygone By-laws

By-law 322, July 30, 1860

No snowballs are allowed in public parks. No archery allowed in public places.

By-law 375, November 10, 1862

All bread sold in the city shall be in loaves of 2 lbs. or 4 lbs. only. Any other size will be seized. This does not include biscuits, buns, rolls, crackers, or fancy cakes.

By-law 467, October 26, 1868

Do not let stud horses near mares in any public place.

By-law 477, October 26, 1868

Jugglers must be charged anywhere from five to 50 dollars for a license to practice in public.

By-law 478, October 26, 1868

No profane or insulting language shall be used in public streets or highways.

June 2001: During a press conference to deal with the fallout from the above comments. "I am truly sorry, and I'm going to say it again: I'm sorry that my comments were inappropriate. And I want to apologize to everyone for my remarks, particularly anyone who was offended by them." Or "I'm sorry I made the remarks. My comments were inappropriate." Or "It was just the wrong thing to say and I am sorry I said it. I mean, what do you want from me, except I'm sorry? I've apologized. I did the wrong thing." All in all, Mel said he was sorry 18 times.

OF COURSE, IF THEY KEPT WALKING LONG ENOUGH ...

In December 1997, *The Utne Reader* included the intersection of College and Clinton in its list of North America's 15 coolest neighbourhoods. It also advised readers in search of the "soon-to-be-hot" to "walk five minutes west to Kensington Market." Let's hope no one tried to take them up on it because, of course, Kensington Market is actually *east* of Clinton. Back in those days, if *UR*'s American editors had actually bothered to check out their recommended spots, they might have noticed the spooky coincidence that Clinton shares an intersection with Gore. The streets are probably not named after our friends to the south, but for Henry Clinton, Secretary for the Colonies (1852-1854) and Sir Francis Gore, Lieutenant Governor of Upper Canada (1806-1817).

Collapsible City

It's no secret homelessness is on the rise in Toronto. Since the late 1990s, apartment rents have gone up 35% while welfare has been cut 21%. That, and a rumoured 12-year wait for social housing, leads to something like Tent City, a squatter's community at the derelict industrial area at Lakeshore Boulevard East and Cherry Street. Tent City had as many as 110 homeless people living there at any one time. They hauled wood and cooked over open fires. There were long-term residents; one young couple even had a baby born there in June 2002. But prostitution was constant, five-dollar crack common. Still, for many, it was preferable to dirty, overcrowded shelters. Not so preferable, however, in the eyes of Home Depot, which owned the land. After intense news coverage (the *New York Times* reported that a shantytown existed in the shadow of Canada's richest banks), private security and the police raided Tent City one late September morning in 2002. Residents were forcibly removed, often without their belongings, and the land was bulldozed. However, the city did establish a rent supplement program for 100 squatters, providing an opportunity for some Tent City folks to live in their own apartments.

William Henry Jackson might have led the most interesting life you've never heard of. Born May 13, 1861, in Toronto, his family moved to Prince Albert, Saskatchewan and opened a farm implement business. Young Will, involved with farmer's rights, joined the local Settler's Union and helped to forge an alliance with the Métis and their fiery leader, Louis Riel. Jackson, who had a strong sense of justice, was so taken with the Métis cause that he became Riel's secretary. After the Northwest Rebellion in 1885, Jackson, wearing a Métis headband, was arrested by Canadian troops and sent to a lunatic asylum near Winnipeg. He soon escaped and fled to the United States, where he renounced his race and Protestant upbringing by changing his name to Honoré Jaxon.

He settled in New York City and for the last 30 years of his life, he haunted the libraries and bookshops there as he accumulated enough material to write the definitive history of Riel and Canadian Native people. On December 1951, the 90-year-old Jaxon was evicted from his tenement apartment for failure to pay the rent. Three men worked six hours to remove the tons of printed matter from the place. Out on the street, with much of his archive lost, he still held out hope of producing his history. He claimed the information was still locked up in his head but, alas, the key was lost when Jaxon died on January 10, 1952.

Photo City of Toronto Archives, Fonds 1267, 149

A CRACK IN THE GLASS CEILING

In 1893, William P. Hubbard (1842-1935) ran for alderman of what was then know as Toronto's Ward 4. The former master baker lost that year, but won the following year and was returned to office 13 times in the next 13 years. He spent eight years on the Board of Control, and served as Acting Mayor in 1906 and 1907. A champion of public energy (recent deregulation probably has him rolling in his grave) and small Chinese laundries, Hubbard was responsible for convincing the City to acquire the Toronto Islands. And, oh yes — he was black, the son of freed slaves from Virginia. The City has named a Race Relations Award in his honour.

Father Time

Photo: Glenbow Archives NA-1494-6

IN THE WORST OF TASTE

The proprietor of W.K. Drug Store, one William Knapp Buckley, is probably the most successful pharmacist in the history of this city. Back in 1919, he formulated an evil-tasting mixture of natural cough remedies, and the following year he began to sell it under the name of Buckley's Mixture. The number-one cough medicine in Canada stayed in the family for more than 80 years, passing from William to his son Frank. In 2002, it was sold to Swiss-based pharmaceutical giant Novartis; nonetheless, Buckley's continues to be manufactured locally, and will always be known for the fact that "it tastes awful. And it works."

Known as the "Father of Standard Time," Sir Sandford Fleming was responsible for gathering the appropriate authorities in Washington in 1884 to organize a standard mean time in North America and to divide the continent into time zones. The railways, who needed such a system most, actually adopted his measure before everybody else, in 1883. (Before that, every region set its own time according to local criteria, which clearly made for scheduling chaos.) Since he was in charge of the surveying, Fleming is one of the top-hatted gentlemen pictured at the driving of the last spike in the Canadian Pacific Railroad tracks. He also invented Canada's first postage stamp, worth three cents, with a picture of a beaver on it, to speed up the post offices. There's a plaque on Richmond Street East at Berti to commemorate the fact that "In a building which stood west of this site, Sanford Fleming (1827-1915) read a paper before the Canadian Institute on February 8, 1879, outlining his concept of a worldwide, uniform system for reckoning time."

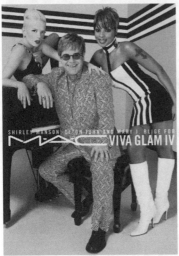

SHIRLEY MANSON, ELTON JOHN AND MARY J. BLIGE FOR
M·A·C VIVA GLAM IV

Now available in 36 countries, M·A·C· Cosmetics is a *force majeur* in the makeup world, but it started out at 233 Carlton Street back in 1985, when Toronto makeup artist Frank Toskan teamed up with marketing genius Frank Angelo to create and sell a line of cosmetics for industry professionals. Gordon Espinet, now Chief Makeup Artist for M·A·C· internationally, was one of a trio of freelancers who joined the company at the end of the '80s. Then, it had only twelve locations worldwide, including the flagship U.S. store on Christopher Street in Greenwich Village. According to Espinet, you could already see where the company was going in those days, especially when the paparazzi photographed Madonna jogging in her M·A·C· T-shirt. Soon, staff at the sole Markham warehouse couldn't turn out products quickly enough to satisfy the snowballing demand. Since 1994, M·A·C· has been owned by Estée Lauder, but it still maintains a distinctive Canadian personality. The company may be based in New York, says Espinet, "but we still spell 'colour' with a 'U'!" (In 2000 the M·A·C· AIDS Fund, whose spokespeople have included RuPaul, k.d. lang, Mary J. Blige, Elton John, and Lil' Kim, donated $250,000 to U.N. efforts to combat AIDS in Africa. The charity has raised more than $20 million since it was incorporated in 1994.)

RUNWAY SUCCESS

When she's not strutting the runway for Chanel, St. Laurent, Gucci, or Oscar de la Renta, top model Yasmin Warsame heads home to Toronto. Born into a family of 20 in Somalia, she began modelling in 2002; as soon as the industry caught a glimpse of those almond eyes, that generous mouth, and her finely-drawn figure, she was being booked by the likes of *Vogue* (Italian, British, *and* American), *Harpers Bazaar*, and The Gap. Despite her whirlwind international success, she still finds time for some local work: look for her in the pages of *Flare* and *Toronto Life Fashion*.

Photo: Thierry Legoues, Antik Batik Catalogue

We Can Dig It

They may not have gone equipped with bullwhips, but Toronto archaeologists have been exploring Egypt and other Middle Eastern destinations for more than 100 years. It started at the turn of the last century with Charles Trick Currelly, founder of the Royal Ontario Museum. As a young man, he learned about basic crafts like pottery and weaving from Native peoples and European settlers on the Prairies. Then he got a position on an Egyptian dig with the renowned British archaeologist Sir Flinders Petrie, acquiring further knowledge and the first of many artifacts. Much of the rest of his career was divided between trips to Toronto to convince wealthy patrons to sponsor more acquisitions, and travels to remote locations to bring them home. At one point, when the revolution was bringing great historical treasures out of China through highly irregular channels, Currelly was brought, blindfolded, to a London warehouse. As the blindfold was lifted, he caught a glimpse of the richest trove of Chinese antiquities he had ever seen – but suddenly the alarm was sounded and he was bundled out of the building, never to learn what became of them.

More recently, the University of Toronto's Donald Redford has become famous as the excavator of the fabled temple of the pharoah Akhenaten in East Karnak. Jack Holliday stood in the legendary footsteps of Moses and the Israelites at Tell el-Maskhuta in Lower Egypt, while former ROM Director Cuyler Young, born in Iran of missionary parents, returned there to dig at Godin Tepe, later excavating in Iraq and Turkey. Although the focus of field excavation in the modern era has moved away from treasure collecting, younger generations of scholars at the ROM – where Currelly's ghost is said to walk – and the University of Toronto are learning to read history in a potsherd, a fragment of bone, or a discoloured course of mud brick, and it's likely that Toronto will be sending archaeologists into the field for at least another 100 years.

YOU OUGHTA BE IN PICTURES

She may have been born in Australia (where she and her brother were the survivors of a quadruplet birth), but Etobicoke resident Cara Wakelin is such a Torontonian now that she posed in hockey gear for her Playmate shoot for *Playboy*. The blonde and perky Miss November of 1999 likes animals, and keeps a collection of dog and cat statuettes. She also had a small part ("Princess") in the filmed-in-Toronto *Death to Smoochy* (2002).

Everybody enjoys a good ghost story, but Albert Durrant Wilson of 10 Euclid Avenue maintained a particularly spirited interest in the next world. The poet/doctor, who lived from 1859 to 1926, published a number of books on the subject, including *Mediums and Mystics: A Study in Spiritual Laws and Psychic Forces*. More recently, author John Robert Colombo has documented lots of supernatural stories around Toronto, and the practical-minded Toronto Ghosts and Hauntings Research Society (*torontoghosts.org*) carries out site visits to follow up on reports of ghostly manifestations around the area.

Toronto provides lots of grist for the paranormal mill, with dozens of haunted buildings, of which the best known is probably University College. When the ornate building was being constructed, a rivalry sprang up between two stonemasons, Ivan Reznikoff and Paul Diabolos, who both loved the same woman. The fiery Russian Reznikoff is said to have taken up an axe and attacked Diabolos. (As proof, believers point to the scar in the outer door of Croft Chapter House at the southwest corner of the building, said to mark the place where Reznikoff swung and missed.) But Diabolos, apparently keeping a cooler head, defended himself capably and stabbed Reznikoff to death (or pushed him to a fatal fall; take your pick). Reznikoff's body was hidden, and a skeleton presumed to be his was discovered after a fire in the building in 1890. Now Reznikoff's bearded ghost haunts University College. (Apparently he sat down for quite a long chat at one

Photo: John Hood

point with lawyer Sir Allan Aylesworth.) Diabolos is supposed to have carved likenesses of himself and Reznikoff into two gargoyle masks outside Croft Chapter House; there's even a student café named for Diabolos.

A more touching story is that of Jemima Howard, wife of the John Howard who donated the land that is now High Park to the City. While she was fatally ill, Mrs. Howard lived at Colborne Lodge, which still stands. She would often go to the window to look out over the land,

HEAD HUNTER

Bill Jamieson has a head for collecting. Actually, he's got ten of them; among the tribal art dealer's incredible collection is a series of authentic shrunken heads. Two of them, with shaggy hair and dopey, sewn-shut eyes, he calls the Ramones. Another, with white skin and red hair, is Dr. Livingstone. They're displayed, along with Amazon hunting spears and throwing knives from Nagaland, in his two-storey condo-museum in the downtown fashion district.

Jamieson hunted down his first head in 1995. His *Globe and Mail* ad, "Wanted: authentic shrunken heads. Serious calls only," generated some press coverage and an encouraging phone call. An antique dealer had a head for sale and, a couple grand later, Jamieson was on his way.

Photo: Ontario Tourism, 10\90

including the family burial plot. Since she died in 1877, the ghost of Jemima Howard has often been seen at the upper window of Colborne Lodge, pointing to her own last resting place.

The Elgin Theatre has a phantom presence that likes to ride the old-fashioned elevator, usually calling it to the fifth floor. (This has been particularly noticed, since the Elgin is one of the very few buildings in the city – along with the Flatiron Building at 49 Wellington East and the Ontario Heritage Centre building at 10 Adelaide East – that still employs elevator operators.) But whether the ghost is that of an Edwardian lady thought to have been stabbed to death in a washroom, or of a theatre technician who died on the job, or of a young child who fell from one of the boxes, no one can agree.

Many private homes are also haunted. One of the spookiest tales is told of 121 Walmer Road in the Annex, where the owner of a cocker spaniel is supposed to have stabbed himself to death. Now, horrified visitors to the house apparently report seeing him re-enact his suicide, as the dog runs around him in circles.

Another haunted private home – albeit one that is now a public museum – is Mackenzie House at 82 Bond Street. In fact, the residence of Toronto's first Mayor, rebel leader William Lyon Mackenzie, is reputed

to be the scene of more ghost activity than any other building in the city. Both the firebrand himself, in clothes of his period, and his wife Isabel, with flowing hair, have been spotted. Some of the reputed activities include playing with the plumbing and other machinery, and clumping up and down the stairs.

Another coup came in 1998, when Jamieson bought the Niagara Falls Museum and its 19th-century collection of curiosities. Some of the goodies included a whale skeleton, now donated to the Royal Ontario Museum, and nine Egyptian mummies. Following up a hunch with some research, he discovered one of the mummies was the remains of Pharaoh Ramses I. So after 140 years in Niagara Falls, Ramses was sent off to Emory University in Atlanta, Georgia for study, before being sent back home to Egypt.

The Truth is Way, Way Out There

Where were you on October 20, 2002 at 11:30 p.m.? Were you staring up at the night sky? If so, you might've seen a strange, orange-coloured object zip through the clouds at tremendous speed. And you wouldn't have been alone. A couple driving north on Jane Street saw it, as did a High Park man while smoking a cigarette in his back yard. Multiple witnesses make UFO sightings more irrefutable, according to Ufology Research of Manitoba, which recorded 34 separate incidents around Toronto in 2002.

All of which makes sense to Commander X, mysterious author of *Underground Alien Bases*. According to the Commander, aliens have set up secret bases inside the planet Earth. Entrances exist in major cities and are connected by an ancient tunnel system. In Toronto, there is supposed to be an entrance off Parliament Street, "between two buildings" and then down a sewer. The centre of Toronto's secret base lies below the intersection of Church and Gerrard, which is why, the Commander explains, there is a very high accident rate at that corner. Seems powerful alien equipment emits such a strong magnetic field that many motor vehicles above ground run haywire.

Born Again, and Again and Again

Charles Spiegel was a born leader. Or perhaps, he was a reborn leader. His 1985 autobiography, *Confessions of I, Bonaparte*, reveals his previous lives. Napoleon. Pontius Pilate. Tyrantus, an emperor from the Orion star system. So even though he entered our material plane in Toronto in 1922, Spiegel has the perfect resumé for the Unarius Society. Founded in 1954 by Ruth and Ernest Norman, the Unariuns are a southern California group who are awaiting the arrival of aliens. Spiegel, who became the Unariuns' director after the 1993 death of Ruth Norman, expected the lost city of Atlantis to rise out of the Caribbean in 2001. Then, aliens from the planet Myton would land and offer great knowledge to the people of Earth. Alas, this doesn't appear to have happened. Was Spiegel disappointed? No way of knowing. He died just days before the start of the 21st century. His journey continues.

HERE TO STAY

Toronto has attracted some pretty notable residents over the years, and we think that the kind of people who pick this city as their home says a lot about the character of this place.

• The author of the revolutionary 1961 book *The Death and Life of Great American Cities* — which radically changed the way city planners look at urban design — would have been welcomed in any town in North America. But Jane Jacobs chose Toronto, and her diminutive silver-haired figure can be seen making its way around the Annex neighbourhood in a characteristic, and somewhat ragged, striped poncho.

• Maybe he doesn't feel the lurking menace of the "undertoad" here as badly as some other places. For whatever reason, John Irving, author of such deeply appreciated books as *The World According to Garp*, has spent long periods of time as a resident of Toronto and a teacher at The Bishop Strachan School.

Just Visiting

Toronto has seen its share of famous visitors of all descriptions. Nonetheless, a few stand out from the tourist throng....

• Charles Dickens included Toronto on his North American tour in the 1840s. He was pleased to note "a good stone prison" among the amenities, and remarked that "In the College of Upper Canada ... a sound education in every department of polite education can be had, at a very modest expense...." (Which may still be true of the quality of the education, but not the cost!)

• In 1919, Marcus Garvey founded Toronto's Universal Negro Improvement Association Building at 355 College Street (now the home of a chiropractic clinic). Prominent touring black musicians used to stay there in the days when many Toronto hotels were not so hospitable to them.

• Anarchist Emma Goldman spent the end of her life in Toronto. When she died here in 1940, her body lay in state in the Labour Lyceum on Spadina near Kensington Market until it could be moved to Chicago for burial.

• When beloved film star Gina Lollobrigida's son was born in 1957, the Italian government refused to grant him citizenship (her husband, Milko Skofic, was Yugoslavian). Much miffed, La Lollo flounced straight to Toronto, where she lived happily until the flap was sorted out. She even had her own private policeman.

• In February of 1977, the Rolling Stones thought it would be fun to play a small club gig, so they arranged with the group April Wine that the Canadian rockers would headline a show at the El Mocambo on Spadina, while the Stones would appear lower down on the bill under the assumed name of The Cockroaches. Things didn't go exactly as planned. First Keith Richards was arrested at the Toronto airport for drug possession. Then Margaret, bored wife of then-PM Pierre Trudeau, took it into her head to have a bit of a party with the band, and what had been envisioned as a quiet little rock 'n' roll in-joke turned into one of the most notorious club dates in Canadian history. (In a remarkably enlightened judicial decision, Richards was sentenced for his crimes to perform a benefit concert for the Canadian National Institute for the Blind, which took place on April 22, 1979, not in Toronto but in neighbouring Oshawa's Civic Auditorium.)

• Kim Phuc may have done as much to end the Vietnam War as any activist when photographer Nick Ut recorded his unforgettable image of her at the age of nine, naked, terrified, and burned with napalm as she fled the bombing of Trang Bang. Now a UNESCO Goodwill Ambassador, Kim lives in Ajax, just outside Toronto.

• We've seen princes come and go, but the only one reported to have bought a home here is Prince Rogers Nelson, he of the various former names, including a symbol. In 2002 the royal rocker reportedly bought a $5.5 million mansion on the Bridle Path with 19 rooms and a tennis court.

Living

Who Is Toronto? As of the 2001 Census, there were 2,481,494 people living in Toronto proper, and 4,647,955 in the Greater Toronto Area. Over half usually speak English at home; about 8% usually speak Chinese, and almost 5% speak Italian. Seventeen language groups have more than 10,000 speakers. Regardless of what language they speak, more than a quarter of a million people consider themselves to be Chinese, another quarter-million say they're South Asian, and the black population numbers over 200,000.

Those who still think of Toronto as a Protestant stronghold might be shocked to know that Roman Catholics are by far the largest group, with Protestants in second place, and people of no declared religious affiliation not too far behind in third. The number who say they have no religion is growing, but not as fast as the numbers of Muslims, Sikhs, Hindus, and Buddhists, which all doubled – or more than doubled – over the past decade. (We also have a few who officially profess to be Pagans, Wiccans, Satanists, and followers of the Jedi faith.)

The numbers give a sense of what every street, school, and subway car clearly shows. Toronto lives up to its UNESCO designation as the world's most multicultural city, and that means that everybody who lives here has an amazing choice of things to do, eat, see, and experience.

Dollars and Sense

Everyone likes a little bang for their buck. The good folks in the St. Lawrence 'hood get more than most. Residents from the area at Jarvis Street and The Esplanade swap their regular money for Toronto Dollars and spend the alternative currency at any of the 200 stores and restaurants that accept them. Merchants then turn the Toronto Dollars back into cash, with 10% going to charity. Since 1998, when the Toronto Dollar Community Project (*torontodollar.com*) was launched, almost $40,000 has been raised for youth programs, church groups and food drives. Now that's smart shopping.

seasons of life

It's a truism that living in a multi-ethnic city exposes you to other cultures, but Toronto actually does immerse its residents — sometimes boisterously and unexpectedly — in the street festivals and religious ceremonies of many nations. One minute you may be strolling to the corner store for milk; the next you're part of a Felliniesque carnival, or maybe confronting a lion dancer. Some celebrations are mostly carried out inside private homes. (This would apply to the Muslim Eid, the Persian new year No Ruz, which falls on the first day of spring, and most of the Jewish holidays. Although, if you have Jewish friends, you might be lucky enough to be invited to see the inside of an outdoor *succah*, the "tabernacle" where the family eats during the autumn Succoth, which commemorates the wandering of the Jews in the desert.) But many celebrations are much more public.

Chinese New Year

The rules for calculating the date of Chinese New Year are a little bit complicated; let's just say that it always falls on a new moon between January 21 and February 21. So: 2004 is a Monkey year, 2005 is Rooster, 2006 is Dog, and so on through Pig, Rat, Ox, Tiger, Rabbit, Dragon, Snake, Horse, Sheep/Goat, and back (in 2016) to Monkey again. Around the New Year you'll see restaurants and shops decorated with pictures of coins, the animal of the year, and the decorative red paper envelopes that are given as gifts (containing money, of course). If you're walking in certain neighbourhoods at the right time — like Gerrard Street at Broadview, Spadina around Dundas, or in the Chinese malls — you may be lucky enough to encounter the clashing cymbals and drumbeats that herald the arrival of Chinese lion dancers, hidden under the movable head, body, and tail of an ornate fabric beast. (Most often these are performed by members of a martial arts academy, because the disciplines are linked; watch the careful leg postures of a good ensemble.)

Easter

Leading up to Easter, Italian shops become festive with shelves of football-sized, foil-wrapped, toy-filled chocolate eggs for children, bread embedded with

TOP 20 HOME LANGUAGES

1. English: 2,902,975
2. Chinese: 190,295
3. Italian: 51,805
4. Punjabi: 49,180
5. Portuguese: 37,055
6. Tamil: 36,225
7. Spanish: 27,520
8. Polish: 25,535
9. Russian: 22,915
10. Farsi: 21,020
11. Urdu: 20,255
12. Vietnamese: 19,660
13. Korean: 18,950
14. Tagalog: 17,500
15. Arabic: 15,520
16. Greek: 12,635
17. Gujarati: 11,635
18. French: 9,870
19. Romanian: 5,975
20. Hindi: 4,980

coloured eggs, and sugar or marzipan lambs. (The same phenomenon occurs on the Danforth, but the Greek Orthodox Church celebrates Easter one week later.) At 3 p.m. on each Good Friday, St. Francis' Church (*72 Mansfield Ave.*) holds its legendary annual procession depicting the final hours of Jesus Christ leading up to the crucifixion. The characters of the drama are played with appropriate passion by parishioners, always accompanied by representatives of the many Italian social clubs (*circoli*) sporting colourful, medieval-style sashes and banners. The next day, Easter Saturday, it seems as though every man, woman, and child on Roncesvalles is carrying a pretty little lace-covered basket. These traditional Polish Easter baskets, containing bread, meat, flowers, and so on, will be taken to church to be blessed, then returned to the home to bring blessing and plenty to the household in the coming year. Then on the day itself, the Beaches community celebrates with an Easter Parade on Queen Street that has become a major annual event.

Senhor Santo Cristo dos Milagres

Photo: Sarah B. Hood

'Round about May, the east side of Bathurst at Adelaide sprouts such an array of lights that you'd almost think Christmas was back again. Since 1966, that's been the time when St Mary's Catholic Church (*589 Adelaide St. W.*) organizes this Azorean festival. On Saturday afternoon, the flower-decked image of Jesus Christ takes a brief tour around the block, accompanied by pageantry and huge crowds; on the Sunday there's a longer procession. Senhor Santo Cristo dos Milagres can fall as early as April 26 or as late as May 30; it's always the fifth Sunday after Easter.

Rathayatra, the Festival of Chariots

For the past 30 years, the International Society for Krishna Consciousness (*243 Avenue Rd., 416-922-5415*) has been organizing this mid-July festival, which involves a procession of three gorgeous flower-decked

Photo: Sarah B. Hood

chariots – carrying Lord Jagannatha, Lord Baladeva, and Lady Subhadra – down Yonge Street from Bloor to the harbour. Anyone who takes up a rope to help pull a chariot is endowed with special grace. And anyone who crosses the water with the celebrants is invited to a free outdoor vegetarian feast on Centre Island – not to mention the Indian music and dance.

Diwali

This Hindu festival of lights is another movable feast that falls somewhere in October or November, according to the date of the month of Ashwin. It welcomes Lakshmi, goddess of wealth and prosperity, and – like many other world customs in early winter – is the reassurance that light and goodness will endure against darkness and evil. Every home is lit up inside with the little clay oil lamps called *diyas*, which are sold in crates outside Indian shops. Public businesses decorate themselves with Christmas-type lights, and in Indian neighbourhoods like Gerrard, from Greenwood to Coxwell, sidewalks bustle as music is broadcast into the streets. (Confusingly, some of it sounds like calypso or dancehall reggae; that's because Toronto has a huge Indo-Caribbean population, so the form affectionately known as chutney soca gets mixed in among the bhangra and classical tunes.)

Christmas

If you really rate in the Caribbean community, you may get a Christmastime visit from a Parang group. Like mummering, it's a door-to-door practice. It brings groups of singers to household parties to entertain with traditional Spanish-language songs accompanied by the rhythm of the stringed *cuatro* in return for food and drink (usually rum). For the rest of us, one of the most cheering manifestations of seasonal celebration is in the light displays of homes and businesses. And some people take their Christmas lights very seriously indeed! Take the Musson family of 3360 Spruce Avenue in Burlington. Their overwhelming exhibit is famous, and people drive great distances to see the house swathed in strings of

TOP 10 RELIGIONS

1. Roman Catholic: 771,190
2. Protestant: 520,400
3. No religious affiliation: 463,165
4. Muslim: 165,135
5. Orthodox Christian: 119,365
6. Hindu: 118,765
7. Jewish: 103,500
8. Other Christian: 96,340
9. Buddhist: 66,510
10. Sikh: 22,565

brilliant colours, with manger figures, Santa, and a host of related displays. There are neighbourhoods that almost seem to be in competition, like Cosborn (north of the Danforth) between Woodbine and Coxwell, and the high rises of Jameson Avenue. On Jones Avenue below Danforth, a family in the film business has wowed the neighbours for many years with their Grinch-themed display, complete with swaying Whos. And Cabbagetown is always pretty with cedar swags and red velvet bows. The perspicacious will note, however, that while the one-of-a-kind Jet Fuel Coffee Shop (*519 Parliament St.*) has finally agreed to the cedar, they refuse the bows: the only shop on the strip with the temerity to do so!

News of the World

The are easily 200 ethnic community newspapers and magazines published around Toronto, not to mention neighbourhood papers like *Toronto Voice* in the east end, *Beach Metro Community News*, *The Lakesider*, and the informative *What's On Queen*, covering Queen Street from east to west. There are roughly two dozen South Asian publications, about 15 papers serving each of the Hispanic, Chinese, and Caribbean communities, and about ten each for the Italian, Portuguese, and Greek communities, to name only a few. (Outlets are launched and disappear again, and some are difficult to track, so it's tricky to come up with exact figures.)

Some of the most important community voices are the French-language *L'Express de Toronto*, Daniel Ianuzzi's Italian-language stalwart *Corriere Canadese*, the *Canadian Jewish News*, and the gay/lesbian *Xtra!* The Chinese-language readership is served by not one, not two, but three dailies: *Ming Pao*, *Sing Tao*, and *World Journal*. They make up the paper in partnership with their Asian counterparts, adding local sections in with world news coming from Hong Kong, for example. (Times zone delays make this easier than it might otherwise be.) The Caribbean communities are especially well represented with print media. Among the longest-established are Arnold Auguste's *Share*, *Caribbean Camera*, *Pride*, *Jamaican Weekly Gleaner*, and the urban monthly *Word Magazine*.

Some of the best events in the city are the annual block parties put on by community-minded spirits who like to celebrate on their own doorsteps. On the first Sunday in May, as distinctive golden blossoms burst forth in local gardens, residents of Cabbagetown celebrate the **Forsythia Festival**. Children and their dogs, bedecked with shredded yellow paper and plastic garlands to represent the shrub of the hour, parade through the streets east of Parliament between Carlton and Wellesley, with a big finish among the budding trees at Wellesley Park on the edge of the Don Valley.

It may be Simcoe Day weekend to you, but to the community of Ward's Island, it's **Gala Day** weekend, when the Islanders celebrate their continuing residency with bingo for the grownups and games for the kids. But adventurous city-siders who venture across the water at dusk on the Friday will encounter the wildest and most wonderful part of the festivities: an annual lantern parade through the narrow lanes, ending with a bonfire and drumming on the beach.

The Republic of Rathnally was created in 1967, the year of Canada's Centennial, when the inhabitants of Rathnelly Street (west of Avenue Road, north of the railway line at Dupont) appointed a queen for themselves and broke away from the rest of the nation. Almost 40 years later, they still close the streets for **Rathnally Day** (spelled, like the Republic but unlike the street, with an "a") every second summer.

Finally, it may be only one block long, but that doesn't prevent residents of **Draper Street** (running north off Front Street between Bathurst and Spadina) from putting on their own party every August. In fact, with potluck fare, games, and other entertainment (a full samba band turned up one year), Draperites may have more fun per square foot than any other inhabitants of the city.

GLOBAL GROCERIES

When the recipe calls for *nam pla* or *nori*, an adventurous chef may have to look beyond the corner grocer. **Hua-Sheng Supermarket** (*293-299 Spadina Ave., 416-263-9883*) is a dependable source for a wide range of Chinese and Southeast Asian ingredients. (However, fresh produce and seafood may be cheaper at nearby sidewalk stalls and shops, or at the intersection of Gerrard and Dundas.) As its name suggests, **Korean and Japanese Oriental Food** (*430 Parliament, 416-972-6075*) carries sushi fixings and the like, and so does Japanese shop **Sanko** (*730 Queen St. W., 416-703-4550, toronto-sanko.com*). **BJ Supermarket** (*449 Gerrard St. E.*)

Photo: Sarah B. Hood

Families with the perseverance to use cloth diapers can call upon **Comfy Cotton Diaper Service** in Markham (*905-940-8118, comfycotton.ca*) with the certainty that they'll use environmentally friendly detergents. But even the most diligent families will use disposables some of the time. For them, Torontonian Marlene Conway is a heroic figure. In the late 1980s, she invented the world's first practical system for recycling disposable diapers, as well as some other absorbent fibres that usually end up in landfill. Conway founded the New York-based Knowaste Technologies Inc., but Torontonians can still use her system by having their baby's diapers recycled through **Small Planet** (*905-568-8442, smallplanetinc.com*).

There aren't many activities for newborns, which may be one of the reasons why the **Parent-Child Mother Goose Program** (*416-588-5234, nald.ca/mothergooseprogram*) has spread across Canada and into the U.S. and Australia since it was founded in Toronto in 1986. Mother Goose teaches songs and rhymes as parenting tools for parents of babies up to the age of 2½. From 2½ to 4, storytelling becomes the focus.

Moms and dads seeking a semblance of their pre-baby lives rejoice when they find a welcoming neighbourhood cafe like **Alternative Grounds** (*333 Roncesvalles Ave., 416-534-6335, alternativegrounds.com*). It has a doorway ramp to make stroller access easy, and toys for older kids. **Movies For Mommies** (*905-707-8866, movies4mommies.com*) arranges weekday matinees with amenities like stroller parking, changing tables, free baby wipes, bottle warming, and lower-volume soundtracks at the Fox Cinema, the Music Hall, and the Bloor. The similar **CineBabies** (*416-398-6452, cinebabies.com*) uses the SilverCity theatres at Yonge and Eglinton, and in Richmond Hill and Newmarket, as well as the Coliseum in Mississauga. Parents who miss the gym and the dance floor will find locations where they can work out or even practice Latin dance moves with their infants at the sites *fitmomcanada.com*, *ballroombabies.ca*, and *salsababies.com*.

And yes, the quintessential baby souvenir is still available through **The Baby Shoe Bronzers** (*12921 Keele St., King City, 416-482-6713*).

and other grocers on the Gerrard Indian strip stock a complete range of Indian foods (including boxes of inexpensive ripe mangos in season). The Tamil shops clustered on the east side of Parliament just south of Wellesley extend this range even further. **Nicey's Food Mart** (*621 Vaughn Rd., 416-656-5648, niceysfoodmart.com*) is a convenient outlet for Caribbean groceries; Nicey's has seven locations around Toronto and the surrounding area. Abdulrahmn Ibrahim at **Ethiopian Spices** (*160 Baldwin St., 416-598-3014*) carries tef flour (and the freshest, spongiest rounds of injera bread), along with everything else for the Ethiopian kitchen, including English-language cookbooks.

Photo: Sarah B. Hood

Romantic Torontonians can celebrate their wedding in one of Toronto's beautiful historic buildings, like Spadina House with its sensational gardens, Colborne Lodge in High Park, Cedar Ridge Creative Centre in Scarborough, or Zion Church, which dates from 1873. These spots are the purview of the **City of Toronto's Facility Rental Coordinator** (*416-338-0030*). Those who – like political powerhouse duo Jack Layton and Olivia Chow – fancy an Island wedding need only call the **Algonquin Island Association Clubhouse** (*416-203-0965*) for rates and scheduling. Specializing in contemporary *mandaps* (the archway-and-dais layouts for Indian weddings) is **Modern Mandap** (*416-834-6519, modernmandap.com*). They can customize layout, flowers, candles, and symbology for Hindu, Sikh, or Muslim ceremonies. Invitations? **Pantry Press and Greenstreet Design** (*103 Roncesvalles, 416-537-9977*) uses lovely old presses, and handles the printing of many of the west end's art exhibition catalogues. Ayoma Fonseca of **Ayoma Cake Masterpieces** (*416-225-9442, ayomacakes.com*) is the fanciest wedding cake baker in town. She whips up fabulous creations with hand coloured, handmade edible flowers. The fellow to call for an ice sculpture – say, of the wedding party – is **The Iceman** (a.k.a. Adam Cummings) at 416-504-6615. **Greenery Patch** (*753 Queen St. W., 416-703-1880; 2199 Queen St. E., 416-690-1282*) started out as a really nice florist's shop, but owner Lisa Latour found the boundaries of her business gradually expanding until it encompassed all aspects of wedding planning. Now engaged couples can look to her not just for the bouquet, but for the whole shebang.

Why Have Your Cake? Just Eat It!

Altitude

Dennis Findlay's wonderful cakes must rank among the top ten reasons to venture east of the Don Valley. *1346 Queen St. E., 416-461-7519*

Athena Bakery

For when you're seeking baklava, melomakarona, and other honey-soaked Greek sweets. *598 Danforth Ave., 416-462-1411*

Photo: Sarah B. Hood

Photo: Sarah B. Hood

Danish Style Cakeshop and Delicatessen

Strangely, this east-end establishment bakes *English style* teatime snacks — like Eccles cakes, Chelsea buns, and brandy snaps — on the premises, as well as breads, cookies, and eclairs that aren't half bad. It also stocks herring and other more "Danish style" items, but it's definitely more of a cakeshop than a deli.
1027 Kingston Rd., 416-694-5333

Furama Cake and Dessert Garden

Orgasmic, creamy vanilla cakes alongside Chinese savouries like pork buns.
248 Spadina Ave., 416-504-5709

Ho Do Kwa Ja

Those addictive little walnut-shaped and filled Korean mini-cakes!
656 Bloor St. W., 416-538-1208

There are bulk candy stores all over town, but the original is **Sugar Mountain**. Its founder Sean McCann started out in 1992 selling candy on the sidewalks of Queen West, acquiring his first storefront three years later. His fascination with nostalgic retro candy led him deeper and deeper into what was becoming a vanishing industry of local factories producing their own signature specialties. McCann eventually located sources all across the continent for the candies that we cherished in our childhoods, like licorice pipes, wax lips, Rockets, and black balls.

Then he went one step beyond, actually acquiring the exclusive license to produce certain items that were no longer available – like Black Cat Cigarettes – while his east-end warehouse became a veritable museum of Pez. Now there are four stores in Toronto, with others in Belleville, Ottawa, Waterloo, Winnipeg, and Vancouver, ensuring an ongoing supply of important staples like Chupa Chups, Big League Chew, Garbage Candy, Cracker Jacks, Pop Rocks, and of course Tootsie Pops, for generations to come.

Photo: Sarah B. Hood

Flour

These days everyone knows Ace Bakery, but there are lesser-known wheat wizards around town. Formerly located on Queen Street East, **A Slice of Life Bakery** (*285 Coxwell Ave., 416-463-5974*) bakes on premises daily (Wednesdays are gluten-free!) and makes the best gingerbread people anywhere ... they have cardamom in them. The bread is organic and usually made with honey instead of sugar. **Alchemy Baking** (*938 Bathurst St., 416-531-2471*) creates gorgeous loaves of organic blue corn with jalapeño and other exotic combinations, but we love it because it's the only place we know that makes lavender shortbread.

Sugar

It seems that one of the least explored desserts is *burfi*, the Indian equivalent of fudge. Coloured in soft pinks, pale whites, and the vivid green of pistachio, it's sometimes topped in real silver foil. Some outlets include **Surati Sweet Mart** (*1407 Gerrard St. E., 416-462-3480*) and

Photo: Sarah B. Hood

Punjab Foods and Sweets (*1448 Gerrard St. E., 416-466-4647*). At Christmastime, the Italian **Riviera Bakery Ltd.** (*576 College St., 416-537-3465*) brings out its home-made and gorgeous marzipan fruit, almost too precious to eat. And for the quintessential Canadian sugar hit, you can order maple syrup and leaf-shaped sugar treats online at **ontariomaplesyrup.com**.

Coffee

Coffee drinkers love their morning jolt, but the people who have the really jarring lives are the coffee pickers. Things are slowly changing with the Fair Trade movement, which fosters decent wages and long-term trading relationships between growers and distributors.

Photo: Howard Akler

BAD ON THE NERVES

Annex-area coffee drinkers got a little jittery in 1996, when neighbourhood fave **Dooney's Café** looked to be on the way out. Dooney's owner Graziano Marchese was told his lease would not be renewed. Starbucks was on the way in. But the deal turned into a public relations disaster for the American coffee chain when petitions were quickly signed and protests grew loud. Chants of "Yankee Go Home!" even greeted a Starbucks on Queen West. So the chain backed out of the agreement and paid $40,000 for a full-page ad in the *Toronto Star*, saying they were a good corporate citizen and wouldn't dream of upsetting the neighbourhood. Dooney's would stay. And so would Starbucks, which moved in across the street just a few years later.

The two main local suppliers of Fair Trade coffee are **Alternative Grounds** (*333 Roncesvalles Ave., 416-534-6335, alternativegrounds.com*) and **Moonbean Coffee Company** (*30 St. Andrew St., 416-595-0327, moonbeancoffee.com*). All of Moonbean's and most of Alternative Grounds' blends are organic, too. **Big Carrot** (*348 Danforth Ave., 416-466-2129*) carries several organic and Fair Trade brands, as do **Down Under Health Food** (*491 Church St., 416-928-0807, downunderhealth.com*) and **Baldwin Natural Foods** (*20½ Baldwin St., 416-979-1777*). Meanwhile, the **Merchants of Green Coffee** (*2 Matilda St., 416-778-6600*) offer green (unroasted) Fair Trade, sustainably produced coffee. They'll even sell you a roaster to roast your own beans.

Tea

When teatime rolls around, it's nice to have a choice of blends in the cupboard. **House of Tea** (*1015 Yonge St., 416-922-1226*) and **Ten Ren's Tea & Ginseng Co.** (*454 Dundas St. W., 416-598-7872; Pacific Mall in Mississauga; 103-330 Hwy 7, Richmond Hill*) are the city's best suppliers of teas and herbal teas from around the world. If you prefer to step out to sip a cup, there's the delicious little **Red Tea Box** (*696 Queen St. W., 416-203 8882*), which more than fulfills the promise of the wonky, wonderful marzipan-coated layer cakes in the window. Since it's tiny, and they don't take reservations, be prepared to kill some time. For the most luxurious version of the afternoon pick-me-up, head to **Le Royal Meridien King Edward Hotel** (*37 King St. E., 416-863-3131*), where a complete British high tea is still served between 2:30 and 4:30 p.m. every Thursday to Sunday. At $28 per person, you may not be doing it every day, but the price includes a selection of mini-sandwiches, mini-pastries, and the obligatory fresh scones with Devonshire cream and strawberry preserves, all served in royal style. The experience is guaranteed to make you feel like the Queen herself (reservations are highly recommended). Newer and a little bit more affordable, at $19 for high tea, is the Victorian-style tea room **La Tea Da** (*2305 Queen St. E., 416-686-5787*).

THE LOVE BEAN

Plenty of romances begin over a cup of coffee; this one started with an entire espresso machine. Jackie Zuccarini met Rocco Di Donato at a trade show in 1986. Both were working for the family business: she sold Gaggia espresso machines for Zuccarini Importing Company, he sold for Faema. Their fathers were intense rivals, so any attraction was bound to be a potent brew. They began seeing each other secretly, but the Romeo-and-Juliet romance had to come out in the open when wedding bells began to ring. So they spilled the beans and got a sure sign of acceptance: the two fathers traded sips of coffee at the wedding in 1989. Today, two kids later, Jackie and Rocco still work for rival companies. "At work, we're competitors," says Jackie. "But at home, we're partners."

chocolate heaven

The Belgian Chocolate Shop

Proprietors Eric and Patricia make molded chocolates with a hard, lustrous shell and a soft centre, rather than dipped truffles with a firmer gamache centre, but they're pretty and tasty.
2455 Queen St. E., 416-691-1424

The Chocolate Addict

Only a few years old, this is a comparative newcomer to the world of confectionery, but it's unique for its unusual flavours of chocolate truffles, like basil, wasabe, delicious lavender with white chocolate, and milk chocolate with hot chili pepper. Who orders that one, we ask? Girls, they reply.
185 Baldwin St., 416-979-5809

Ed's Real Scoop

Ed Francis is the most versatile of the chocolate artists. He makes a limited but delectable range of dipped truffles and chocolate-covered orange peel, ginger, and Oreos. He also got himself obsessed at one point with the question as to why the family fudge recipe was so unpredictable, figured out the chemistry in detail, and now offers a selection of fudge as well. But he's probably best loved for his house ice cream, made right in the shop in an array of flavours for cones or take-home tubs.
2224 Queen St. E., 416-699-6100

Simryn

Family-run Simryn tempers its truffles to a hard exterior finish, but the interiors are silky and strongly flavoured, and the shop offers sugar-free dark chocolates.
147A Danforth Ave., 416-778-7978

Stubbe Chocolate & Pastry Ltd.

Here's our favourite. Daniel Stubbe is a sixth generation chocolatier; his great-great-great grandfather started the business back on May 9, 1845 in the town of Meppen, Germany, and his father runs a shop in Ottawa. Patterned after the German Konditorei, his shop sells tortes and cookies, but chocolate is the predominant theme, and there are never fewer than 22 kinds of truffles on hand. (We like their Pear William and Gewurtztraminer.) Home confectioners can drop

Be My Sweet Tart!

Fran's

The once-mighty Fran's empire — for so long a Toronto icon — has shrunk to just one store, but Fran Deck's legacy lives on in the old-fashioned diner-style pies baked on the premises. These days the only year-round home-made pies are apple and lemon meringue. Any others are from outside sources, except seasonal specialities: pumpkin for Thanksgiving and mincemeat at Christmas and Easter.
20 College St., 416-923-9867

Photo: Sarah B. Hood

Nova Era

They pride themselves on their fancy wedding cakes, but we're drawn to the simple, flaky, perfect Portuguese custard tarts (and the crusty buns).
1172 Dundas St. W., 416-538-7700;
490 Rogers Rd., 416-651-5000;
770 College St., 416-516-1622;
980 Bloor St. W., 416-531-1222,
bridal.ca/novaera

in for supplies of raw chocolate, nuts, and fillings, as well as helpful advice from the master on the delicate art of tempering the temperamental treat. Stubbe also molds chocolate figures on request from antique or heirloom molds that customers may own but feel too timid to use at home.
253 Davenport Rd., 416-923-0956

The Queen of Tarts

Once located on Bathurst, the Queen of Tarts continues to make some of the most beautiful savoury and dessert tarts in town. Their "Seasonally Evolving" list makes the fruit and berries the stars (as in Hazelnut frangipane with plums or pears), while their Mexican chocolate and chipotle tart is renowned. They also bake the most sophisticated iced gingerbread and sugar cookies: Maple Leafs, Osmonds, Good and Evil Martha, and so on.
283 Roncesvalles Ave., 416-651-3009

Vienna Home Bakery

A little homier, less fanciful than the Queen of Tarts, Vienna Home Bakery nonetheless bakes up exquisite seasonal pies and tarts, like the excellent autumn pumpkin pies for people with busy schedules and a roster of Thanksgiving guests.
626 Queen St. W., 416-703-7278

just chillin'

The inquisitive ice cream fan will want to drop in to the nearest Indian grocery or paan shop to try *kulfi*, Indian ice cream. Available in flavours like mango and strawberry, it's most often to be found in the form of small, paper-wrapped popsicle-type treats-on-a-stick, but here's a hot tip: very tasty pistachio *kulfi* is available in tubs at a few outlets, including **BJ Supermarket** (*449 Gerrard St. E.*). For the western variety, we've already mentioned **Ed's Real Scoop** (*2224 Queen St. E., 416-699-6100*) for his chocolate; here are some other ice cream geniuses.

Dutch Dreams

This is the ultimate kid's fantasy, with its whacky, colourful sign, home-made ice cream, and fantastically opulent cones and sundaes. (And it appears in the 1998 movie *Half Baked*.)
78 Vaughan Rd., 416-656-6959

Greg's Ice Cream

Greg's natural ingredients and fresh flavours (like coconut) are often one of the first urban discoveries made by new students when they get to the University for the first time.
200 Bloor St. W., 416-961-4734

Ice Cream Junction

An evocative, old-fashioned ice cream parlour adjacent to an antique shop.
2896 Dundas St. W., 416-766-6342

Toto, I Don't Think We're in Outremont Anymore

Photo: John Hood

To paraphrase the famous Montreal bakery slogan, "you don't have to be Jewish" – or Francophone – to crave characteristic Montreal foods in Toronto, and you can always tell a recent ex-Montrealer by her or his wistful recollection of true bagels, excellent deli food, and competent snow removal.

Sadly, we haven't found any place in Toronto that can truly match a smoked meat sandwich on the Main, nor is a knish here the same as a knish there, nor is pepperoni, nor is pizza, nor are subs. Take comfort, though! The most homesick *Montréalais(e)* has to love the croissants baked fresh every morning at **Daniel et Daniel** (*248 Carlton St., 416-968-9275, ext. 15*), one of the few places in town that understands the noble French art of sandwiching the thinnest layers of butter between the finest leaves of pastry. They're only available in the one location, and if you wait too late in the day they'll be gone! Other notable *patisseries* are **Rahier Patisserie** (*1717 Bayview Ave., 416-482-0917*), **Tournayre Patisserie** (*1856 Queen St. E., 416-693-7997*), and **Patachou** (*1095 Yonge St., 416-927-1105*).

For some reason, Torontonians call any donut-shaped bun a bagel. However, a few locations bake the properly twisted sweet, eggy dough in wood-fired ovens, and they distribute to many outlets around town. None is perfect, but three come close: **St. Urbain Bagel Bakery** (*St. Lawrence Market, 416-364-8305; 895 Eglinton Ave. W., 416-787-6955; 7077 Bathurst St.,*

Hemp

The Friendly Stranger

A popular purveyor of goods related to "cannabis culture," the Stranger carries hemp fabric items, as well as books, jewellry, cosmetics, and (surprise) pipes and rolling papers. 241 Queen St. W., 416-591-1570, friendlystranger.com

Photo: Sarah B. Hood

Hempola

They're actually located a little bit north of Toronto, but Hempola Valley Farms retails its yummy hemp massage oils, lip balms, soaps, and salad dressings widely in the city. Watch for their hemp festival late in the summer.

2133 Forbes Rd., RR#1 Barrie, 800-240-9215, hempola.com

Ruth's Hemp Foods

A Toronto-based company producing hemp oil, salad dressings, chips, pasta, and other foods. Their products are available in health food stores and some of the fancier grocery outlets around town.

416-588-4209, ruthsfoods.ca

THC (Toronto Hemp Company)

Hemp-based clothing, papers and pipes, incense, patches, books and comics, and gardening supplies — including *Psilocybe cubensis* mushroom spores — for adventurous souls with green thumbs.

667 Yonge Street, 416-923-3556, torontohemp.com

905-731-8305), **Brick Oven Bagels** (*35-2700 Dufferin St., 416-256-1633*), and the most recently opened **Kettleman's Bagel Co.** (*542 Danforth Avenue, 647-777-0113, kettlemansbagel.com*). (The latter has pretty good smoked meat, too.)

For chopped liver, latkes, gefilte fish, brisket, and of course chicken soup, you can visit **Nortown** (*303 York Mills Rd., 416-447-0310; 892 Eglinton Ave. W., 416-789-2921; 1 Promenade Circ., Thornhill, 905-889-1610; all locations closed on Saturdays*). A fine range of kosher groceries — and great halvah — is to be had at **Daiter's Creamery** (*3535 Bathurst St., 416-781-6101; 5984 Bathurst St., 416-636-8716; 928 Eglinton Ave. W., 416-787-5913*).

Not only at Purim, but all year round you can buy *hamentashen* (the three-cornered pastry named for the hat of the evil Persian functionary Hamen), with traditional prune and poppyseed fillings — as well as cherry and apple — at **Haymishe Bagels** (*3031 Bathurst St., 416-781-4212; 9301 Bathurst St. in Richmond Hill, 905-737-4532*).

And as for May Wests (as in "un Pepsi p'is un May-West"), although its companion cake, the chocolate Jos. Louis, is available in every *dépanneur*, the signature snack of Quebec is very hard to find. It was most recently spotted in cartons of 12 in **Joe's No Frills** (*449 Parliament*).

Photo: Sarah B. Hood

Feel like roasting a whole lamb on the spit? **Loui's Meat Market and Deli** has been selling fresh wholesale and retail lamb, pork, goat, veal, and beef since 1971. They also supply excellent feta cheese, kefalotiri, and other Greek treats (*449 Danforth Ave., 416-465-3364*). If you don't happen to have a spit of your own, **Sinni's Bakery and Deli** (*1592 Queen St. W., 416-538-4527*) will bake a whole pig or lamb for you on Saturdays by appointment. **Cumbrae's** (*481 Church St., 416-923-5600*) is a family-run butcher shop (taken over from former occupant Simon de Groot) that deals in beautifully prepared high-end specialty cuts, all naturally raised and humanely killed, while **The Chopping Block** (*2256 Queen St. E., 416-690-5209*), also high-end, promises naturally raised, drug-free meats.

Roncesvalles is paradise for kolbasa lovers. We like **Copernicus** (*79 Roncesvalles Ave., 416-536-4054*) for their friendly service and **Super Kolbasa Delicatessen** (*83 Roncesvalles Ave., 416-588-3759*) for their now-fading giant sausage "S." (Don't forget to pick up some mackerel, herring, pickles, sauerkraut, and plum jam.) The Mennonite communities of western Ontario prepare exquisite long-aged summer sausage; recognize it by its cloth wrapper and pungent smoky smell. It's available in a few locations around town including **Cheese Magic** (*182 Baldwin St., 416-593-9531*), **Carlo Foods**, the meat counter at the entrance to Zeller's inside Gerrard Square Mall (*1000 Gerrard St. E.*), and, in November, at the **Royal Winter Fair**.

You should get some of **Anton Kozlik's Canadian Mustard** from the St. Lawrence Market to go with that (*416-361-9788*). It's prepared in numerous ways, from a sherry-laced gourmet blend to the no-nonsense "XXX Hot," a narrow step away from straight-up horseradish.

Photo: Sarah B. Hood

SHELL GAME

In the Farmer's Market section of the St. Lawrence Market, you can get yesterday's farm eggs if you go early enough. But if you miss out, go to the store without a sign, **Augusta Egg Market** (*251 Augusta Ave., 416-593-9817*). Besides fresh chicken eggs, you can also get turkey and quail. And because they buy in bulk flats, they'll happily take off your hands any empty dozen-egg cartons you may have saved up.

MAINTAINING A STABLE SOCIETY

On any day of the year up to 60 horses (and riders) are on duty with the Toronto Police Service Mounted Unit, whose stables are located on the north side of the Horse Palace on the CNE grounds, opposite the recently expanded Exhibition GO station. Although they don't particularly advertise their presence, the Mounted Unit officers are generally gracious to drop-in visitors; there's a modest exhibit at the entrance, and official colouring books can be had for the asking. It's usually a tranquil spot, but a few years back there was a bit of excitement when one of the horses bolted. Officers scrambled, and calls were hurriedly placed to CN to alert them of a potential equine emergency on the rail line, but the situation was quickly resolved after the runaway animal galloped straight through the front doors of the then-still-operating Upper Canada Brewing Company — probably in search of a helping of barley mash.

Organic Decisions

• Organic farmers' markets are a coming thing around town. There's a year-round market on Thursday afternoons at Dufferin Grove Park, across from the Dufferin Mall. Riverdale Farm in Cabbagetown runs one on Tuesdays. (This is just a summertime thing at the moment, but may become year-round.) Both locations also have community bake ovens where bread and pizza are cooked and shared; more markets and ovens are expected to spring up, with Parkdale the likely next candidate.

• The non-profit **FoodShare** (*200 Eastern Ave., 416-363-6441 ext. 21, foodshare.net*) co-ordinates neighbourhood distribution points where people can pick up the "Good Food Box" – a pre-packed box of organic produce – as often as once a week.

• **Front Door Organics** (*9-415 Horner Ave., 416-201-3000, frontdoororganics.com*) delivers a large or small box of similarly pre-selected organic produce weekly or every other week. (Or clients can pick up the food themselves.) People usually try just one box at first, then sign on for regular delivery.

• **Green Earth Organics** (*70 Wade Ave., Unit 3, 416-285-5300, greenearthorganics.com*) delivers as often as weekly to homes or businesses; customers have some choice as to what comes in their box, and there's no minimum number of orders. Green Earth donates 10% of profits to like-minded charities, and leftover food goes to Second Harvest.

• **Urban Harvest** is the local source for organic herb and vegetable seeds, plantlets, and garden amendments (as in fertilizer). They're available in garden centres; the number to call to locate the nearest one, or for mail order, is 416-504-1653.

• Now we can raise a glass to sustainable living, since Toronto's first certified organic brewery has opened in Tankhouse 53 of the Gooderham and Worts Distillery Historic District. The **Mill Street Brewery** (*55 Mill Street, Building 63, 416-681-0338, millstreetbrewery.com*) produces tasty craft beers that are available around town as well as at the brewery, where they also run tours and a tasting bar.

For those who long to learn the Chinese *erhu* or secretly practice Indian singing in the shower, **Worlds of Music Toronto** (*416-588-8813, worldsofmusic.ca*) presents ten-week spring and fall workshops in world singing, drumming, dance, and music. Great local musicians like Njacko Backo, Anne Lederman, and Nicolás Hernandez teach these beginner sessions, which range from African drumming to Celtic fiddling to Balkan singing; there's a public performance at the end of each class. **Dance Ontario Association** (*416-204-1083, icomm.ca/danceon*) has the cure for itchy toes: their directory of dozens of dance classes at all levels, like Arabesque Academy of belly dancing, Mississauga's What's On Tap school, and – for those who fancy a little Riverdancing – Celtic Dance Company. Popular health-food store **The Big Carrot** (*348 Danforth Ave., 416-466-2129, thebigcarrot.ca*) teaches macrobiotic and vegetarian cooking classes, with a dinner at the end of each one. Long-established European language learning schools are the **Alliance Francaise** for French (*24 Spadina Rd., 416-922-2014; 1 Elmhurst Ave., 416-221-4684; 111-1140 Burnhamthorpe Rd. W., 905-272-4444, alliance-francaise.com*), the **Italian Cultural Institute** for Italian (*496 Huron St. 416-921-3802, iicto-ca.org*), and **The Goethe Institute** for German (*163 King St. W., 416-593-5257, goethe.de/uk/tor/enindex.htm*). For rarer tongues like Ojibway, the **University of Toronto School of Continuing Studies** (*158 St. George St., 416-978-2400, learn.utoronto.ca*) is the best bet. The **City of Toronto Cultural Division** oversees an eclectic range of activities around museums, galleries, and historical houses. For example, Colborne Lodge in High Park offers courses in basketry, wreath-making, and open-hearth baking. These are compiled in *Toronto Fun*, a big newsprint magazine that's distributed around libraries and community centres several times a year; it also lists community centre classes, and it's the one-stop guide to sports instruction and teams. For inimitable course listings like "How to Open A Tea Shop," "Be Your Own Pet Psychic," and "The Art of Breathing," there's the dependable **Learning Annex** (*416-964-0011,*

Tourist Traps

When you measure the dollar-value to fun ratio, some Toronto landmarks seem overrated, as in:

CN Tower

You can face an incredibly long lineup to get up there, the view is spoiled by any clouds or haze, it's rather costly, and, worst of all, you can have a long wait *to get out*!

Cheap Thrills Alternative: A ferry ride across to the Islands. If you have time, you can enjoy a barbeque, rollerblade, rent a four-person bike, or stroll through parkland. If you actually want to blow some cash, visit Centreville and get on the antique carousel and the log ride.

Tip: The ferry lineup can be long on summer weekends, but if you plan ahead, you can buy advance tickets in lots of ten for a 10% discount; these will let you bypass the line, even on the unbelievably packed Caribana weekend.

learningannex.com). (Now, let us pause for a moment of silence for the Toronto District School Board, which, as of spring 2003, discontinued hundreds of community courses – their complete roster of fitness, cooking, crafts, and computer skills classes – due to budget cuts.)

Eaton Centre

Really, it's just a shopping mall.

Cheap Thrills Alternative: Honest Ed's at Bathurst and Bloor, with its crazy doorcrasher specials, weird, piped-in music, kooky hand-written signs, Royal Alexandra memorabilia and true bargain shopping.

SkyDome

Yes, cheap seats for an afternoon ball game can be idyllic, but the Dome's so big it distances you from whatever action you're there to enjoy.

Cheap Thrills Alternative: the concert stage at Harbourfront Centre (pictured below). There's no retractable roof, but it's outdoors, and you can get right up close to the stage. It books big international acts, especially in the world music, jazz, and blues idioms, and many of the concerts are free.

Herb-ane Comforts

Photo: Sarah B. Hood

There are only five outlets for **L'Occitane en Provence** in Canada, and we've got two of 'em (*150 Bloor St. W, 416-413-4899; 2589 Yonge St., 416-440-3979*). Based in Provence, France, L'Occitane makes exquisite soaps and creams from very fine herbal extracts and shea butter. Their lavender and verbena products are made once a year, like a vintage wine, as the products come into season (lavender in September, verbena in May). Loose herbs, essential oils, and consulting services are to be found at **The Herbal Clinic and Dispensary** (*409 Roncesvalles Ave., 416-537-5303*), **Ottway Herbs & Vitamins** (*3188 Yonge St., 416-487-8307; 2785 St. Clair Ave. E., 416-755-2258; 453 Church St., 416-967-9222; 300 Danforth Ave., 416-463-5125; ottway.com*), and **Thuna Herbalist** (*298 Danforth Ave., 416-465-3366, theherbalclinicanddispensary.com*). Every Chinese shopping district includes at least one herbalist. Like naturopaths, these health professionals work with clients to bring the body into strength and balance through the use of herbal treatments. Word is that the best referral to one of these specialists is from a Chinese auntie. Those lacking in Chinese aunties claim to have had good results in picking a shop by ordinary urban instinct.

Seems like there's so much time to fill when you're a kid – or planning the day for one! One elegantly simple solution is to stop by the **Children's Storefront** (*1079 Bathurst St., 416-531-8151*), a free drop-in with its own toys for girls (and boys) who just want to have fun. For a fee of only $35 per month (or the astonishingly affordable $125 per year), the Downtown YMCA **Family Development Centre** (*15 Breadalbane St., 416-513-1164, ymcatoronto.org*) gives parents and children of all ages access to a library, a solarium, toys, art supplies, dress-up clothes, seminars, and singalongs, as well as the company of other downtown families.

Toddlers aged 3 to 5 years meet with a real live farmer over the course of nine weeks at the Riverdale Farm **Parent & Young Farmer** program (*416-392-6794, friendsofriverdalefarm.com*). They learn about caring for and feeding a different farm animal each week, and then carry out a craft project that relates to the animal they've just visited. The fun, innovative **Avenue Road Arts School** (*460 Avenue Rd., 416-961-1502, avenueroadartsschool.com*) offers courses taught by professional artists for students from nine months old right up to adult level. In the Beaches, **Brenda Ellenwood** (*416-598-1257*) teaches fabulous pottery classes for youngsters in her own home/studio.

The **Royal Ontario Museum Summer Club** (*100 Queen's Pk., 416-586-5549, rom.on.ca*) is one of the best of all the summer camp-type programs. Kids get to meet mummies, learn excellent nature facts, and generally have as great a time as you can at a museum if you're not actually locked in overnight. It even includes sports and swimming. There's a substantial discount for people who have family memberships at the Museum (but the membership price plus Summer Club fees come out to more than the non-member cost.) Posh private girls' school the Bishop Strachan School (*298 Lonsdale Rd., 416-483-4325, bss.on.ca*) runs the sensational summertime **Erin Gilmour Arts Workshop** for boys and girls aged 7 to 18. The choices included a pretty high-level introduction to film production, and lots of other disciplines like dance, photography, singing, and Shakespeare. Best-kept secret: some scholarships are available.

For the books and the great events, **Mabel's Fables Children's Book Store** (*662 Mt. Pleasant,*

Getaways

Photo: Ontario Tourism, 08301

North

In Gravenhurst, you can board the old-fashioned steamships *Segwun* or *Wenonah II* to tour the beautiful lakes Muskoka, Joseph, and Rosseau. Downtown Gravenhurst has enough to offer to amply fill up whatever's left of a day or a weekend. But be warned: locals say that the place that used to have the best blueberry pie still claims they do, but it's not like it used to be!
705-687-6667, wenonah.ca

South

If you arrange to go for a good long visit on a day when they're not overcrowded, the staff at the Mackenzie Heritage Printery Museum will let your family play for hours with antique printing equipment, actually setting type and printing out cards, signs, and other documents. It's situated in the house where William Lyon Mackenzie produced his first newspaper (*The Colonial Advocate*), and has been restored as

416-322-0438; 2939 Bloor St. W., 416-233-8830) is a fine destination, and **A Different Booklist** (746 Bathurst St., 416-538-0889, adifferentbooklist.com) carries books for and about kids of all cultures. There's also a plethora of great information at the exhaustive website **helpwevegotkids.com**, related to the popular resource guide of the same name. And for families about town on Sundays and holidays, the TTC charges only $7.75 for an all-day pass for up to six people (maximum of two adults).

a museum of the history of printing.
1 Queenston St., Queenston, 905-262-5676, mackenzieprintery.ca

Photo: Wayne Eardley

East

4th Line Theatre, near Millbrook (outside Peterborough) is a unique professional theatre that performs plays inspired by the history of the region on a former working farm. Some of the shows are set up in the barnyard; others are staged in the adjacent woods and fields. The setting can be heart-stoppingly beautiful and the shows are consistently fine. They're generally suitable for children while still satisfying for adult theatregoers. *800-814-0055, 4thlinetheatre.com*

West

The Home County Folk Festival is one of the Ontario's best. It takes place each July at London's Victoria Park, with an open stage and an array of crafts markets, all for free. *519-432-4310, homecounty.com*

Furry, Feathery, and Leathery Friends

The **Toronto Humane Society** (11 River St., 416-392-2273, torontohumanesociety.com) takes in over 10,000 ownerless dogs, cats, and rodents every year, along

Photo: Sarah B. Hood

with some stranger pets. For $20 (rabbits) to $125 (dogs), you can adopt a loving and healthy animal and save it from the eventual euthanasia that comes to about 300 dogs and ten times as many cats annually. Especially gentle families are candidates for the fostering program, which places sick, sad, or simply immature animals with temporary homes until they're strong enough to go to a permanent placement. (And remember that the Humane Society is always in need of extra blankets, towels, and dog biscuits.)

Whereas Toronto has pretty much eliminated stray dogs in the city, we have a huge population of ownerless cats. Recognizing that the average lifespan of a stray cat is under two years, and that many die in miserable circumstances, several groups of volunteers have come together to feed feral cats, rescue, shelter, and foster strays, and promote spaying and neutering of pets. These organizations, which have a no-kill policy, are **Annex Cat Rescue** (416-410-3835, annexcatrescue.on.ca), **Kensington Market Stray Cat**

Rescue (*416-596-2331, freeanimals.org*), and **Toronto Cat Rescue** (*416-538-8592, catstoronto.com*).

For those who have their hearts set on acquiring a non-mammal pet, **Menagerie Pet Shop** (*549 Parliament St., 416-921-4966*) is a responsible and well-informed source of exotic birds, fish, and reptiles. They'll also board smaller pets, like birds, rodents, and reptiles – but not fish. **Port Credit Pet Centre** (*219 Lakeshore Rd. E., 905-274-8018*) deals specifically in reptiles and amphibians. **Pet Sitters of Toronto** (*416-252-3863*) will take temporary care of your mammals, birds, or fish while you're away.

Finally, the stall known as **Uncle George's Place** sells organic sprouts on Saturdays in the St. Lawrence South Market (*lower level B17, 416-601-2112*), but kitty lovers know George best as the city's premier purveyor of fresh, live catgrass, which he also distributes to pet stores and convenience stores around town.

Picture Perfect

If you want to get great photo developing, enlargements, and transfers from one format to another, go where the pros go. Considered the top of the line by many is the esteemed **Chas Abel** (*5 Lower Sherbourne St., 416-364-2391, chasabel.com*), in business since 1906. **Steichenlab** (*500 Richmond St. E., 416-366-8745, steichenlab.com*) and **Toronto Image Works** (*207-80 Spadina Ave., 416-703-1999, torontoimageworks.com*) get the thumbs up from many, while **West Camera** (*514 Queen St. W., 416-504-9432*) is particularly popular with people around the music and film industries. The only place in town for 8mm film processing is **Exclusive Film and Video** (*50 Portland St., 416-598-2700*), where you can also have your old home movies transferred to video. For custom framing, there's no better place than **Akau** (*742 Queen St. W., 416-594-5990*), which is pronounced like their sign, which has a picture of … a cow.

Double Fun

The cheapest neighbourhood for photocopying documents is College Street just south of the University of Toronto, where you can go as low as three cents per copy at locations like **Alicos Digital Print and Copy Centre** (*203A College St., 416-599-2342, alicos.com*).

Where to Rent Movies

Apart from the selections listed below, of course, there are shops that stock international films in original languages in every neighbourhood with a large community of, for example, Chinese, Tamil, Polish, or Vietnamese residents. In some cases, non-English-language videos are a sideline for a grocery; in others they complement a "mainstream" selection.

After Dark Video

Cult films, monster movies, odd TV stuff … kinda what you'd expect from the name.
1043 Bathurst St., 416-533-7500

Balfour Books

A small rental collection, mostly foreign and "artsy" films that can be hard to find elsewhere, including the best edition of *Nosferatu* we've come across.
601 College St., 416-531-9911

Canadian Filmmakers Distribution Centre

CFMDC handles distribution to film festivals, schools, and so on for over 550 independent filmmakers. They stock more than 2,300 films in Super 8, 16mm, and 35mm. Rental fees are designed for organizations, not individuals, but if you're looking for local independent films, you'll find them here. *220-37 Hanna Ave., 416-588-0725, cfmdc.org*

China Book Store

Chinese-language films including Hong Kong action. *623 Gerrard St. E., 416-469 2110*

Fair Deal Audio Video

An extensive Bollywood collection on VHS and DVD, plus lots of related audio tapes and CDs. *1430 Gerrard St. E., 416-778-4646*

The Film Buff

Aptly named, this is the premiere spot for film noir, with a little café, a great website, and informative literature (like their annual December "Best of the Year" pamphlet). It's so dedicated to the cause that it stocks a shelf of impossible-to-find films acquired from non-standard sources (known as "The Black Vault"), which may be borrowed at no charge. *73 Roncesvalles Ave., 416-534-7078, thefilmbuff.com*

You can get DVDs anywhere; here are some places that sell VHS, so you can stock up before it becomes as obsolete a format as Betamax.

BMV Bookstore

Particularly at the Yonge Street store, a staggering array of obscure used videos from the '80s, as well as a goodly range of more recent fare. (They're also a more-than-decent used book and magazine store.) *2289 Yonge St., 416-482-6002; 10 Edward St., 416-977-3087*

Monster Records

Lots of watchable second-hand video, including some of the rarer film buff fare (Marx Brothers, spaghetti westerns, and so on). *664 Yonge St. 416-975-1829*

National Film Board

The NFB sells their own videos, including many Oscar-nominated films, at their shop and online. *150 John St., 416-973-3012, nfb.ca*

World's Biggest Bookstore

The best new retail selection we've found, especially when it comes to documentary videos (science, nature, history, biography, and so on). *20 Edward St., 416-977-7009*

Photo: Sarah B. Hood

The **Festival Cinemas** (*festivalcinemas.com*) are the six comfortably dilapidated neighbourhood repertory houses that share a single member card guaranteeing $6 admissions ($4 on Tuesdays). Their programming is eclectic, to say the least, and – even though you can get most of this stuff on video nowadays – it's great to watch on a big screen in the correct proportions. Special events include premieres of local films, Oscar nights, and cult experiences like late-night *Rocky Horror* screenings and Kung Fu Fridays. The participating theatres are the **Fox** (*2236 Queen St. E., 416-691-7330*), **Kingsway** (*3030 Bloor St. W., 416-690-2600*), **Music Hall** (*147 Danforth Ave., 416-778-8272*), **Paradise** (*1006 Bloor St. W., 416-537-7040*), **Revue** (*400 Roncesvalles Ave., 416-531-9959*), and **Royal** (*608 College St., 416-516-4845*). The **Bloor Cinema** (*506 Bloor St. W., 416-516-2330, bloorcinema.com*), once a leader within the festivals group, is now independent, but it still uses the same kind of card system.

Programmed by the Toronto International Film Festival Group, **Cinematheque Ontario** (*bell.ca/cinematheque*) screens important films from around the world, often in the form of director retrospectives. Prices are lower than first-run rates (especially for members), but you need to line up early if you're buying tickets at the door. Screenings take place at the Art Gallery of Ontario's Jackman Hall. As of late 2002, the **National Film Board Mediatheque** (*150 John St., 416-973-3012, nfb.ca*) programs public screenings of gems from its

MVP (Master Video Productions)

A sensational selection of Italian language video, including classics of Italian cinema with English subtitles, as well as contemporary fare from Italy, and Hollywood movies dubbed or subbed into Italian.
604 College St., 416-534-6121

Queen Video

Many would call this the best all-round video rental outlet, with a wide selection of contemporary, classic, foreign, and rare movies.
412 Queen St. W., 416-504-3030; 480 Bloor St. W., 416-588-5767

Revue Video

A serious rental catalogue of international films – including Latin American and African – and the rarer works of Hollywood directors like Ford, Capra, Welles, and Altman – put Revue squarely on the cinephile map. They carry a very short list of DVDs, too.
207 Danforth Ave., 416-778-5776, revuevideo.com

Photo: Sarah B. Hood

collection. Even more fun are the personal viewing stations for individuals and couples, where – for a mere $3 an hour – you can use a touch-screen to choose and view your picks from among 600 NFB films.

Probably no one in the history of this city has pasted up more handbills than maverick film curator **Reg Hartt**, who has spent the past several decades screening rare cartoons, silents, and unusual landmark films like Leni Riefenstahl's *Triumph of the Will*. Opinionated, deeply knowledgeable, and an indisputable Toronto icon, Hartt shows the films at his own space, identified in red neon as "Cineforum" (*463 Bathurst Street, 416-603-6643*).

And they don't call us the city of festivals for nothing. In late September, after the overwhelming smorgasbord that is the **Toronto International Film Festival** (*416-967-7371, bell.ca/filmfest*), we have the **Planet in Focus Toronto International Environmental Film and Video Festival** (*416-531-1769, planetinfocus.org*). October brings the innovative **Moving Pictures** festival of dance on film and video (*movingpicturesfestival.com*). Late November/early December sees the **Toronto Reel Asian International Film Festival** (*416-703-9333, reelasian.com*). March is the month of the **Toronto Jewish Film Festival** (*416.324.9121, tjff.com*), and, later, of the French-language **Cinefranco** (*416-928-9794, cinefranco.com*). April showers bring the multicultural **Reel World Film Festival** (*416-598-7933, reelworldfilmfest.com*), then the experimental **Images Festival** of independent film, video, new media, performance, and installation (*416-971-8405, imagesfestival.com*). At the beginning of May, it's **Hot Docs, the Canadian International Documentary Festival** (*416-516-3320, hotdocs.ca*), and **Sprockets International Film Festival For Children** (*416-967-7371*), curated by the Toronto International Film Festival team, which shows kids' films in their original languages, with subtitles read aloud. Late May welcomes the **Inside Out Toronto Lesbian and Gay Film and Video Festival** (*416-977-6847, insideout.ca*), followed in early June by the Canadian Film Centre's **Toronto Worldwide Short Film Festival** (*416-445-1446, ext. 815, worldwideshortfilmfest.com*) and in mid-June by the **Italian Film Festival** (*416-657-0100, italianfilmfest.com*). August ushers in **Filmi – The South Asian Film Festival** (*filmi.org*), and in early September the independent filmmakers congregate at **Planet Indie** (*planetindie.com*) … just in time for another edition of TIFF.

To our taste, there isn't a more simpatico fitness facility than **Liberty Village Spa and Fitness Studio**. It's a haunt of the film, music, and design house types around Liberty Village, and – although it's a fine place to sweat and bulk up – it's very welcoming to women and has none of the cheesy singles bar ambiance of so many chain gyms. Liberty is run by cheerful ex-musician Mike, who prepares for his own road and mountain bike competitions in between personal-training sessions; his hair colour varies like seasonal foliage. It's a small space, but it offers extras (hot tub, towels, great massage pros) that many larger places don't.

When all is not as it should be, you can turn to a healing hand at **Health Focus** (*355A College St., 416-922-4909*). Under the direction of the tiny powerhouse that is chiropractor and acupuncturist Anita Shack, Health Focus offers a wide range of therapeutic treatments, including shiatsu. Its atmosphere is so positively charged that merely taking a seat in the waiting room will do you good. When it's sheer luxury that you're after, **Pure + Simple** (*2375 Yonge St., 416-481-2081, pureandsimple.ca*) beckons with detoxifying facials and other spa services, including the fabled Nirvana Facial, which is based on Ayurvedic principles and employs not one but two therapists who work on your whole body from the scalp on down. Meanwhile, **Jean Pierre Aesthetics and Spa** (*Upstairs at 530 Yonge St., 416-964-2505*) is not run by a French gentleman but by a Caribbean lady who trained as a nurse, and who has special expertise in skin care. Jean specializes in the needs of African skin and hair, and has created her own line of cosmetics, Obsidian, designed for a full spectrum of skin tones.

Beyond Goodwill

Everybody knows that you can donate your no-longer-needed clothing and housewares to Goodwill and the Salvation Army Thrift shops. But how do you pass along a gently-used bay window or a dead Dodge?

BIKES

The **Community Bicycle Network** (*761 Queen St. W., 416-504-2918, onelesscar.ca*) will accept (and sometimes pick up) children's or adult bicycles and bike parts, even if they're not in great shape. Some may go to a neighbourhood club, where people of all ages learn bike repair skills. Others may become "yellow bikes," available free to people with a Bikeshare membership.

CARS

When good cars go away, they end up in **Car Heaven** (c/o Ontario Automotive Recyclers Association, 224-845 Upper James St., Hamilton, carheavenhelps.com). When you recycle a car through the program, you get free towing, a minimum $60 charitable tax receipt, a chance to win prizes, and the knowledge that every part of the car that can be salvaged and reused will be.

CELL PHONES

The **Daily Bread Food Bank** can turn phones into food. There are several hundred public drop-off points around town, including some community centres and fire stations, and all Purolator outlets. The Food Bank also collects laser toner cartridges and inkjet cartridges; in their hands, one single item can be transformed into a carton of milk, a jar of peanut butter, or a whole meal.

The list of drop-off locations is available online at *think-food.com* (for toner cartridges) and *phonesforfood.com* (for phones), and by phone (*888-271-3641*). (People can also order a collection box for their school or workplace.)

Good Hair Day

Gone are the days of "shave and a haircut, two bits," but Chinatown East still offers the $6 haircut, and a good one too, capably achieved with a freehand electric razor. Among other spots, try **New Salon Hair Design** (*302 Broadview Ave., 416-778-7418*) or **Daily Salon** (*right next door at 304 Broadview Ave., 416-461-6099*). And if Clairol just doesn't make enough colours to suit you, take a trip to **Cosmetic World** (*623-A Yonge St., 416-964-6188*) for the city's most comprehensive array of hair colouring products in all shades and degrees of permanence. Their selection of products for African hair – straightened, braided, or dreaded – is also pretty good, and they stock a great range of general cosmetics and related equipment in a capacious storefront that you could pass a thousand times without picking it out from among the surrounding dollar stores and martial arts boutiques.

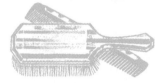

Flower Power

The most gorgeously minimalist and exotic floral arrangements and house plants come from **poppies plant of joy** (*1094 Queen St. W., 416-538-2497*), newly established in the hopping almost-Parkdale section of Queen Street. For cheap, bulk flower purchases, go where the sidewalk vendors go: **Flower King Inc.** (*597 King St. E., 416-364-2222*). Walk into the warehouse for mostly cut-rate roses, but they carry some other blooms as well. (You don't have to buy in any particular quantity.)

How Can You Mend a Broken Heart?

Alas, we do not know. As your elders always told you, you just can't expect anyone to walk into your life and fix everything – but sometimes you can find that dependable someone who'll fix *something*: your trusty old TV, the heirloom necklace you borrowed and broke, or that three-speed you've discovered at the back of the garage.

• **George Brown College** has a sensational Jewellery Arts program, but few non-students know that the department offers inexpensive and trustworthy jewellery repair and modification. If you take a piece in, be sure to ask when the next student sale is planned, since this is your big chance to buy a real treasure from one of this city's up-and-coming designers. (*George Brown College, Casa Loma Campus, 160 Kendal Avenue, 5th floor, 416-415-5000, ext. 4463*)

• In business for close to a century, **Novelty Shoe Rebuilders** is the place to go for old-school resoling, reheeling, and other shoe repairs. (119 Yonge St., 416-364-8878); not quite so venerable, but venerable enough is **Alex Shoe Repair** (*213 Roncesvalles Ave., 416-532-7580*).

Photo: Sarah B. Hood

• Not all bike repair shops are created equal. Regular everyday cyclists will find the warmest greetings at **Urbane Cyclist**, Toronto's only co-op bike shop (*180 John St., 416-979-9733, ucycle.com*), or **Ideal Bike**, where they'll encounter the unflappable Maggie (*1178 Queen St. E., 416-463-2453*). Impossible to categorize, **Cavern Cycles** (*179 Queen St. E., 416 203-2565*) was started by bike couriers with a love of track and road racing. It's actually a storefront spinoff from the back-alley west-end warehouse shop known as Courier Cavern. The Cavern can handle anything from fixing a flat to sourcing the perfect replacement components for a

COMPUTERS

reBOOT Canada (*reBOOT Canada: 110-136 Geary Ave., 416-534-6017; reBOOT reTAIL: 1314 Queen St. W., 416-532-4983, reboot.on.ca*) has already refurbished over 20,000 computers for redistribution to charities. Mind you, they probably don't want your old Kaypro, but if your office is refitting its entire system, they'll be glad to hear from you. (They have been known to find grateful re-users of related items, like telephone systems.) What they can't give away goes into their retail outlet for sale at very low prices to the general public.

DOORS AND WINDOWS

Habitat ReStore (*29 Bermondsey Rd, 416-755-7353 ext. 3; 1120 Caledonia Rd, 416-783-0686, torontohabitat.on.ca/restore.shtml*) is a registered charity and a self-styled "thrift-shop for reusable building materials." Builders can donate used and salvaged items like doors and windows, lumber and trim, appliances and fixtures, tiles and flooring, paint, and nuts and bolts. Resale prices run about 50% of normal cost, and proceeds go to Habitat for Humanity to build houses for those who can't afford them. Similar materials will be received at **Home Again Recycling Depot** (*89 Research Rd., 416-467-4663*).

FOREIGN CURRENCY

Mount Sinai Hospital (*600 University Ave., 416-596-4200*) has a donation station in their patient admissions room for that spare change you've had sitting around your dresser drawer since your last foreign escape. Through the good offices of Thomas Cook, those leftover lira and drachmas will turn into Canadian currency that the hospital can spend on its many needs.

vintage Italian racer. Also courier-owned is the newly-established **The Bike Joint** (290½ Harbord St., 416-532-6392, thebikejoint.com).

• Wayne, at the tucked-away **Toronto Furniture Refinishing** (*37 Hanna Ave., Laneway Door #5, 416-588-5888*), lovingly rebuilds and refinishes wooden furniture, while **Angel Interiors & Custom Upholstery** (*683 Bloor St. W., 416-537-9169*) makes house calls to pick up a piece for reupholstering.

• If something comes with a power cord, sooner or later it will stop working. Some Toronto appliance heroes include **Ring Audio**, loving restorers of classic sound systems, including stereos with tubes (*742 Queen St. E., 416-693-7464*). As soon as you see the collection of electric and human-powered machines at **Central Industrial Sewing Machine Co. Ltd.** (especially the beautifully decorated models from China), you know yours is in good hands with mechanic Mike. For a few dollars, he can also sell you an extra drive belt for a treadle machine (*491 Queen St. W., 416-504-2500*). From the solid and pleasing late-'50s sign over the door to the alluring hint of machine oil within, even the ambiance of **R.A. Butler's Appliance Service Inc.** (*249 Coxwell Ave., 416-463-1164*) instills confidence. They repair everything from vacuum cleaners to VCRs, and they also stock oddments like replacement carafes for coffeemakers. The comforting experts from **Gate Electronic Services** (*416-766-8744, a-ideas.com*) make house calls to repair all kinds of electronics (even telephones) for a reasonable hourly rate. They're great with the software side too, and can handle programming, networking, virus protection, or simply removing and installing programs.

Photo: Sarah B. Hood

Giving Back

People volunteer because they want to feel good about themselves, because they want to learn new skills and network for a better job, or because they want to meet people and get invited to good parties. Volunteering works for all of these, and opportunities abound. Any charity or arts organization or health cause – and even some businesses – will try to find a place for a volunteer who turns up offering to help. Same goes for festivals and special events, like the Film Festival, Caribana, and Pride Week (as long as the potential volunteer turns up at least a few weeks ahead of time). The **Volunteer Centre of Toronto** runs a website that lists opportunities of all kinds weekly (*volunteerstoronto.on.ca*). **Harbourfront Centre** has its own volunteer office (*416-973-4944*). The **City of Toronto** (*city.toronto.on.ca/involved/index.htm, 416-392-0146*) has a number of volunteer groups: the Task Force to Bring Back the Don; the boards of the Hummingbird Centre and the Toronto Atmospheric Fund; committees on lesbian, gay, bisexual, and transgendered issues; children and youth; aboriginal affairs; bingo; race and ethnic relations; the status of women; cycling; pedestrian affairs. When positions become vacant, notices are posted in the newspapers; applicants must usually attend an orientation meeting before submitting their name for consideration. Terms of office run from about one to three years.

Running for City Hall

It's not much harder to become a candidate for City Hall than it is to get a library card. Candidates have to be Canadian citizens over the age of 18, but apart from that, if they can show ID and proof of an address within the city, they're more or less in. There's no fee, but there are certain rules, the strictest of which is to submit professional financial statements after the election.

Elections come up every third year: 2003, 2006, and so on, and the election is always the second Monday in November. Anyone who wants to run needs to present forms to the folks at City Hall sometime between January 1 and Nomination Day, which is 45 days ahead of the election. To find out how to do this, call 416-338-1111

HOUSEPLANTS

The **Yonge Street Mission** (*416-925-6069, ysm.on.ca*) will come and collect your beloved plants when they outgrow their present accommodation; they'll be loved and cared for (small ones go to seniors, and the big ones cheer up the Mission's public spaces). For more than 100 years, the Mission has been alleviating poverty and alienation in the downtown core; they run the Evergreen street youth centre, drop-ins in low-income neighbourhoods, seniors' services, and the **Double Take Used Clothing Store** (*310 Gerrard Ave.*). Therefore they'll also collect household items for youth and seniors, and they always have an urgent need for food, toiletries, and vitamins.

PERISHABLE FOOD

What the Daily Bread Food Bank is to canned and dried foods, **Second Harvest** (*416-408-2594, secondharvest.ca*) is to fresh produce, bread, and cooked food. They collect fresh food every day from shops and restaurants and redistribute it to a list of 135 shelters, hostels, day programs, and other places where there are hungry mouths to feed. They'll cheerfully pick up unserved portions after weddings or office parties, if they have advance notice and there's enough to feed 50 or so.

When quantities are smaller, or leftovers can't be accurately predicted or stored, organizers can call a day ahead to be referred to an agency that will accept food at any hour. (People have been known to cab fruit baskets, cheese platters, sandwiches, or lasagnas to waiting recipients in the middle of the night.)

WEIRD AND WONDERFUL

If it doesn't seem to fall into any other category, but it's just too great to toss, take it to **Garbage Palace** (*970 Queen St. W., 416-530-5850*), where it'll either be sold as is or transformed into a fabulous craft item by being melted, glued to something, or covered with decoupage.

or download the helpful *Candidate's Guide* from *toronto.ca/elections*. Once the person has registered as a candidate, they get a kit that includes excellent maps of the area they're campaigning in, and a list of voters by address so they can plan door-to-door canvassing, phone blitzes, literature drops, the usual. Their name will automatically be given out to media and community groups who want to meet the candidates.

Then the candidate and their team – usually including at least a Campaign Manager and a Chief Financial Officer – must open a business bank account in the name of the campaign. Every donation of cash or supplies must be recorded. No individual is allowed to contribute more than $2,500 to a mayoral campaign or $750 to a councillor campaign. The people who contribute money get a sizable rebate from the city, as long as the candidate issues an official receipt. Candidates have campaign spending limits, too: about $20,000 for a councillor and about $1 million for mayor.

The candidate will probably spend some of the money on signs. (Signs can only go up 25 days ahead of the election, and must be removed three days ahead.) More money will probably go towards campaign literature; it's normal for a candidate to drop at least three pieces of literature in each door over the course of the campaign.

More than money, a political campaign requires lots of volunteers. One of the effects of amalgamation has been to make the wards so large that it's not really possible for a truly independent candidate to run and win, as it once was. If someone seriously wants to get into politics, they'll have to work on other people's campaigns first. (Although, officially, citywide municipal parties don't exist, pretty much everyone who has taken office in the past ten years got started through connections to an existing party.)

But the energetic person who just wants to make a statement can easily run an inexpensive mayoral campaign on chutzpah and imagination – just look at the Hummer Sisters, street musician Ben Kerr, artist Jenny Friedland, Enza Supermodel, or environmentalist Tooker Gomberg. And anyone who wants to make the Unknown City their own can choose no more vital way than by working on a campaign, whether it's theirs or someone else's.

index

index

index

index

index

index

index

index

index

index

index

index

index

index

index

index

HOWARD AKLER is a life-long resident of Toronto. He has written for *Lola*, the local art magazine, and is currently at work on a novel set during the city's centenary.

SARAH B. HOOD is the author of *Practical Pedalling*, has contributed to *Toronto Life*, *NOW*, and *eyeWeekly*, and is the editor of *Performing Arts in Canada*. In 1990 she received an honourable mention at the National Magazine Awards.